ROUTLEDGE LIBRARY EDITIONS:
THE ECONOMY OF THE MIDDLE EAST

Volume 18

LIBYA: AGRICULTURE AND ECONOMIC DEVELOPMENT

LIBYA: AGRICULTURE AND ECONOMIC DEVELOPMENT

Edited by
J. A. ALLAN, K. S. McLACHLAN AND
EDITH T. PENROSE

LONDON AND NEW YORK

First published in 1973

This edition first published in 2015
by Routledge
2 Park Square, Milton Park, Abingdon, Oxon, OX14 4RN

and by Routledge
711 Third Avenue, New York, NY 10017

Routledge is an imprint of the Taylor & Francis Group, an informa business

© 1973 J. A. Allan and K. S. McLachlan

All rights reserved. No part of this book may be reprinted or reproduced or utilised in any form or by any electronic, mechanical, or other means, now known or hereafter invented, including photocopying and recording, or in any information storage or retrieval system, without permission in writing from the publishers.

Trademark notice: Product or corporate names may be trademarks or registered trademarks, and are used only for identification and explanation without intent to infringe.

British Library Cataloguing in Publication Data
A catalogue record for this book is available from the British Library

ISBN: 978-1-138-78710-0 (Set)
eISBN: 978-1-315-74408-7 (Set)
ISBN: 978-1-138-81180-5 (Volume 18)
eISBN: 978-1-315-74495-7 (Volume 18)
Pb ISBN: 978-1-138-82021-0 (Volume 18)

Publisher's Note
The publisher has gone to great lengths to ensure the quality of this reprint but points out that some imperfections in the original copies may be apparent.

Disclaimer
The publisher has made every effort to trace copyright holders and would welcome correspondence from those they have been unable to trace.

LIBYA:
AGRICULTURE AND ECONOMIC DEVELOPMENT

EDITED BY

J. A. ALLAN

K. S. McLACHLAN

EDITH T. PENROSE

RESEARCH DIRECTED BY

K. S. McLACHLAN

M. M. BURU

FRANK CASS : LONDON

First published 1973 in Great Britain by
FRANK CASS AND COMPANY LIMITED
67 Great Russell Street, London WC1B 3BT, England

and in United States of America by
FRANK CASS AND COMPANY LIMITED
c/o International Scholarly Book Services, Inc.
P.O. Box 4347, Portland, Oregon 97208

Originally published with the assistance of
The University of Libya
The School of Oriental and African Studies
in the University of London
The British Petroleum Company Limited

© J. A. ALLAN and K. S. McLACHLAN

ISBN 0 7146 2946 4

All Rights Reserved. No part of this publication may be reproduced in any form or by any means, electronic, mechanical, photo-copying, recording or otherwise, without the prior permission of Frank Cass and Company Limited in writing.

Printed in Great Britain
by W & J Mackay Limited, Chatham

PREFACE

The discovery of oil in Libya and the subsequent rapid exploitation of reserves is the most important economic and social factor to affect Libya since the Italian colonial occupation of the country after 1911. National and per capita income have been rising rapidly since 1962 and the impact of this new wealth has been felt very much in the agricultural areas of the country. This volume sets out the results of three years of research (1966-1969) by the Libyan-London Universities Joint Research Project into changes in land use and crop management, investment and migration, and labour and wages in the agricultural sector in Libya, which have taken place since the early 1960s. Where data are available, the volume attempts to put recent changes within the context of agricultural development since the turn of the century and specific comparisons are introduced to determine changes, among other items, in land use and wages during the period 1955 to 1968.

Only a limited amount of statistical data has been included here for reasons of economy, though all the material used by contributors in preparing this volume can be consulted at the School of Oriental and African Studies, University of London, or at the University of Libya, Benghazi.

The project was formally set up in October 1966 and was run for three years under the joint auspices of the University of Libya and the School of Oriental and African Studies, University of London. A managing body was established in the form of a joint liaison committee, the members of which were Professor M. Hassan, Dr. M.M. Buru and Dr. H. Balugma for the University of Libya and Professor E.T. Penrose, Dr. K.S. McLachlan and Mr. J.A. Allan for the School of Oriental and African Studies. Over-all academic guidance was given by Professor Penrose, while Dr. McLachlan was the technical director of the project and Dr. Buru acted as chief Libyan liaison director. Mr. Allan worked as full-time research officer based in Libya with special responsibility for local project administration.

The project was originally devised by Dr. Buru and Dr. McLachlan who, jointly with Mr. Allan, designed and implemented the fieldwork programmes of 1967 and 1968. Field enumeration was completed by students of the Department of Geography, University of Libya, and no less than 75 students and demonstrators took part in the survey, which encompassed work on four separate occasions. Statistical data gathered by the 1967 surveys were processed under the supervision of Dr. B.K. Dasgupta of the School of Oriental and African Studies, while Mr. K.E. Rosing of King's College, London, supervised the processing of data for the 1968 survey programme and was also responsible for the production of the computer maps. Mr. R.E. Mabro, now at the University of Oxford, was co-opted as a member of the joint liaison committee in early 1968 and, with other contributions to the project, designed the questionnaires used in the 1968 fieldwork programme. Mr. M. Lamlum was co-opted on to the joint liaison committee in late 1968 to act as the Libyan University's representative in London.

Opinions expressed in this volume are those of the authors concerned and do not represent the views of either the University of Libya or the School of Oriental and African Studies, University of London.

ACKNOWLEDGEMENTS

We are under a great obligation to and wish to thank warmly a large number of individuals and organisations who generously assisted the project and thereby made its successful conclusion possible: particularly those who provided finance; those who gave help in preparing and conducting fieldwork in Libya; those who advised on or contributed to the processing of the data; and, finally, those who helped to make this publication possible.

The Project is extremely grateful to the University of Libya and the School of Oriental and African Studies who jointly financed research work with assistance from the British Petroleum Company Ltd.

In Libya generous facilities were made available to the London staff in respect of accommodation and transport in Tripoli, Benghazi and Gharyan. For these we are grateful to the former Minister of Education, Mr. Mustafah Baiou, Mr. A. Daghman, former Rector of the University of Libya and Mr. Sadawiyah, the Vice-Rector. Other individuals also gave help and we should like to thank Mr. A. Abaidi, Mr. S.Y. Mansuri, Mr. A. Massoudi and Mr. A. al Tayyar. The staff of the Science and Engineering Faculties in Tripoli deserve our thanks for accommodation, and for transport in particular we are indebted to Dr. K. Sgaier and Mr. I. Shaban. Members of the Geography Department in the University of Libya were essential in supervising three of the periods of fieldwork, namely, Dr. H. Balugma, Dr. G. Dannassuri and Dr. A. Shahin, while Professor M. Hassan, head of department, co-operated closely with project administration. Much useful background information concerning geology and hydrology was provided by Dr. C. Grey and Dr. A. Cate of the Department of Geology, Tripoli.

The Libyan students from the Department of Geography in Benghazi carried out the land use and crop surveys as well as the questionnaire surveys. Their hard work, intelligence and integrity in asking questions and making records have brought high levels of accuracy and consistency to the maps and field data. Meanwhile, the project acknowledges its debt to the university drivers, Jumah, Musah, Salem, Sa'ed, Mohammed and Haj for their patience and good humour.

Many senior members of the administration of the School of Oriental and African Studies have given help and we are very grateful for the considerable work which they have done on our behalf. We owe thanks to Mr. J.R. Bracken, Secretary of the School and his staff for their support to Lt. Col.T.W. Baynes and Mr. J.A. Boxhall for help in arranging printing; to Mr. M. Gatehouse in planning travel for project members; to Miss S.E.H. Smith and her assistants Mrs. M. Delabye, Mr. A.K. Dey and Miss M.M. Hughes in arranging our accounts; and to Mrs. B.Z. Phillips for advising on purchases.

We should also like to record our appreciation of the help given to the project by Professor C.A. Fisher and the late Dr. J.H.G. Lebon.

The project would also like to express its gratitude to the Director of the School of Oriental and African Studies for his sympathetic support.

The British Petroleum Company Limited guaranteed generous financial support for research work and also gave additional assistance to tide the project over the problems created by the devaluation of sterling in 1967. Special thanks are offered to Mr. A.J. Willcocks who gave invaluable assistance on many occasions, particularly in production of Volume 4 of this report. At the same time, British Exploration (Libya) Limited did much to aid administration of the project in Libya and it is a pleasant duty to thank Mr. H.E. Norton, Mr. K.J. Bradley and Mrs. O. Ballard in Benghazi and Mr. R. Holmes, Mr. L.J. Hobson and Miss J. Davis in Tripoli.

In addition to the bodies noted above, considerable assistance was given to the project by other institutions and individuals. Particular indebtedness is acknowledged to Professor W.B. Fisher, Professor H. Bowen-Jones and Professor J.I. Clarke of the University of Durham, whose earlier work in the area was a source of the project's inspiration. During the initial period of project formulation practical aid and encouragement was forthcoming from both Dr. J.A.N. Brehony, who also made available written sources on Libya, and Mr. S. Cody. Mr. A. en Na'as, of the Ministry of National Economy, Mr. A. Sassi, former Minister of Housing and State Property, Mr. H. Jowheri, former director of the National Agricultural Settlement Authority, Mr. I. Ghiblawy, Director of the Institute of Planning and Development, and Mr. N. Rahumah, officer in charge of N.A.S.A. in Eastern Libya, were all long-standing friends and supporters of the project's work in Libya and the considerable debt to them is acknowledged with gratitude. Other help given during preparation and implementation of fieldwork in Libya came from Mr. A. Misurati, Mr. S. Atkinson, Mr. P. and Mrs. A. Noble in the Ministry of Housing; Mr. M. Gilban and Mr. A. Gaarta at the Ministry of Municipalities; and Mr. A. Amish, Mr. S. Ghanem and Dr. S. Sarafy (consultant) at the Ministry of National Economy.

At the Ministry of Planning, particular mention must be made of the assistance given by Dr. A. Attiga, the former minister and a contributor to this volume and to other members of his staff including Mr. A. Balu, Mr. M. Tarabullisi and Mr. Sultan, the latter at the Benghazi office. Mr. S. Zenati, librarian of the Bank of Libya, is to be thanked for his co-operation in use of the library by project staff. An especial mention should be made of the contribution of Mr. A. Sassi of the Ministry of Communications who ensured smooth relations for the project with the Libyan civil administration in Tripoli and who assisted in the maintenance of contacts between project officers in Tripoli and Benghazi.

Important field supervision was provided by Mr. R.G. Ferguson and Mr. J.M. Roberts, the latter acting as the project's field manager in Gharyan. Mr. Ferguson also contributed to the preparation of field maps and to the text.

Work in the field was made more efficient through the help of local administrators, police officials and directors of education in the many mutassarifiyahs which we visited, especially at al Khums, Misuratah, Sabhah, Hun and Brak. Local headmasters were also most helpful, especially Mr. M. Qatus at al Khums and Mr. A. Tamer at Hun, and the headmaster of the Misuratah secondary school.

We must thank Mobil (Libya) for printing one of our questionnaires and for copying services, facilities made available by Mr. R. Williams and Mr. R. Lesseued.

Thanks are due to the British Council in Tripoli for their co-operation and particularly to Mr. W.H. Covington, the representative, Mr. C.K. Smith, Mr. R. Budd and Mr. E. Pugh and, in Benghazi to Mr. B. Potter. At the

British Embassy, Mr. C. Smelley and Mr. A. MacDonald were notable for their assistance in assembling map series for use in the project's fieldwork programme and this debt is acknowledged with thanks.

Full acknowledgement is given here of the help given by a number of air survey companies in providing air photos and advice. Individuals are too numerous to mention; however, the companies which they represented were as follows: Aero Service Corporation (U.S.A.), Aero Exploration (Frankfurt, West Germany), E.I.R.A. (Florence, Italy), Fairey Surveys Limited (Maidenhead, England) and Hunting Surveys Limited (Boreham Wood, England). We are grateful for permission to use the air photo illustrations and for the photograph on the cover. Other advice and assistance was obtained from the Royal Air Force of the United Kingdom, the Directorate of Military Survey of the British Army and the staffs of the map library of the Instituto Agronomico d'Oltremare (Italy).

Translation of questionnaires and other documents was completed for the project by Mr. A. Tawil and typing by Miss F. Tawil, while very important assistance in translation and printing of questionnaires was given by Mr. G. Araibi.

Other individuals were generous with time and advice and our data were greatly supplemented through discussions with Mr. A. Gargour and with his managers Sgr. L. Trigila and Sgr. D. Paulini. We are indebted to numerous farmers throughout Libya, too many to mention by name, but who gave generous help during the period of the field research programme and who are warmly thanked for their co-operation.

University of London computers were used to run our programmes and we are grateful to the staff of the University of London Atlas Computer Centre and to Dr. P. Samit and Mr. D. Sturt and their staff responsible for the University College, London IBM 360 computer. The contributions of Mr. P. Cox, Mr. A. Driver and Mr. R. Hope were important in completing data collation and processing. Mr. M. Lamlum gave essential advice in connection with place-names and was responsible for the art-work for the Arabic names, titles and notes on maps.

Cartography was carried out by David L. Fryer, Henley on Thames, England. Printing of the colour maps was completed by the Dringport Press, Portsmouth, England. Typing of this volume was completed with patience and accuracy by Mrs. K. Jones, and proof-reading undertaken by Mr. F.J. Burch.

CONTENTS

	PAGE
Preface	v
Acknowledgements	vi
Contents and List of Figures and Tables	ix
Abbreviations	xix
Glossary of Arabic words	xxi
Administrative Boundaries and Place Names	xxii

CHAPTER 1. INTRODUCTION

1.1 The Economic Setting	1
1.2 The Economic Impact of Oil on Libyan Agriculture	9

CHAPTER 2. PHYSICAL RESOURCES RELEVANT TO AGRICULTURE

Introduction	19
2.1 Geology and Surface Form	20
2.1 Climate and Weather	26
2.2.1 Rainfall	28
2.2.2 Temperature	28
2.2.3 Humidity	30
2.2.4 Climatic Regions	30
2.2.5 Seasonal Characteristics	33
2.2.6 Climate and Water Resources	34
2.3 Water Resources	34
2.3.1 Surface Water	35
2.3.2 Underground Water	36
2.3.3 Artesian Aquifers	38
2.3.4 Quantity of Underground Water	39
2.3.5 Decline in Ground-Water Levels	40
2.3.6 Water Conservation	42

CHAPTER 3. AGRICULTURAL LAND USE AND CROP PATTERNS 1911-1960

3.1 Agricultural Land Use	45
3.1.1 The Italian Colonial Period, 1911-1942	48
3.1.2 The Post-Colonial Period, 1942-1951	51
3.1.3 Period of Independence Before Oil, 1951-1960	52
3.2 Crop Patterns by Farm Type, 1912-1960	54
3.2.1 Traditional Gardens	54
Cereals	54
Tree crops	56
Vegetables	57
3.2.2 The Modern Sector	57
3.2.3 Grazing and Livestock	60

		PAGE
CHAPTER 4.	LAND USE AND CROPPING PATTERNS: PRESENT POSITION AND RECENT CHANGES	
	4.1 General statement regarding the survey and air photo coverage	67
	4.2 Agricultural Land Use in Libya Against a Background of Rising Oil Revenues 1961-1968	70
	4.3 Western Libya	
	4.3.1 Geographical Distribution of Land Use	73
	4.3.2 Size of Farms	74
	4.3.3 Extent of Cultivation of Farms	78
	4.3.4 Irrigation	82
	4.3.5 Orchards	85
	4.3.6 Cereals and vegetables	89
	4.3.7 Detailed Analysis of Six Selected Areas	
	1. Talbighah (including changes in housing	97
	2. West of Ajaylat	101
	3. Suwani bin Yadim	104
	4. Gefara	104
	5. Jabal Nafusah	108
	6. Wadi Ki'am	110
	4.4 Eastern Libya	
	4.4.1 Geographical Distribution of Land Use	116
	4.4.2 Extent of Cultivation of Farms	117
	4.4.3 Detailed Analysis of Three Selected Areas	
	7. Al Marj	120
	8. Farzugah	122
	9. Al Qubbah	124
	4.5 Southern Libya	
	4.5.1 General Introduction	124
	4.5.2 Extent of Cultivation of Farms	124
	4.5.3 Detailed Analysis of One Selected Area	
	10. Sabhah	126
	4.6 Notes on the Air Photos and the Diagrams derived from them	
CHAPTER 5.	INVESTMENT IN LIBYAN AGRICULTURE	
	5.1 Introduction - some comments on the survey	130
	5.2 Investment and the Size of Farm	131
	5.3 Investment and the Type of Farm	134
	5.4 Regional Pattern of Investment	135
	5.5 Summary and Conclusions	136
	Tables showing details of investment in Western Libya	138

		PAGE
CHAPTER 6.	EMPLOYMENT AND WAGE RATES	
	6.1 Introduction	157
	6.2 Quantitative Supplies of Labour	
	6.2.1 Total Population	158
	6.2.2 Participation in Labour Force	158
	6.2.3 Utilisation of the Labour Force	
	(Employment/Unemployment)	159
	6.3 Wage Rates	160
	6.4 Qualitative Aspects of the Labour Force	165
	6.5 Conclusion	166
APPENDIX 1.	THE CROP SURVEY - LIBYA	
	1.1 Introduction	173
	1.2 Criteria considered in selecting case study areas	176
	1.3 Comments and results	176
APPENDIX 2.	THE GENERAL AGRICULTURAL LAND USE MAP OF NORTHERN LIBYA	
	2.1 Definitions and sources	182
	2.2 The maps and the patterns of land use	182
APPENDIX 3.	COMPUTER MAPS - WESTERN LIBYA	
	3.1 Introduction	186
	3.2 The data	186
	3.3 An explanation of SYMAP	186
	3.4 Comments and results	188
APPENDIX 4.	AN INTERPRETATION OF THE VARIABLES PRESENTED IN SYMAP FORM	
	4.1 The method treatment	188
	4.2 The SYMAPS in relation to the farm classification	189
	4.2.1 The distribution of irrigated and non-irrigated farming	189
	4.2.2 The distribution of traditional and modern farming	189
	4.3 Some general trends in agriculture in Western Libya as indicated by the SYMAPS	192
	4.4 Conclusions	194
APPENDIX 5.	FIGURES IN APPENDICES	
APPENDIX 6.	TABLES IN APPENDICES	

	PAGE
APPENDIX 9. COMPUTER MAP SERIES	195
INDEX	208

LIST OF FIGURES

	PAGE
Libya - Administrative Areas	xxiii
Selected Important Determinants of the Money Supply Libya 1960-1968	5
Indices of Money Supply and Prices Libya 1960-1968	6
Libya - Topographic Map	21
Libya - Simplified Geology	22
Libya - Physiographic Units	25
Libya - Rainfall	27
Rainfall & Relative Humidity at Selected Stations	29
Temperatures at Selected Stations	31
Libya - Water Resources	37
Water Levels in Wells in Western Libya	41
Western & Eastern Libya - Lands scheduled for Agricultural Development by the Italian Administration, State Agencies, Companies and Private Individuals	49
Libya - Field Areas - July-August 1967 & February 1968	66
Libya - Changes in Agriculture	71
Libya - Western Provinces, Sample Points 1968	75
Al Khums (Sahal/Valdagno) 1953	77
South of Sabratah - Air Photo 1953	86
South of Sabratah - Air Photo 1966	87
Talbighah - Changes in Farming	96
Talbighah - Air Photos 1953 & 1968	98
Talbighah - Changes in Rural Housing	100
West of Ajaylat - Changes in Farming	102
West of Ajaylat - Air Photos 1953 & 1966	103

	PAGE
Suwani bin Yadim - Changes in Farming	105
Suwani bin Yadim - Air Photos 1953 & 1968	106
Gefara Plain - Changes in Farming	107
Tighrinnah - Changes in Farming	109
Tighrinnah - Air Photos 1953 & 1969	111
Wadi Ki'am - Changes in Farming	113
Wadi Ki'am - Air Photo 1953	115
Al Marj and Farzugah - Air Photos 1957	119
Al Marj Plain - Changes in Farming	121
Farzugah - Changes in Farming	123
Al Qubbah & Sabhah - Changes in Farming	125
Al Qubbah 1949 & Sabhah 1958 - Air Photos	128

LIST OF TABLES

		PAGE
1.1	Gross National Product 1967	2
1.2	Value of Exports 1968	2
1.3	Sectoral Distribution of the Labour Force 1964	2
1.4	Balance of Payments 1963 and 1967	3
1.5	Expenditures Planned in the Development Budgets for Selected Items	7
3.1	Estimates of Areas of Land Use 1933-1960	46
3.2	Population by Status 1917	48
3.3	Numbers of Animals 1926, 1933 & 1946	52
3.4	Land Use 1960	53
3.5	Arab Wheat and Barley Production in Western Libya 1931-36	55
3.6	Estimates of Barley and Wheat Acreage and Output Eastern Libya 1945-1965	56
3.7	Distribution of Traditional Fruit Orchards - Jabal Nafusah 1960 and Showing the Percentage of Traditional as Opposed to Other Plantings 1960	59
3.8	Italian Plantations of Olive, Almond & Vine 1937	59
3.9	Livestock in Libya 1925-1965	62
3.10	Livestock Products in Libya 1959	63
4.1	The Extent to which Libyan Farming Types have been Covered by the Detailed Examination of Air Photographs for Selected Areas	68
4.2	Western Libya - a Comparison of the Proportions of the Farming Types Defined by the 1968 Systematic Sample with those of the Areas Selected for Detailed Examination, Using Air Photos	70
4.3	Areas of Particular and Mixed Land Use by Farm Type Shown on the Libya Land Use Map (Map 8, Appendix 8)	72
4.4	Size of Farm by Farm Type - Western Libya 1967/68	76
4.5	Area of Farm Cultivated 1967/68 - Western Libya (including orchards)	78

		PAGE
4.6	Area of Farm Cultivated by Farm Type - Western Libya 1967/68	79
4.7	Proportions of a) Uncultivated Land b) Total Fallow plus Grazing c) Total Cultivated Land and d) Cultivated Land as % of Cultivable	80
4.8	Irrigated Area of Farms by Region - Western Libya 1967/68	83
4.9	Irrigation of Farms - Western Libya 1967/68	83
4.10	Irrigated Area Of Farm by Farm Type - Western Libya 1967/68	84
4.11	Trees in Areas of Settled Agriculture - Western Libya 1967/68	85
4.12	Number of Trees by Region - Western Libya 1967/68	88
4.13	Number of Trees on the Farm by Farm Type - Western Libya 1967/68	89
4.14	Per Cent of the Farm Under Cereals on Settled Farms - Western Libya 1967/68	90
4.15	Area Under Cereals by Region - Western Libya 1967/68	90
4.16	Area Under Cereals by Farm Type - Western Libya 1967/68	91
4.17	Vegetable Cultivation on Settled Farms - Western Libya 1967/68	92
4.18	Area Under Vegetables by Region - Western Libya 1967/68	92
4.19	Area Under Vegetables by Farm Type - Western Libya 1967/68	93
4.20	Analysis of Farming Types and the Extent of Cultivation 1949/1953/1957/ to 1966/68	94
4.21	Changes in the Number and Size of Buildings in an Area ($\frac{1}{2}$ km^2) Ten Kilometres to the East of Tripoli 1953-1968	101
4.22	Rainfall at Gharyan 1952/3 & 1967/8	108
4.23	Rainfall - Sahal al Ahmad in Agricultural Years 1952/53 and 1964/65	114
5.1	Frequency Distribution of Farms According to Size, Type of Farming and Region - Western Libya 1968	138

		PAGE
5.2	Expenditures per Farm According to Size and Items of Expenditure for the Entire Sample - Western Libya 1968	139
5.3	Expenditure per Hectare of Cultivated Land According to Size and Items of Expenditure for the Entire Sample - Western Libya 1967/68	140
5.4	Investment per Farm According to Size and Type of Farming for the Entire Sample - Western Libya 1967/68	141
5.5	Investment per Hectare of Cultivated Land According to Size and Type of Farming for the Entire Sample - Western Libya 1967/68	142
5.6	Expenditure per Farm According to Size and Items of Expenditure for TRADITIONAL IRRIGATED FARMS - Western Libya 1967/68	143
5.7	Expenditure per Farm According to Size and Items of Expenditure for MODERN IRRIGATED & SEMI-IRRIGATED FARMS - Western Libya 1967/68	144
5.8	Expenditure per Farm According to Size and Items of Expenditure for TRADITIONAL NON-IRRIGATED FARMS - Western Libya 1967/68	145
5.9	Expenditure per Farm According to Size and Items of Expenditure for MODERN NON-IRRIGATED FARMS - Western Libya 1967/68	146
5.10	Expenditure per Farm According to Type of Farming for the Entire Sample - Western Libya 1967/68	147
5.11	Expenditure per Farm According to Size and Items of Expenditure for JABAL GHARBI - Western Libya 1967/68	148
5.12	Expenditure per Farm According to Size and Items of Expenditure for ZAWIYAH - Western Libya 1967/68	149
5.13	Expenditure per Farm According to Size and Items of Expenditure for TRIPOLI - Western Libya 1967/68	150
5.14	Expenditure per Farm According to Size and Items of Expenditure for al KHUMS - Western Libya 1967/68	151
5.15	Expenditure per Farm According to Size and Items of Expenditure for MISURATAH - Western Libya 1967/68	152
5.16	Investment per Farm and per Hectare by Muhafadahs and by Farm Size - Western Libya 1967/68	153
5.17	Percentage Share of Various Size Categories in Cultivated Land and Investment - Western Libya 1967/68	154

		PAGE
5.18	Percentage Share of Various Farm Types in Cultivated Area and Investment - Western Libya 1967/68	155
5.19	Percentage Share of Various Muhafadahs in Cultivated Land and Investment - Western Libya 1967/68	156
6.1	Characteristics of the Wage Distribution in Agriculture - 1968	161
6.2	Average Wages in the Main Sectors - 1968	162
6.3	Statistics of the Wage Distribution in the Oil Industry	163

ABBREVIATIONS

c	'about' with reference to dates
°C	Degrees Centigrade
Co.	Company
constr.	construction
ENTE	Ente per la Colonizzazione della Libia
EWM	Employment, Wages and Migration Questionnaire 1968
E.P. or E. Prov.	Eastern Muhafadat
GDP	Gross Domestic Product
GNP	Gross National Product
ha.	hectare (100 metres by 100 metres)
HP	horse power
I.N.P.S.	Istituto Nazionale della Previdenza Sociale
Kg	kilogram/s
Km^2	square kilometre/s
L.A.J.S.	Libyan American Joint Services
L.P.D.S.A.	Libyan Public Development and Stabilization Agency
£	pound sterling
£L	pound Libyan
m	metre/s
m^2	square metres
mm	millimetre/s
mn	million/s
NASA	National Agricultural Settlement Authority

ABBREVIATIONS (continued)

No. .... number

Obs'n's ...... observations

Pt. .... part

Q. .... question

S.P. or ...... Southern Provinces or Southern
S.Prov. ...... Muhafadat, formerly Fezzan

Trad. .... traditional

W.P. or   Western Provinces or
W.Prov. ...... Western Muhafadat.

GLOSSARY OF ARABIC WORDS

'dalu' traditional well

'ginan' a small inundation garden in Western Libya

'mudiriyah' subdivision of a 'mutassarifiyah'

'muhafadah' ('muqataah') one of ten major administrative subdivisions of Libya

'muhafadat' plural of 'muhafadah'

'mutassarifiyah' subdivision of a 'muhafadah'

'suani' traditional irrigated garden, generally under two hectares in size

Administrative Boundaries.

The map opposite shows the administrative boundaries of Libya in 1968. Libya is divided into ten muhafadat (provinces) and these have been grouped and referred to as 'The Provinces of Eastern Libya', 'The Provinces of Western Libya' and 'The Provinces of Southern Libya'. These names appear on the map opposite and in the text in the abbreviated forms, 'Eastern Libya', 'Western Libya', and 'Southern Libya'. It should be noted that on some maps the main divisions of the country have been shown as 'Eastern Province', 'Western Province' and 'Southern Province'. These three groupings of the muhafadat can be taken to refer to the same areas as Cyrenaica, Tripolitania and Fezzan, names used more generally before 1951. Boundary changes introduced since mid-1969 have not been incorporated in the map of administrative areas following.

Note on Place Names

Place names used in this report are standardised following the method of the U.S. Board of Geographic Names, Department of the Interior, Washington D.C., Gazetteer No. 41 June 1958, where their locations are also defined. The most useful map series for reference to place names mentioned in the text is the Libya 1:50,000 P761, U.S. Army, 1962, while the North Africa 1:250,000 AMS P502, U.S. Army, 1954 series offers a more convenient but less comprehensive guide.

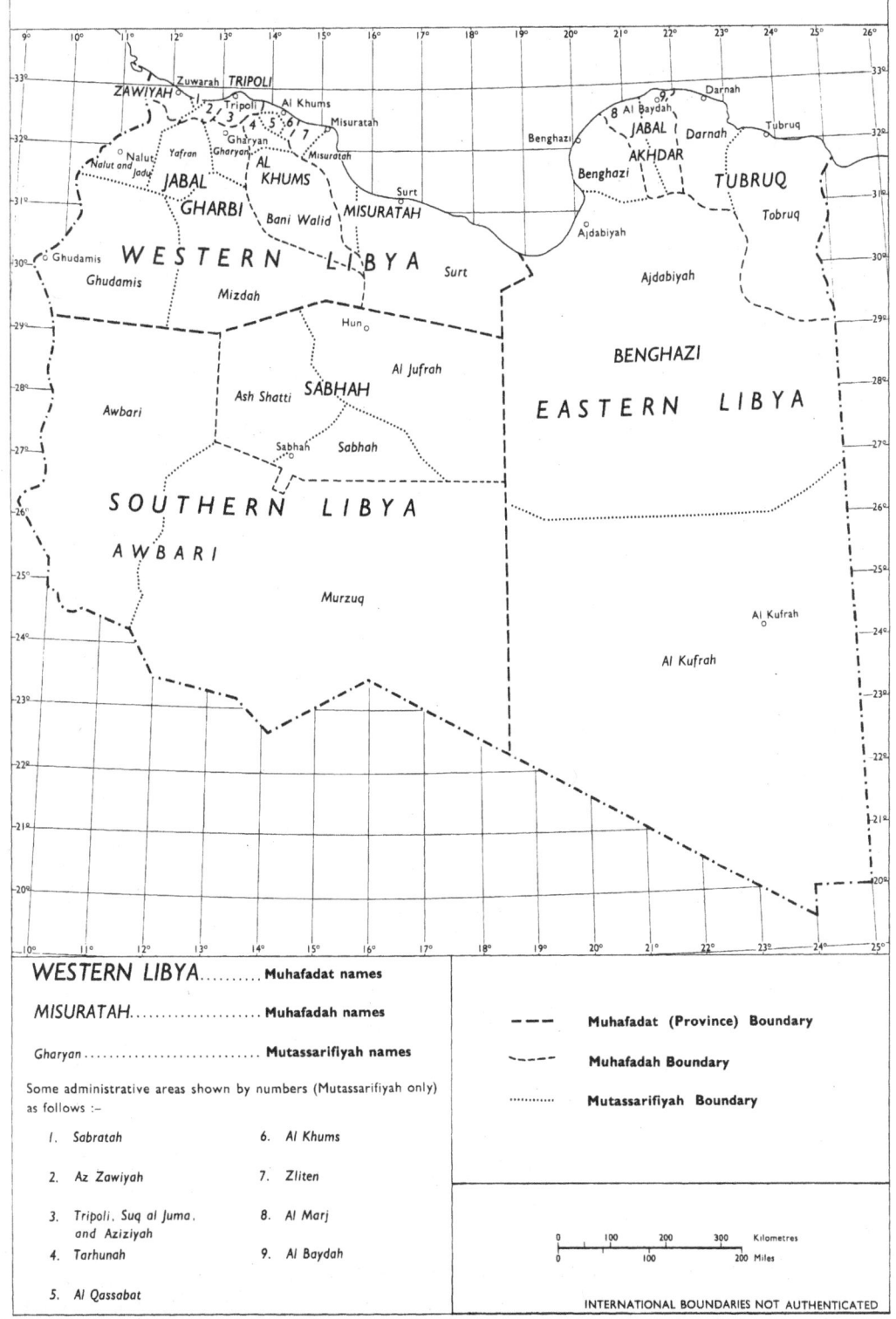

Chapter One

INTRODUCTION

1.1 The Economic Setting

This volume, covering the work of the Libyan University/London University project, has two purposes. The first is to present briefly the economic, physical, and historical background which has shaped the Libyan countryside, and thus created the context against which the present position must be interpreted. The second is to report and analyse the results of the surveys of land use in Libya and of certain economic conditions closely associated with land use, which were conducted in the two years 1967 and 1968 under the auspices of the two Universities. Chapter 1 through 3 present the background, and Chapter 4 through 6 analyse the results of the surveys. In this introductory chapter we shall very briefly outline the broad economic setting.

At the time of its independence in 1951, Libya was considered to be one of the poorest countries of the world, with few known natural resources, a difficult natural environment, and a population which was small, poor, illiterate and backward in almost every respect. The people had endured considerable hardship under Ottoman and Italian rule. Education had been almost completely neglected and what economic development had been encouraged had been largely for the benefit of the foreign colonizers. To be sure, the Italians had left a number of good farms in the Western Provinces and a small infrastructure, much of which, however, was destroyed in the Second World War. No effort had been made to unite the various parts of the country, which were separated by difficult country and hundreds of kilometres of desert. On independence, therefore, the economy was in poor shape and depended on outside aid. The resources of the country simply were not adequate to support the very large investments needed to construct the transport and communication links required to unify the country geographically, or to create the educational and health facilities required to develop the native abilities of the people, or to build the foundations for a productive and growing agriculture and industry.

This bleak picture was dramatically changed with the discovery and development of the country's oil resources. Before World War II the existence of oil in the country was suspected, but the Italians lacked both resources and time to carry out successful exploration. Independent Libya turned its attention to the problem in the early 1950s, and late in 1953 reconnaissance permits were issued. Activity effectively got under way in 1955 after the first Petroleum Law was signed in June and the first concessions granted in November. Four years later oil had been discovered, and by 1961 exports had begun. In 1962 the Libyan Government received over £L 14mn in oil revenues.

From then on there was no looking back. Production rose from less than a million tons in 1961 to over 125 million in 1969 and revenues exceeded £L 270mn. Libya became the third largest producing country in the Middle East, the sixth in the world. Per capita income increased ten or twelve times, roads and airlines spread across the country linking it together, schools and school enrolment increased very rapidly, and the main centres of the country became hives of bustling activity. The economic and social changes were due to oil, since oil contributed over 60% of the national income and nearly 100% of the value of exports, as shown in the following tables. But the industry employs less than 4% of the country's labour force.

Table 1.1

Gross National Product. 1967

	£Lmn.	%
Agriculture	18.5	3.1
Petroleum	356.8	60.1
Industry	15.3	2.6
Construction	38.6	6.5
Transport	23.3	3.9
Services	141.5	23.8
	594.0	100.0

Source: Ministry of Planning

Table 1.2

Value of Exports. 1968

	£Lmn.
Oil	666.43
Non-oil	2.59
	669.02

Source: I.M.F., International Financial Statistics

Table 1.3

Sectoral Distribution of the Labour Force. 1964

		%
Agriculture	144,853	35.74
Petroleum	14,259	3.52
Industry	29,377	7.25
Construction	31,434	7.75
Transport	22,748	5.6
Services and unclassified	162,587	40.14
Total	405,258	100.00

Source: Population Census, 1964

The sectoral distribution of income shown in Table 1.1 not only brings out the importance of oil but also indicates the weight of the services sector which is itself sustained by oil revenues. The other productive sectors account for a mere 16% of the GNP with about a third of this attributable to agriculture and industry. This type of distribution of the national income is not unexpected in an oil economy. Construction and transport are, of course, necessary to develop infrastructure for industry and also, especially for a country like Libya with its very great distances, to establish the necessary communications. The oil companies, too, have had to invest heavily in roads, pipelines, terminals and other facilities required for the production and transport of oil. Construction also produces a large demand for building materials; for example, the index of cement consumption rose from 100 in 1958 to 1100 in 1968. The c.i.f. value of imports rose from less than £L 75mn in 1962 to over £L 170mn in 1967 and £L 230mn in 1968. As would be expected, the composition of imports also changed, with a fall in the proportion of total imports accounted for by food and a rise in the proportion of manufactured products.

The nature of the change in the structure of the Libyan balance of payments can be seen in the following table showing the position in 1963 and 1967, in particular the large and growing surplus on trade account.

Table 1.4

Balance of Payments

1963 and 1967

£Lmn.

	1963 Credits	1963 Debits	1967 Credits	1967 Debits
Goods and Services				
Trade balance (c.i.f.)	34.0		248.2	
Investment income		.8		97.6
Central government (n.i.e.)	.5		?	7.8
Transfers				
Private		5.6		14.6
Central government	10.4			27.6
Current Account	44.9	44.3	248.2	227.2
Capital (n.i.e.)	6.7		4.3	
Banks and monetary authorities (net)		9.5		14.3
Errors and Omissions (net)	2.2			11.0
	53.8	53.8	252.5	252.5

Source: I.M.F. *International Financial Statistics*, July, 1969

The increasing surplus in the balance of payments, which is indicated by the rising net debit of the banks and monetary authorities, has been reflected in the rapid increase in the gold and foreign exchange assets of the Bank of Libya, which rose from US$92.7mn in 1962 to $118.2mn in 1963 and $543.0mn in 1968. The increased revenues of the country are reflected in the money supply, which rose nearly six times between 1962 and 1968. The figure opposite shows the changes between 1960 and 1968 in the assets and liabilities of the Libyan monetary system which together determine the net changes in the money supply.* It can be seen that the assets acquired by the monetary system rose very steeply indeed, but that increase in claims on the private sector (primarily credit extended by commercial banks) went up almost as fast as foreign assets. The effect of the acquisition of these two types of assets on the money supply was partly offset by the rise in "quasi-money" (almost half of which were time and savings deposits in commercial banks), and the rise in government deposits in the Bank of Libya, which are not treated as part of the money supply. The rise in claims in the private sector indicates the strong part played by this sector in economic activity, while the increase in government deposits reflects budget surpluses due to the rapidly rising government revenues in relation to an inflationary effect on prices, and in the figure facing page 7 is shown the rise in the index of consumer prices and foodstuffs in relation to the money supply.**

---

* *Money, here defined as demand deposits and currency outside banks, is the chief liability of the monetary system together with savings and time deposits of various kinds (quasi-money), and government deposits. All of these are claims of the public or of the government on the monetary institutions. In creating these liabilities the monetary institutions acquire assets for which they pay out the currency or create the bank deposits. The assets may be foreign exchange or other claims on foreigners, or domestic government and private securities of all kinds, or other claims on the public. The figure opposite shows two kinds of assets: foreign assets and claims on the private sector, in the acquisition of which the liabilities have been created - money or quasi money and government deposits, as well as miscellaneous variety of other liabilities which are not shown. In 1968 the "monetary balance sheet" was as follows:*

	Assets	£Lmn	Liabilities
Foreign Assets (net)	190.06	Money	157.50
Claims on the Private Sector	73.46	Quasi-money	46.77
		Government Deposits	42.87
		Other items (net)	16.39

Source: As for Table 1.4

** *As noted above the money supply includes demand deposits as well as currency because the former are also used as means of payment. It excludes time and savings deposits on the assumption that these are "idle balances" and not held as means of payment. It is likely, however, that some part of the demand deposits are held for the same reasons as time and savings deposits and should be excluded from the money supply, especially when the relation between money and prices is considered. For this reason, many economists think that currency is a better measure of the holding of money for payments purposes. In Libya the ratio of currency to the total money supply did not change much between 1960 and 1968, although it fluctuated slightly. The figures are given below.*

Ratio of Currency to Money

Year	C/M	Year	C/M	Year	C/M	
1960	.47	1963	.53	1966	.51	
1961	.50	1964	.55	1967	.50	Source: as for figure opposite
1962	.53	1965	.50	1968	.45	

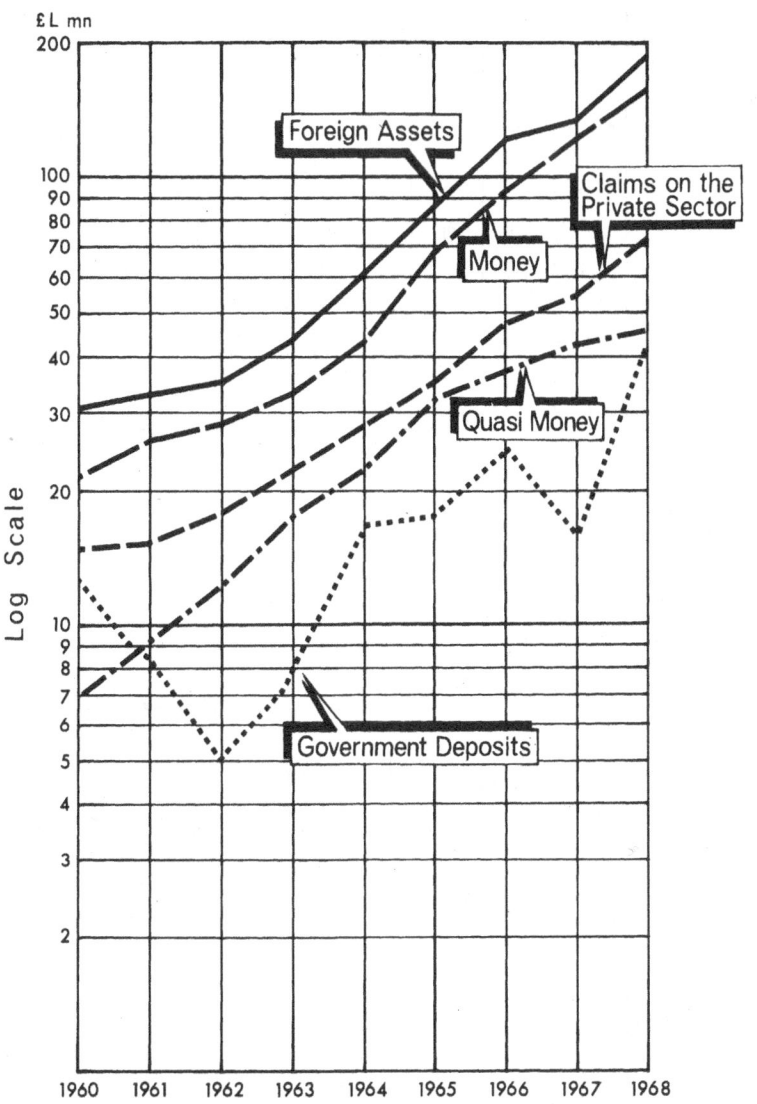

Figure 1 Source: International Financial Statistics, various years.

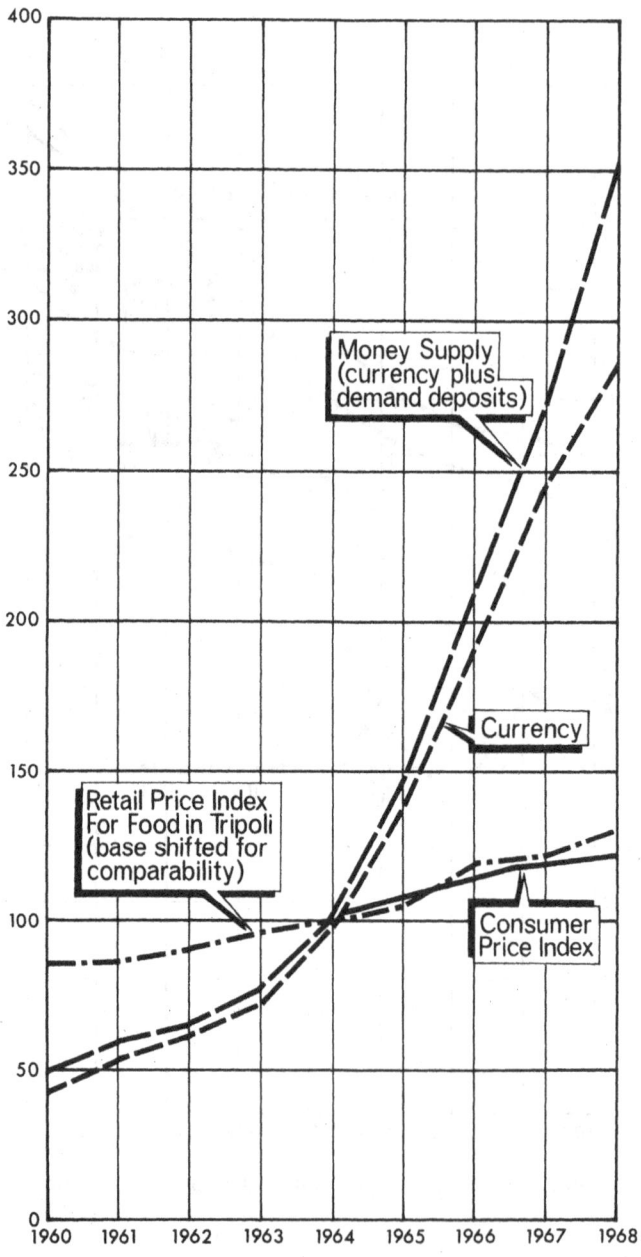

Figure 2   Source: International Financial Statistics

It can be seen that prices rose steadily, but not nearly so fast as the money supply. The effect of the increases in the supply of money on prices will depend very much on the supplies of goods coming on the market for people to spend their money on, and of these goods, imports supply a large proportion in Libya. Imports more than doubled between 1964 and 1968, but since the money supply more than tripled, there was bound to be some pressure on prices in the absence of a large increase in the domestic production of goods for the domestic market.

In an economy where the greater part of the national income comes from oil revenues which accrue directly to the government, a special burden and responsibility is imposed on the government which it cannot escape. Having received the revenues it must distribute them, and such things as education, housing, health, transport and communications, other public works and projects for economic development will have a high priority in a developing country. The rate and distribution of expenditure by the government will, therefore, have a decisive influence on the economy.

In Table 1.5 are presented selected items from the First Five-year Development Budget for the two years of the agricultural survey to which this report is devoted and for 1969/70, the first year of the Second Five-year Development Budget, as well as the budget for the whole five years of the Second Development Plan. Altogether the Second Five-Year Plan calls for an expenditure in the period 1969/70-1973/74 of £L 1,149,500 millions under all heads (including those not selected here). From these figures can be seen the great and growing attention that the government is paying to agriculture directly, and also to education, housing, transport and communications, much of which goes into the rural areas.

Table 1.5

Expenditures Planned in the Development Budgets for Selected Items

£Lmn

	First 5 Year Plan ('64-'69)		Second 5 Year Plan ('69-'74)	
	1st Year	Total	1st Year	Total
Agriculture	7,918	11,100	16,420	150,000
Education	9,800	13,850	14,600	116,250
Housing	19,000	12,000	24,900*	128,500*
Communications	19,506	23,750	22,650	162,544
Industry	5,300	7,700	7,860	90,556
Health	2,720	13,850	7,420	56,000

Including government property

Source: Government of Libya, Development Budgets.

Between 1967/68 and 1968/69 the rise in the total expenditures earmarked for agriculture represented an increase of from 7% to 9% of the total development budget, while in the period of the Second Five-Year Plan (1969/70 to 1973/74), it is planned to spend more than 13% of the total on agriculture, including animal resources.* In addition to this, of course, the favourable financial position allows farmers easier access to credit for improvement of their holdings, mechanisation, irrigation, etc. As will be seen, however, our survey indicates problems relating to water supplies and to the availability of labour. In spite of the efforts made, farmers will have incentives to move to the city. We discuss these problems in Chapters 4 and 5 especially.

It can be seen from Table 1.5 that significant, although smaller, sums are being devoted to industrial development. Commonly in the developing countries, the processing of agricultural products provides a basis for the growth of industry, especially food and textile industries which are among the earliest that tend to develop. In this respect, industry in Libya is handicapped by the relative weakness of the agricultural sector, and investment in agriculture, therefore, should strengthen the base for the growth of industry. But conditions differ markedly in the different parts of the country, and in the following pages we present a detailed discussion of land use and agricultural developments in the Western, Eastern and Southern Provinces in recent years, together with a brief description of the historical background.

---

* *See Part 1.2, Chapter 1, which follows.*

1.2 The Economic Impact of Oil on Libyan Agriculture

The discovery of oil and its rapid development and exploitation have had a profound impact on Libyan society in general and on the economy of the country in particular. Since the base of the economy, before oil, was agriculture, it was natural that the economic impact of oil would be felt most acutely in that sector. The purpose of this section is to describe, in general terms, how oil has affected the relative position of agriculture in the Libyan economy.

Before the discovery of oil the physical resources that were identified for development were agriculture, fishery and tourism, in this order of priority. At that time, nearly 80 per cent of the population lived in the rural and nomadic sectors of the economy and most of the labour force was engaged in these sectors. Apart from the few modern farms, which were largely owned and managed by Italians, the agriculture of the country was in the subsistence sector, except for cereals and livestock, of which there were significant marketable surpluses in some years. About 65% to 80% of per capita expenditure was on food.

Agricultural production was, and still is, largely determined by the amount of rainfall, which is very unpredictable. (See Chapter 2. Section 2.2.1) In an average year, such as 1950, barley production was 85,000 metric tons, wheat 8,000, dates 40,000 and olive oil about 8,000 tons. In the same year the total number of sheep was estimated at 767,000, goats 690,000, cattle 63,000, and camels 83,000. While there are no reliable figures on the annual livestock production in terms of meat, milk, wool, and hair, it can be safely assumed that per capita output was very low, due to poor breeding, feeding, and management conditions. (See Chapter 3, Section 3.2.3 for further details) The same is true for productivity of the labour force in agriculture. In fact, there was substantial seasonal unemployment and permanent underemployment in agriculture and nomadic activities.

Yet, in spite of such a poor state of development, agriculture was the backbone of the economy. It engaged about 70% of the active labour force and produced about 60% of the GDP. Except for scrap metal, remaining from the Second World War, exports consisted of agricultural products, including esparto grass. These facts pointed to the necessity of giving agricultural development top priority. But the implementation of such a strategy was handicapped by the extreme shortage of skills in agriculture and the scarcity of capital. Infrastructure was almost entirely lacking in the rural areas and was badly damaged during the war in urban areas. There was also lack of essential technical and economic data needed for the formulation of adequate agricultural development projects. It is true that during the Italian colonisation, considerable agricultural research and planning was undertaken, but it is equally true that Libyans had no place in that planning, except as an input factor. This basic fact, coupled with the destruction and dislocation of much of the Italian documents on Libya's agriculture during the war and the following eight years of British and French Administrations, made it necessary to undertake new studies of the agricultural potential of the country. (See Chapter 3)

It was against this background that various plans were formulated to develop the agricultural sector. But the shortage of funds and technical know-how as well as the lack of adequate government machinery to formulate and execute co-ordinated national agricultural plans made it extremely difficult to gain speed in that direction. However, a start was made and some progress was

achieved in introducing the essential elements of modern agriculture among
the rural people. At that time, people looked upon agriculture as the main,
and in most cases, the only means of livelihood. Yet, even with such positive
attitudes, it was extremely difficult to raise productivity in agriculture,
due to the various physical and human obstacles mentioned above. But when
oil was discovered, agriculture suddenly became a very unattractive and un-
profitable occupation.

The immediate economic impact of oil exploration was the injection of substantial funds in the urban sector of the country. Thus, money supply increased
from £L9.8 million at the end of 1955, when the first oil concessions were
given, to £L18.8 million at the end of 1959, when oil was discovered in commercial quantities. By the end of 1961, when oil was first exported, money
supply reached £L26.1 million and £L35.7 million two years later. Such a
rapid monetary expansion, concentrated in the main urban centres of the country
created a new economic situation. The first manifestation of this development
was a significant increase in the level of effective demand for goods and
services, which attracted the attention of the rural population. As agriculture was highly underdeveloped, it could no longer provide an acceptable
form of employment. Before the sudden oil prosperity, agriculture was acceptable as the only available means of livelihood for the majority of the population, but oil opened up easier and more lucrative forms of employment.

This development created a rapid wave of rural-urban migration. While in the
economic development of Europe, the United States and Japan, such migrations
were brought about partly by technological innovation and increased productivity in agriculture, this was not the case in Libya. On the contrary, people
did not leave farming because they were being pushed by the adoption of new
technology in agriculture, but rather because their earnings were far less
than prevailing wages in the urban areas. This rush for the "black gold"
attracted far more people from agriculture than the oil industry could absorb.
The result was deserted farmland in many parts of the country, and crowded
urban centres. One immediate result of this situation was a sudden increase
in the demand for foodstuff in these centres. This came about both as a
result of increased urban population and of higher per capita consumption,
due to higher disposable income among Libyans and foreigners serving the oil
industry and related activities. Under normal conditions this would provide
a strong stimulus for agricultural production to increase in response to
higher prices for foodstuffs. But such a healthy development could not take
place because of the low state of technology in agriculture. Another reason
was the higher profits on investment in the trade and service sector of the
economy.

It is well known that even in the highly developed economies of today, agriculture is too weak to stand on its own feet if the market mechanism were
left free to allocate resources and distribute income. The nature of the
production process in agriculture, the number of firms engaged, the scale
of operation and the use of the labour force are very different from what
they are in industry and in the service sectors. These basic differences
make it impossible for agriculture, no matter how efficient it may be,
successfully to compete with integrated modern industries, and have given
rise to various farm support programmes and agricultural subsidies, now
common in the advanced economies of Europe and the United States.

The inherent weaknesses in agriculture in general were reinforced, in the
case of Libya, by very low productivity due to technological backwardness
and lack of capital, as well as to the high degree of uncertainty associated

with agricultural production in arid areas. Thus, in the face of increased earnings and brighter prospects in the trade sector and the construction and service industries, brought about by the discovery of oil, both labour and capital moved away from agriculture. With this movement, Libyan agriculture was left to stagnate in its low level of development, and the consumer turned to the world markets for the purchase of his daily food. Oil-induced prosperity provided him with increased income for such purchases and it also provided the country with the essential foreign exchange for significantly increased imports. A few figures will illustrate the magnitude of this development. The total value of imported food and food products in 1956 (the beginning of oil exploration) was about £L5 million, but it increased to £L7.6 million in 1962 and to £L27.6 million in 1968. On the other hand, agricultural exports declined from a value of £L1.23 million in 1956 to £L600,000 in 1961, and to only about £L32,000 in 1968. This last figure is not enough to pay for Libya's import of food for one-third of a single day.

The availability of food from abroad filled the gap created by the sudden increase in demand in the cities. Many people tended to look upon this source as an adequate and relatively easier alternative to the development of domestic agriculture. Thus, gradually, the urban, and later on even the rural population, became more and more dependent upon foreign agriculture for the production of its food requirements. The increased income and prices brought about by the discovery of oil further added to the inefficiency of agricultural production by increasing the cost of labour and other inputs. The relative ease with which agricultural commodities were imported diminished the rate of increase of domestic food prices in relation to income in the urban areas. This situation further increased the unattractiveness of agriculture, especially in its traditional form.

Such a situation clearly calls for strong government intervention to subsidise agricultural production and protect rural income. But, unfortunately, such a policy could not be followed at the proper time because of two basic limitations. The first was simply lack of public funds, with which to support a large-scale programme of agricultural subsidies. The second was the necessity to keep food prices as low as possible, in the face of an inflationary situation, created by the injection of funds by the oil companies. As the Libyan consumer became more and more dependent on imported foodstuff, tariffs became less and less applicable as a means of protecting domestic agriculture. Moreover, the treasury at that time depended heavily upon customs duties as a form of indirect taxation. Thus, between 1955 and 1962, a situation was created in the economy which led to a drastic decline in traditional agriculture. At the same time, the introduction of modern agriculture could not take place, as has already been mentioned, because the level of agricultural skills was low and the level of earnings and profitability was much lower, even on efficient farms, than they were in trade, services, and real estate. The government was unable to play a significant role in dealing with the situation, because it lacked the necessary skills and funds, as well as the determination to use fiscal measures to favour agricultural investment and discourage relatively unproductive activities, such as real estate speculation. Politically, this was not feasible, and technically it was difficult to use modern fiscal and monetary instruments to redirect the allocation of resources towards agricultural development.

Under such circumstances, the market mechanism performed its traditional function of allocating resources and distributing income in favour of the economically stronger and more profitable forms of activities in the tertiary sector.

The net result of the above developments was the abandonment of traditional agriculture and nomadic activities in many parts of the country. Although the more modern farms, near the city of Tripoli and mainly operated by Italians, remain in production, their relative position in the economy was rapidly deteriorating. Thus, during the period 1956-62, the economic forces released by the discovery of oil produced their greatest adverse impact on agriculture. The latter simply could not withstand the great pressure of economic forces generated by the injection of substantial funds in the urban areas.

At the invitation of the Government, the World Bank surveyed the economy in 1958/59 and presented its findings and recommendations in 1960.[1] The report of the Bank placed special emphasis on the development of agriculture. The main problem facing agriculture as identified in the report were as follows:

1. Land ownership and tenure, with particular reference to the system of tribal ownership which still prevails over much of Eastern Libya and parts of Western Libya;

2. The supply of adequate credit to farmers;

3. The wider dissemination of knowledge of modern farming and livestock practices – essentially a matter of agricultural training and extension services;

4. Marketing facilities and related questions of agricultural prices and protection against imports;

5. Government organisation for the administration of agriculture.

The Bank Mission proposed a public national programme designed to tackle the above-mentioned problems at an estimated cost of £L5.130 million over the five years 1960/61 - 64/65, giving an average annual expenditure of £L1.026 million. This level of expenditure was actually little less than total public investment in agriculture during the previous years. However, the Mission felt that, with proper planning and efficient execution, such investment would be sufficient to initiate a programme of satisfactory agricultural development in the country. This programme, of course, was formulated as an integral part of an over-all development programme for the whole country, extending over a period of five years and costing about £L25 million at 1959 prices. The Mission also recommended an additional expenditure of £L1.575 million for the five-year period, covering the establishment cost of a new Federal Ministry of Agriculture and Natural Resources, an Agricultural Development Board for Eastern Libya, a Land Survey Department and a Federal Department of Geology and Hydrology.

Although the World Bank presented its report to the government several months after the first major oil discovery, it was not able properly to evaluate the impact of that event on Libyan agriculture. It generally assumed that the impact of oil on the Libyan economy would not be greatly felt during its proposed Five-Year Development Plan. Subsequent developments show that this was, perhaps, the most unrealistic assumption in the entire report. In fact, when the Mission made its survey in 1959 the impact of oil exploration on the country's traditional agriculture was already showing its harmful effects.

It took three years after the presentation of the World Bank Report before the government was able to approve a national development plan. In the meantime, the proposals of the World Bank regarding agriculture remained unimplemented, except for the creation of a Federal Ministry of Agriculture in 1961. At the same time, several major institutional changes took place, during the period 1960-63, which had a profound effect on the government in agriculture. In addition to the creation of a Federal Ministry of Agriculture in 1961, the government issued the necessary legislation to abolish the Bilateral Development Agencies (LPDSA, LARC, LAJS), which were established at the beginning of independence to administer development aid, largely from Britain and the United States. The functions of these agencies were entrusted to a National Development Council representing the Federal and the Provincial governments. Another major event, during this period, was the elimination of the Federal System of government and the reorganisation of development administration in accordance with this fundamental reform.

Although the objective of all these changes was to strengthen the role of government in development administration, their actual impact in this direction was not felt until several years later. In the meantime, the impact of oil on the economy in general, and on agriculture in particular, continued unabated. In addition, at this critical point the government initiated, in 1961, long-term agricultural loans on easy terms, for the purchase of agricultural land from the Italian settlers who had acquired it during the Italian colonisation. This policy began with a credit scheme of lending up to 50% of the estimated sale price of the farm, but a year later it was modified to lend up to 100% of the value of small farms, the value of which did not exceed one thousand pounds. Although this credit policy helped to transfer the ownership of many farms to Libyan nationals, the economic and social price paid for this achievement was very high and could have been avoided.

The first result of this credit policy was the sudden increase in the value of agricultural land owned by Italians. Liberal credit terms encouraged many people to enter the market as competitive buyers, while the supply side was relatively organised and inflexible. This had the effect of further raising the cost of agricultural production and diminishing its competitive position in the economy. Another detrimental aspect of this policy was the tendency to grant these long-term credits to urban people who had neither the experience, nor the necessity to maintain and improve the productive capacity of their newly acquired farms. Since they had other sources of income, either in government or in the tertiary sector, they generally looked upon their purchases of these farms as good investment outlets in the face of rising inflationary trends initiated by the oil industry. Another motive for buying these farms was the recreational environment associated with agriculture and highly valued by urban people. In other words, production was not a primary objective in the purchase of these farms. In the case of small lots of land, where long-term credit was extended for the whole value of the purchased farm, the result was excessive fragmentation of economic farm units, adding to the sale price of agricultural land and further diminishing its productivity.

The above-mentioned aspect of government intervention in agriculture during the period 1960-63, combined with the adverse impact of oil on the agrarian sector, caused a great deterioration in the position of agriculture in the Libyan economy. Yet, in any serious consideration of Libyan development prospects, apart from oil, agriculture still offered an attractive potential as well as a necessary condition for the balanced growth of the economy. The fact that between 1960-63 there was no systematic national development programme for agriculture pointed to the urgent need for immediate government intervention on a large scale. Fortunately, by that time, the government began to receive significant revenues from oil exports, thus giving it an opportunity, for the first time, to invest these funds in such a way as to mitigate the adverse effects of oil on agriculture. This happy development, as well as the centralisation of development planning and administration, referred to earlier, encouraged the government to formulate a new development plan, partly based on the recommendations of the World Bank, but taking into consideration the relevant changes that were not foreseen in the Bank's report.

In August 1963 the country's First Five-Year Development Plan was officially approved at an estimated cost of more than £L169 million covering the period 1963-68. The share of agriculture in this total allocation was £L29.275 million or 17.7%. This level of planned expenditure was nearly seven times the proposed World Bank programme for the period 1960/61 - 65/66, which was not implemented. Allocation for agriculture under the new Plan was nearly six times the level proposed by the Bank. Some of the main objectives of the agricultural development programme, as stated in the Plan, were as follows:

1. To provide food for the whole population and improve nutrition by raising the level of agricultural production, quantitatively and qualitatively;

2. To improve the economic conditions of farmers by establishing the prices of certain main products and providing farmers with suitable means of farm credit;

3. To provide education and training for farmers and to promote modern methods of research and experimentation in suitable farming methods.

In general, the new agricultural programme was designed to raise the productivity of the agrarian sector by the provision of financial incentives in the form of easy credit and price support, on one hand, and the promotion of research, training and extension, on the other. In practice, however, the implementation of this programme during the first three years of the Plan was hindered by the critical shortage of qualified personnel, lack of much needed technical and economic data, and excessive administrative routine. Actual expenditure for agricultural development during these years was lagging behind allocations. Moreover, the rapid development of the oil sector intensified the trend towards investment in real estate and the tertiary sector, where profits were phenomenally high. But, in spite of all this, the worst aspects of the impact of oil on agriculture were beginning to diminish by 1965. Prices for fresh food, especially meat, fruits and vegetables, were rising very rapidly, due to higher per capita consumption and certain protection measures against foreign competition. At the same time, foreign labour was beginning to come from neighbouring countries for agricultural employment to replace the national labour force, which had migrated to the cities in search of easier and more lucrative employment. With increased income in agriculture, the use of farm machinery and fertilizers was rapidly increasing in agricultural production. At this time the urban farm owners who had bought their farms under the long-term credit scheme began to get interested in putting their land into modern production, using some of their savings from profitable activities in the urban areas.

The government agricultural programme responded to this development in several ways, although it tended to do this without a consistent and co-ordinated policy, due to lack of experience and to inadequate evaluation and supervision of its role in agriculture. Fortunately, from a financial point of view, oil revenue had increased by more than twice that estimated in the Plan, because output was greater than foreseen and because of an amendment of the arrangement with the oil companies which raised the government revenues per barrel from the independent oil companies from 10 to 35 Libyan piastres (28 to 100 U.S. cents).

The greatly improved financial situation enabled the government to increase its allocation for development from £L 169.7 to £L 336 million for the Plan period, while agricultural allocation increased from £L 29.3 to £L 49.9 million. The rapid expansion of government programmes to subsidise agricultural production in the form of farm machinery, fertilizer, well drilling, feeds and seeds, and interest-free credits, enabled the agricultural authorities to spend more of their planned expenditure. Price support for such crops as cereals, olive oil, almonds and ground-nuts absorbed another significant portion of public funds allocated for agricultural development. These significant expenditures on farm subsidies and price support, largely incurred during the period 1965-68, provided a further stimulus to agricultural production, which had been showing signs of improvement since 1963. At the same time, the rate of profitability on non-agricultural investment was beginning to diminish compared to earlier periods, thus further reducing the adverse impact of oil on agriculture. If at that time the country had had a proper taxation system, it would have been wise to tax non-agricultural activities at a much higher rate than was the case. Such a step could have given agricultural development a further push in the right direction. The basis of such a taxation system, however, was not enacted until 1968 and its implementation began only in January 1969.

The following figures give a general idea of the changing place of agriculture in the national economy during the period 1957/58 to 1967/68:

	1958	1962	1967
	£L million		
Total value of agricultural production (1964 prices)	20.0	17.3	21.0
Value of food exports (current prices)	2.7	1.8	0.6
Value of food imports (current prices)	5.1	8.4	19.2
Food deficit (value)	2.4	6.6	18.6
Value of petroleum exports	0	49.0	417.3

	1958	1962	1967
	Per cent		
Value of petroleum production as per cent of GDP	6.9	28.5	54.7
Value of agricultural output as per cent of GDP	26.1	9.4	3.4
Agricultural labour (per cent of total labour force)	70.0	50.0	33.9

The above figures support the conclusion reached earlier in this section that the worst impact of oil on agricultural production was during the period 1958-62, when the value of agricultural output, at 1964 prices, declined from £L20 to £L17.3 million, representing a decrease of about 4% per year. But from 1962 to 1967, the trend was reversed, as production at constant prices increased from £L17.3 to £L21.0 million, giving an annual increase of about 4.5%. This means that the worst is over for agriculture, as far as the impact of oil is concerned. From now on, oil in the form of development funds and greater disposable income in urban areas, can provide agriculture with the necessary modern infrastructure and a secure market at favourable prices. This will not happen, of course, by itself. But based on the experience of the last few years, it is reasonable to conclude that if greater efforts are made in modernising agricultural production and rural institutions, and at the same time improving the efficiency of agricultural marketing, the oil-based prosperity will be a great stimulus to agricultural production.

As production data show, agricultural output has increased by 4.5% per annum from 1962-67, after having declined, under the initial impact of oil, at the rate of 4% per year during the previous five years. The fact that such significant improvement in agricultural output went unnoticed, in the general context of the economy, was due to the very high increase in oil production, which recorded an annual increase of 45.6% for the period 1962-67. Some of the other fast-growing sectors during this period were construction, which grew at a rate of 30.1% and trade and banking, which grew at 23.6% per annum. It is natural that, with such unusually high growth rates, the modest 4.5% growth in the agricultural sector would not be easily recognised, but when viewed against the performance of agriculture during the period 1958-62, it represents an important achievement and a significant shift in the direction of healthy economic growth.

But, however significant these promising agricultural trends may be, they represent very little compared with the needs of the domestic market for food. Thus, in addition to the appreciable increase in food production during the years 1962-67, the total value of food imports increased by more than 22% per annum, reaching a level of £L19.2 million in 1967, which is almost equal to the value of domestic agricultural output for the same year. At the same time, food exports declined from £L1.8 to £L0.6 million, thus raising the net food deficit from £L6.6 to £L18.6 million. Undoubtedly, the absolute value of these figures will increase during the years to come, but if agricultural production could be raised by 7 or 10% per year, the relative position of the agrarian sector would improve considerably. This should be the primary objective of agricultural planning and development during the next decade.

In order to achieve this level of development in agriculture, it is essential to achieve significant progress in the creation of economic farm units through a programme of land consolidation and the distribution of tribal land to individual ownership. Agricultural research, education and extension would have to be greatly improved in quality and expanded in scope and coverage. Agricultural credit, marketing and price support as well as various forms of agricultural subsidies will all have to be organised systematically with periodic evaluation and follow-up of their actual impact on agricultural production. Assured revenues from oil during the next decade provide a secure source of financing for all these schemes, and at the same time, mean that the impact of oil on agriculture, which was negative in the beginning, can now be a positive force behind its steady development. The growing need for food in the domestic market as well as the necessity to diversify exports calls for immediate and steady efforts in this direction, in order to reinforce the promising start, which has already been made.

CHAPTER 1

References

1   *The Economic Development of Libya*

Report of a Mission organised by the International Bank for Reconstruction and Development.

The John Hopkins Press, Baltimore 1960.

Chapter Two

PHYSICAL RESOURCES RELEVANT TO AGRICULTURE

Introduction

Libya is 1,700,000 square kilometres in extent, or almost twice the size of Egypt, five times that of France and one third that of the United States.

There are few areas of high ground, and these are located in the extreme south of the country. The northern half of Eastern Libya, and the part of Western Libya to the east of Misuratah lie below 300m. South and west the ground rises gently but rarely reaches above 1000m. (see map facing page 20).

As rainfall averages less than 50mm. per year for 90% of the country (see map facing page 26) the landscape is of the arid type, characterised by broken country forming basins of inland drainage with ephemeral streams and dry valleys (wadis), and deserts of both the rock and sand types. Sand seas cover approximately one third of the provinces of Eastern, and Southern Libya. (see map facing page 24).

Two upland areas though only 600 m. in height, and small in extent are very important. There are the Jabal Akhdar in Eastern Libya, and the Jabal Nafusah in Western Libya. (see map facing page 20). They are relatively well watered with over 300 mm. mean annual rainfall, and support a Mediterranean scrub vegetation. Grazing and limited dry farming are possible on these hill areas.

The Mediterranean coast of the provinces of Western Libya is low lying (under 50 m. except just to the west of al Khums), and the 200 mm. mean annual rainfall in the areas westwards from Misuratah supports limited drought-resistant vegetation, some pasture and discontinuous settled agriculture, the latter frequently dependent on irrigation. The triangle of the Gefara Plain inland of Zuwarah (see map facing page 24) is almost as arid as the interior of Libya, as is the coast between Misuratah and Benghazi, and the Marmorica area to the east of Darnah (see map facing page 24).

For the area south of the Jabal Nafusah, and south of the Oasis Depression in the Eastern Provinces of Libya very little information on the geology, and even less on geomorphology, meteorology, climate or water resources, had been collected before the 1960s. The most prolific scientific writers on the physical environment of Libya have been Italian. During the 1930s, Italian geologists such as Desio and Lipparini, and climatologists such as Fantoli, grasped the scientific opportunities offered by so wide and so poorly known an expanse of land. Their work in the northern, more accessible, parts of Libya was thorough and precise. However, they dealt with the southern parts of the country in only the most general terms. It was not until the interests of the international petroleum companies were aroused, that deep and persistent penetration of southern Libya for scientific data began to be published by the field geologists working in Libya, and that meteorological data were collected by the air pilots serving the oil-men in southern Libya. In the study of the physical environment, as in almost every other field in Libya, the oil-boom has led to immeasurably valuable developments which might not otherwise have occured for a number of years.

Among the many advances in knowledge brought about by intensified petroleum development has been that relating to water resources. In a country the climate of which varies between the arid margin of the humid temperate region and the arid extreme of the hot desert, the provision of water at the land surface is of greatest importance for population distribution, human occupations and future economic development.

2.1 Geology and Surface Form

A basement of Pre-Cambrian rocks underlies the whole of Libya at a variety of depths, but outcrops are few and difficult of access. Klitzch[1] noted evidence for two orogenic periods in the slates of the Pre-Cambrian, both folding periods being associated with magmatic activity.

Subaerial rather than marine planation of the Pre-Cambrian rocks may be assumed from the continental environment in which the Cambrian rocks were laid down unconformably on the basement. The deposits are predominantly coarse sandstones and conglomerates. The major structural basins of Libya were beginning to develop even in this period, and Cambrian sediments reach immense thicknesses in places, for example, there are 1,700 metres of Cambrian sediments on the north-east flank of the Murzuq Basin.[2]

Activity along the flexures forming the sedimentary basins culminated in an end- Cambrian folding period, and the sub-aerial erosion of the Lower Ordovician landscape was followed by a marine transgression of all of Libya except the Kufrah Basin by the Middle Ordovician sea. The deposits of the Silurian period indicate renewed marine transgression which covered the western part of the Kufrah Basin. The greater part of the Basin remained under the influence of sub-aerial landscaping agencies, but off the shores of the landmass, sediments were deposited which today exceed some 500 metres in thickness.

Late Silurian and early Devonian times saw the development of the north-north-west/south-south-east Caledonian structural axes, which continued the development of the major structural basins. The Tibesti-Tripoli uplift reflects renewed activity along the axis separating the Murzuq and Kufrah Basins. Similar renewed movements occurred along the Calanscio-Uwaynat Arch, which was responsible for repelling the marine transgressions of Lower Paleozoic times into the eastern part of the Kufrah Basin. The South Haroudj Axis seems to have been a more violent uplift associated with intense magmatic and volcanic activity.

The Lower Devonian sediments of Libya are predominantly continental in origin, while the Upper Devonian are mainly marine. Upper Devonian sedimentation was interrupted from time to time by stages in the Hercynian Orogeny. Hercynian fold-axes in Libya trend north-east south-west, in contrast with the typical Caledonian trend. Uplift along these axes in places reversed the depositional trend, notably along the major Tibesti-Surt axis, and by the development of the Ben Gnema trough on the former site of the Dor al Gussa axis.

Marine planation of the Hercynian folds was followed by the deposition of thick marine shales over most of Libya in the Lower Carboniferous period.

LIBYA
TOPOGRAPHIC MAP

1	Sabratah
2	Az Zawiyah
3	Ayn Zarah
4	Al Qasabat
5	Tarhunah
6	Al Aziziyah
7	Shakshuk
8	Na'imah
9	Ad Dafiniyah
10	Al Marj
11	Taknis
12	Massah
13	Beda
14	Suluntah
15	Yafran

Legend:
- Escarpment Edge of Jabals
- Sand Sea Areas
- Hard Surface Roads
- Provincial Boundaries

Scale: 0–300 Kilometres / 0–200 Miles

INTERNATIONAL BOUNDARIES NOT AUTHENTICATED

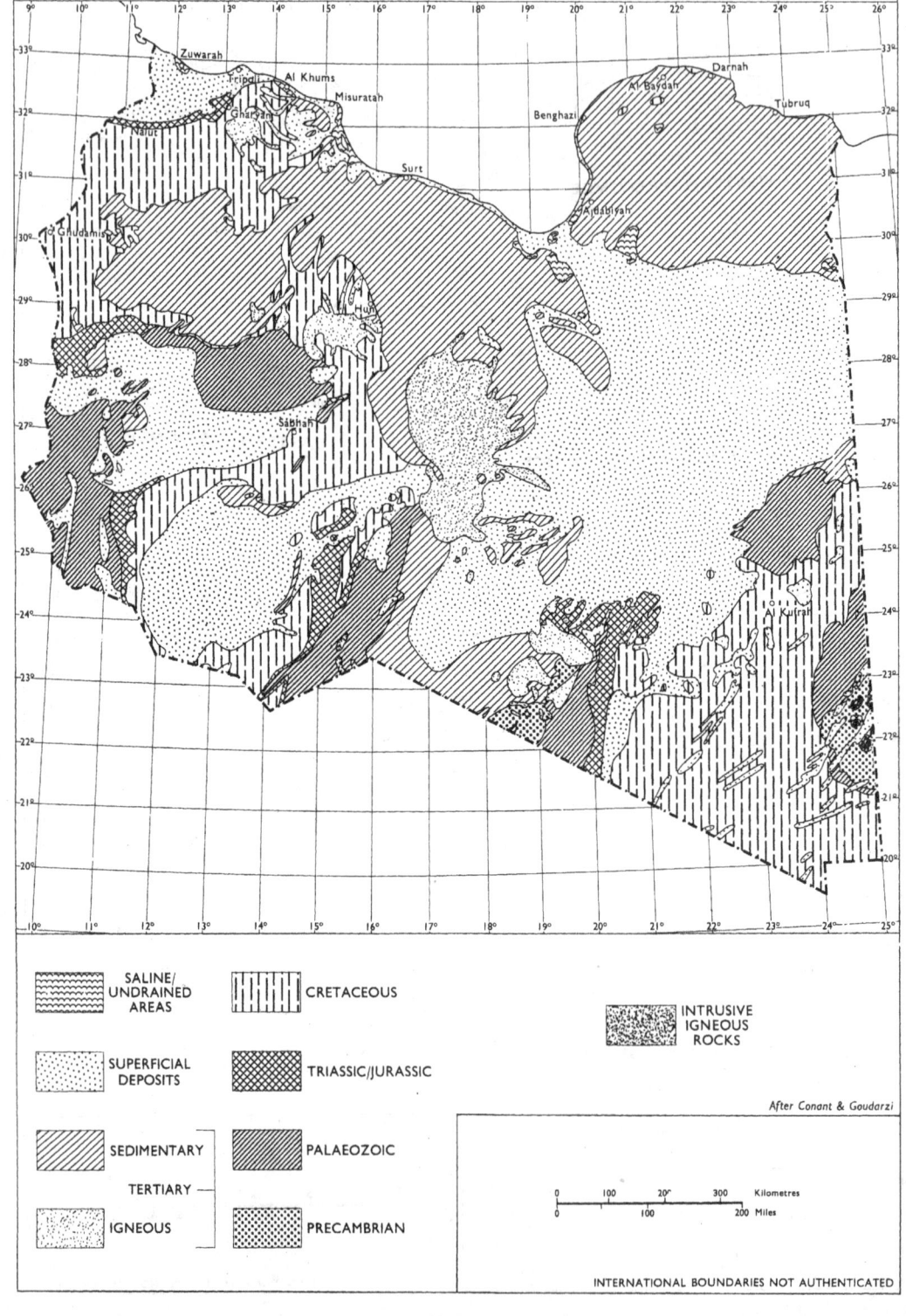

By the Upper Carboniferous, however, the coastline had retreated from much of Libya east of the Tibesti-Surt axis, and even south-western Libya experienced only relatively shallow marine conditions in this period.

Continental conditions returned to almost the whole of Libya through Post-Tassilian times. The term 'Post-Tassilian' refers to rocks occuring stratigraphically between the post-Carboniferous unconformity and the base of the Nubian Sandstone series of Upper Cretaceous age. Only in the north-western part of Western Libya do marine Mesozoic rocks occur in Libya. The stratigraphic record indicates that a marine environment persisted here from Lower Permian through Tertiary time. The Mesozoic elements include lagoonal clays and silts, coastal evaporite series, glauconitic sandstones representing marine transgression, and carbonate rocks representing the occurrence of shallow shelf sea conditions. In all its transgressions and regressions, however, the sea penetrated little further inland than the line of the present jabal crest.[3]

The continental Post-Tassilian deposits are overlain unconformably by the Nubian Sandstone series, south of the 26th parallel. McKee's interpretation of the lithologic and bedding characteristics of the Nubian Sandstone in the Fezzan indicates that the greater part of the 545 metres thick series accumulated on the delta-fronts of lakes and lagoons fed by northward-flowing streams.[4]

Middle Cretaceous times saw extensive earth movements in the northern parts of Libya also, movements which represented posthumous activity along Caledonian lines of weakness. These movements accelerated significantly the development of the Surt Basin. The Tertiary paleogeography of northern Libya is dominated by the periodic extension and regression of the Surt Gulf, Desio's term for that branch of the sea in the Surt Basin at this time.[5] Early in the Eocene period, the Surt Gulf was probably linked to a Paleo-Nilotic Gulf via the tract which now forms the 'Cyrenaican Oasis Depression'. Into this Gulf drained the streams responsible for the deposition of the sands and gravels of the serirs and sand seas of Central Libya. With the passage of time, the Surt Gulf extended westward to cover most of Western Libya. During the Danian period, however, the tectonic uplift of the Jabal Akhdar in Eastern Libya and of the Hamada al Hamra and the Jabal in Western Libya restricted the area of the Gulf. The Gulf was even more drastically restricted by the Alpenide orogenic movements of Middle and Upper Tertiary times, which resulted in the violent volcanic activity which formed the Jabal Haroudj al Asuad. The precise date of the opening of the volcanic period in the Jabal Haroudj is controversial. The traditional view was that this took place in Oligocene times. K-Ar dating of the oldest lavas by Pesce places the occurrence as no earlier than Pliocene, and he visualises volcanic activity in Central Libya proceeding until after the end of the last pluvial period.[6]

If the earliest lavas of the Jabal Haroudj are of Pliocene age, it seems probable that the region formed an upland limiting the incursion southwards of the remnant of the Surt Gulf. The Miocene deposits of Libya are restricted in their distribution to the northern part of Eastern Libya, 'Sirtica', north of the Jabal Haroudj and north of the Jabal Nafusah in Western Libya. By the Upper Miocene, the sea had been repelled from the rising Jabal Akhdar, and through Plio-Pliestocene times the coastline of Libya took on its present form.

The principal single factor in the history of the Quaternary period in North Africa was the series of climatic changes associated with the glaciations of the higher latitudes. The presence of more water on the land surface for a longer and more effective time than before, affected the rapidity with which valleys were deepened and widened, the degree to which their former shape was changed and the rate at which the valleys were infilled with sediment. The second most significant factor was the series of changes of the sea level, which characterised the Pleistocene, although the limited area of the fluvial basins draining into the sea from Libya rendered changes in sea level of geomorphic importance over only a limited region. Pleistocene conditions were seldom uniform over the whole of Libya at any one time, any more than conditions are uniform over an equivalent one-third of the United States today. It is not surprising, therefore, that the Quaternary history of Libya varies from place to place.

An absolute chronology has not been constructed for the south-eastern regions of Libya through the Pleistocene, though the pattern of geomorphic development has been clarified, notably by Klitzch, working in the Sarir as Sabhah. In situ rotting of the Nubian Sandstone during Tertiary times prepared the surface for aeolian winnowing which left a lag-gravel surface in the south, the true serir, and permitted the development of dune-fields to the north. Two generations of dunes are apparent; the earlier, wider, degraded dunes trending north-north-east/ south-south-west have been overrun by more recent seif dunes trending north-east/south-west parallel to the prevailing winds.

In the eastern part of Southern Libya Ziegert was able to reconstruct the occurrence of three pluvial periods and a later (c.4000 B.C.) wetter subphase, on the basis of the valley-fills of the area, and from the periods of domination by aeolian agencies which occurred between fill-deposition periods.[7] In the Jabal as Sauda, Knetsch was able to trace three Tertiary erosion surfaces across the lavas.[8] Within the wadis, the incision of which represents the most recent erosion cycle, a series of cemented scree-fills are overlain by uncemented screes, the screes being referred by Knetsch and Butzer to a period coincident with the Würm glacial of Europe.

In the al Jaghbub Sand Sea, a series of four pluvials has been postulated[9] on the evidence of four series of wadi-fills, each winnowed in the formation of the three Ancient Ergs during the three interpluvial periods. The last pluvial is believed to have extended into the 'period of the climatic optimum', since deposits related to the fourth pluvial are associated with the Neolithic implements.

The late Tertiary and Quaternary history of the Jabal Akhdar, in Eastern Libya, has been more thoroughly investigated than that of any other part of Libya. The lack of deposits of later date than the Lower Miocene period indicates that the uplift of the Jabal occurred through late Tertiary times. This hypothesis is supported by the nature of the upper two of the three escarpments on the scarp face of the Jabal. The foot of neither of the escarpments exhibits altitudinal uniformity, but Hey indicates that this is due to warping of the scarp-foot during the discontinuous uplift of the Jabal from beneath the sea. The origin of the escarpments, in other words, is probably marine, though influenced in their alignment in places by the faults which today coincide with the foot of the escarpments.[10]

Hey relates the lowest escarpment to the Calabrian stage, and the Sahal below the scarp face of the Jabal exhibits six or possibly seven marine benches of Pleistocene age. The 6 metre bench is associated with extensive tufas, both benches and tufas being overlain by the Younger Gravels, which form the upper of two valley fills debouching from the wadi-mouths across the Sahal. The Younger Gravels include Levalloisian-Mousterian implements, dated to a period between 40,000-50,000 years ago. A second period of fluvial activity and

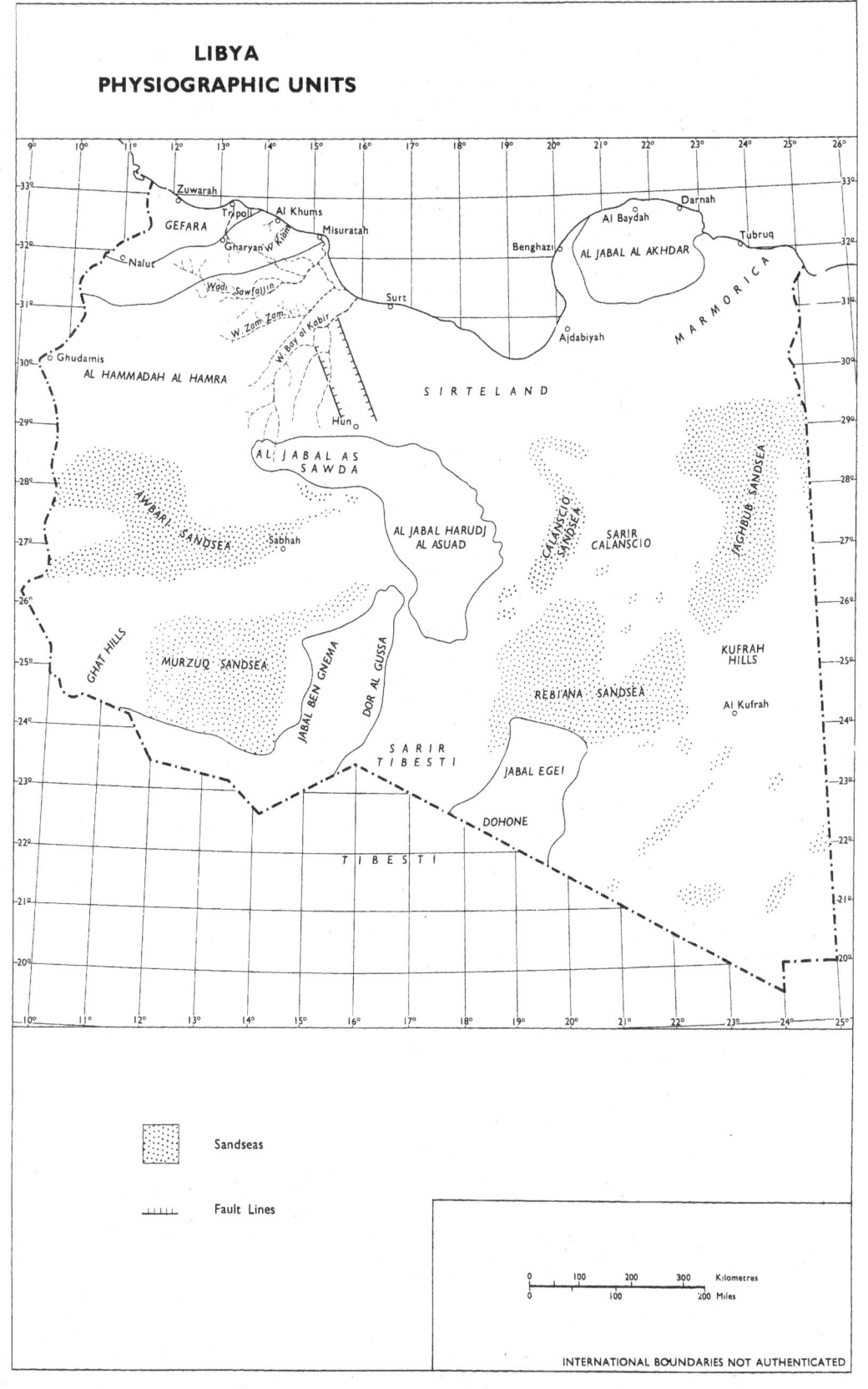

seasonal frost shattering is represented by uncemented relict screes which overlie the Younger Gravels and are dated to the period 4,000-10,000 years old.

The origin of the Jabal Nafusah seems to have been comparable to that of the Jabal Akhdar, in that its scarp face appears to have been formed by marine agencies which removed the northern limb of the 'jaballian' anticline. A number of subaerial erosion surfaces are recognisable on the crest of the Jabal and in the wadis, but the number of stages apparently varies from three in the Jabal Tarhunah, to four in the Jabal Gharyan, two in the Western Jabal Nafusah, and as many as five in the Jabal Nafusah around Jadu. This variety in the number of surfaces is only apparent, the true picture awaiting further investigation. On the other hand there may indeed be different numbers of surfaces in different parts of the Jabal, related to the distribution of regionally differential uplift-stages of the Jabal during its rise from the late Tertiary seas, comparable to the warping of the escarpment on the face of the Jabal Akhdar.

In the Jabal Gharyan, the later erosion surfaces were warped by a phonolite intrusion, the emplacement of which was associated with the extrusion of basalt streams into the Wadi Gan. The latest flows are interdigitated with material which Hey considers to be of 'laha' origin. Middle Paleolithic artifacts from this deposit permit its dating to Upper Pleistocene times. The 'laha' material is overlain by aeolian-transported silt-grade material, through which the wadis were incised prior to the deposition of the upper valley fill. The upper valley fill of the Jabal Nafusah lacks the roundedness of the Younger Gravels of Eastern Libya, and seems to have been deposited under conditions not very different from those of the present. The upper fill pre-dates, and is widely overlain by, the subsequent slopewash fill, in which Vita-Finzi has found Roman sherds, attesting to the influence of Roman agriculture on the rate of sediment production and removal from the slopes of the Jabal.[11] It is likely that the slopewash fill both pre-dates and post-dates the Roman period, however.

North of the Jabal, the Gefara Plain is formed of undifferentiable debris carried down from the Jabal face and deposited in the broad fans of the Gefaric Series through Tertiary and Quaternary times. At the coast, the Gefaric Series is interdigitated with marine deposits, indicating the instability of sea level through much of the Pleistocene. No pre-Tyrrhenian deposits have been found, however, and this may be taken to indicate that the area was being uplifted by tectonic forces through the period prior to the last interglacial in Europe. The uplift was differential in Western Libya, the sub-Tyrrhenian floor declining in elevation east and west from Tripoli. The Würm period of Europe is represented by a regression of the sea on the coast of Western Libya before a weak transgression in Flandrian times which notched the coastal dunes but was too short-lived to leave any sedimentological record.

2.2 Climate and Weather

Remarkably full records exist of the climate and weather for a number of centres in the country, but there are gaps because meteorological stations are unevenly scattered throughout the country.

Much is being done to fill these gaps but as yet the whole of Libya south of the Oasis Depression is unrealistically treated as one undivided climatic zone for lack of detailed records.

LIBYA-RAINFALL

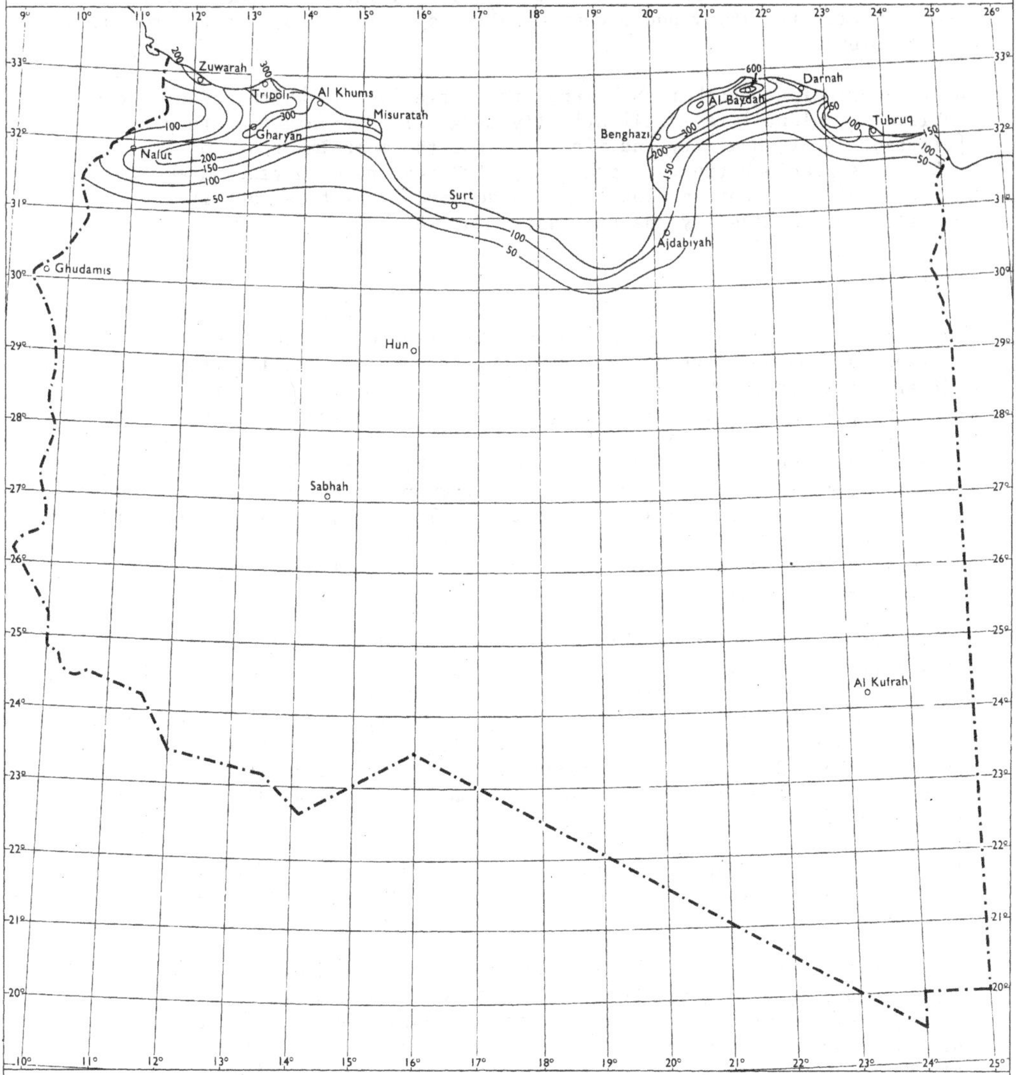

ISOHYETS IN MILLIMETRES

After A. Fantoli

0 100 200 300 Kilometres
0 100 200 Miles

INTERNATIONAL BOUNDARIES NOT AUTHENTICATED

For a study of Libyan agriculture, therefore, one must go beyond the basic statistics of Libyan climate. The following sections contain a brief description of the more important weather phenomena, including the climatic zones of northern Libya, and a consideration of rain as part of the resource base of Libya.

The four principal weather phenomena, the variations in which affect the viability of plant-life in climatically marginal environments, are precipitation, heat, humidity and wind. By far the most important of these in Libya is precipitation. Libya enjoys two seasons each year, one warm and one cool. The warm season is a dry season, it is true, but it would be misleading to classify the cool season as wet.

2.2.1 Rainfall

The rainfall at the coast is caused to a minor extent by the elevation of the land, and more important by lift along advancing frontal surfaces. Mediterranean air in the wake of a cold front is commonly rendered unstable by its passage southwards across the sea, and readily deposits its precipitation. Intense thunderstorms occur in association with cold fronts in the rear of which Arctic air has swept quickly across the Mediterranean with little modification. Snow is fairly common in the Jabal Nafusah and by no means unknown in the Jabal Akhdar, and it is usually associated with orographically induced lift of the Arctic air at the jabal face. Snow seldom lies longer than 24 hours but may be a minor disaster for the unwary shepherd.

The importance of the orographic effect associated with the face of the Jabal Nafusah is indicated by the variations in the mean annual precipitation along a line between Tripoli and Mizdah. The line passes from a zone in which mean annual precipitation of about 350 mm. may be expected, to a zone of less than 275 mm. in the Gefara. At the jabal crest, mean annual totals of about 325 mm. are experienced, and the totals decline regularly southwards down the dipslope of the jabal until, around Mizdah, about 50 mm. are expected.

"The most important aspect of Libya's particular climatic character is its extreme changeability which stems from the alternative predominance of the two great natural influences: the sea and the desert." [12]

This changeability is greater in central and southern Libya than in the north. At Awbari and Brack, in southern Libya, a 300% variation in annual precipitation is experienced. Even at Yafran, in the Jabal Nafusah, however, the total annual precipitation in the drought years 1946-7 and 1947-8 was only 25% of the mean annual total. In the winters of 1937-8 and 1938-9 double the mean annual total was received. In the agricultural zone of Western Libya 55% of the years for which records are adequate received less than the average precipitation, while 45% received more than the average, and the excesses above the average were greater than the deficits were below it. In the Gefara Plain, however, one writer estimated that total failure of the harvest occurs in three out of four years.[13]

2.2.2 Temperature

The temperature records indicate the importance of the influence of the sea and the desert on the weather and climate of Libya. The effect of the desert on temperature is paramount, however, and the highest temperatures are

RAINFALL AND RELATIVE HUMIDITY AT SELECTED STATIONS

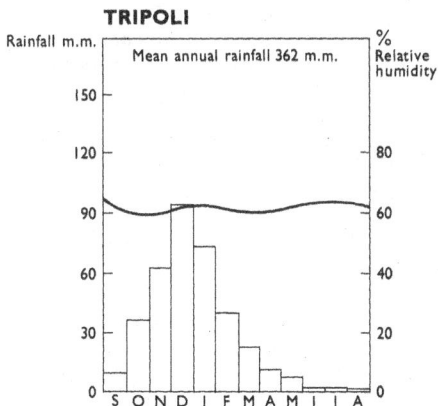
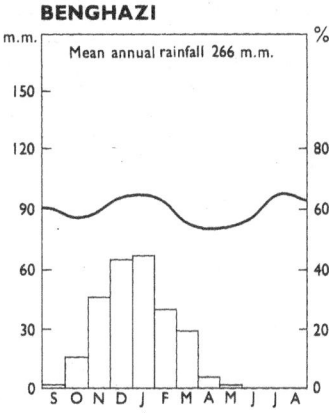
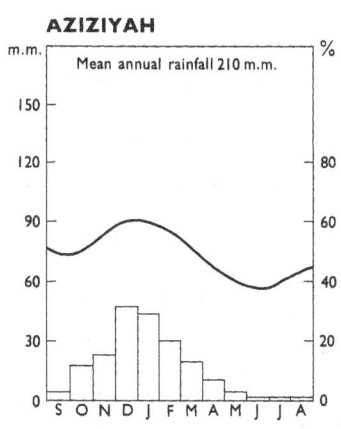
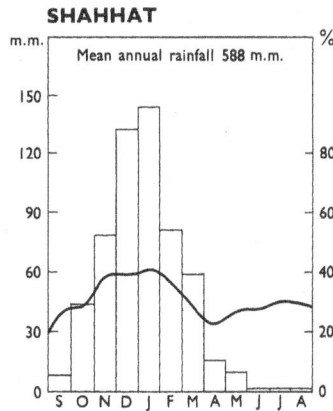
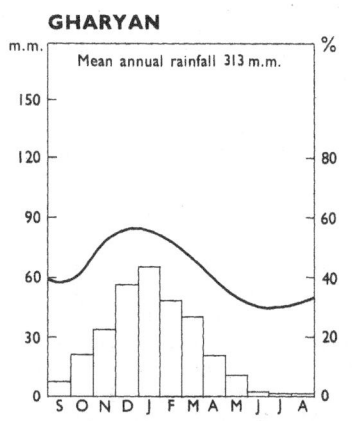
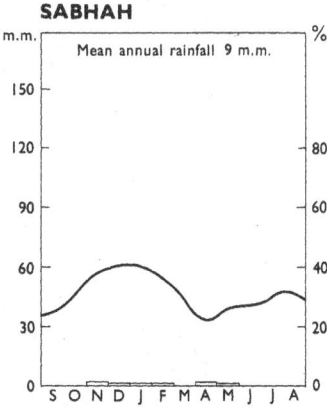

(Source : - Ministry of Communications, Meteorological Service. "Monthly and annual climatological data".)

experienced with southerly airstreams. The sea wields an important influence for only a relatively short distance inland. At the coast, the land and sea breezes are very significant. The extent of the penetration of the sea breeze appears to be a function of its depth; the greater the depth of the airstream the deeper its penetration. The land breeze is simply the draining of the air from the radiation-cooled land surface, and its influence is closely related to topography. The sea breeze may cause a temperature change of $10°$ to $20°C$. in the hot season, when its influence is most appreciated. A strong effect on the relative humidity is noticed with the reversal of the breeze.

Altitude has a small but significant influence on temperatures in the northern jabal in Libya. The influence is greater in the cool than in the warm season. Little is known of the local climates of central and southern Libya, but it is to be expected that the significance of local variations of topography would have a very significant effect on climatic, and especially temperature, variations.

Relative humidity varies with the prevailing airstream and, not surprisingly, the contrast between humidities in airstreams from the desert and those from the sea is extreme. Though the diurnal range of relative humidities varies between 20% and 95% at the coast, the mean monthly relative humidity on the coast is commonly fairly uniform through the year, the range of variation increasing with distance from the sea. Advection fog is common on the coasts of Western Libya and Surt, and radiation fog commonly occurs in the wadis of the scarp face of the Jabal Nafusah.

2.2.3 Humidity and evapo-transpiration

After precipitation, the extremely low relative humidities brought to the agricultural zone by the hot Saharan wind, associated with the passage of an intense depression, are the most significant features of the Libyan climate. The local name for the desert wind is 'ghibli', and Stewart wrote of the ghibli:

"Whenever the transpiration requirement is extraordinarily high for just a few days and the soil moisture available to the plant roots falls considerably short of meeting this demand, annual plants will suffer serious damage. That is why a two or three day hot, dry ghibli coming after a 30-day rainless period will ruin a promising grain crop."[13]

Ghiblis can last five days but seldom persist for more than 24 hours. Winds from the south that are insufficiently dry to be termed ghiblis may raise sudden dust-storms which can affect travel strongly. Airfields may be closed down with little warning when the wind is off the sandy or dune areas, and remain closed until the wind-direction changes. Tripoli Airport, 25 kilometres south of Tripoli, suffers a reduction of visibility to some 100 metres in 'force 6' winds off the dune-fields to the south of the airfield.

2.2.4 Climatic regions

The Libyan Meteorological Department has proposed a series of climatic regions which are noticeably smaller in Libya north of the Oasis Depression than in the region to the south.[12] The regions are demarcated on the basis of climatological variations very closely related to coastal alignment and topography. The effect of topography on precipitation in Western Libya has already been examined. The effect of coastal alignment is significant. The dominant wind in winter is from the north-west, hence Tripoli, on a north-

TEMPERATURES AT SELECTED STATIONS

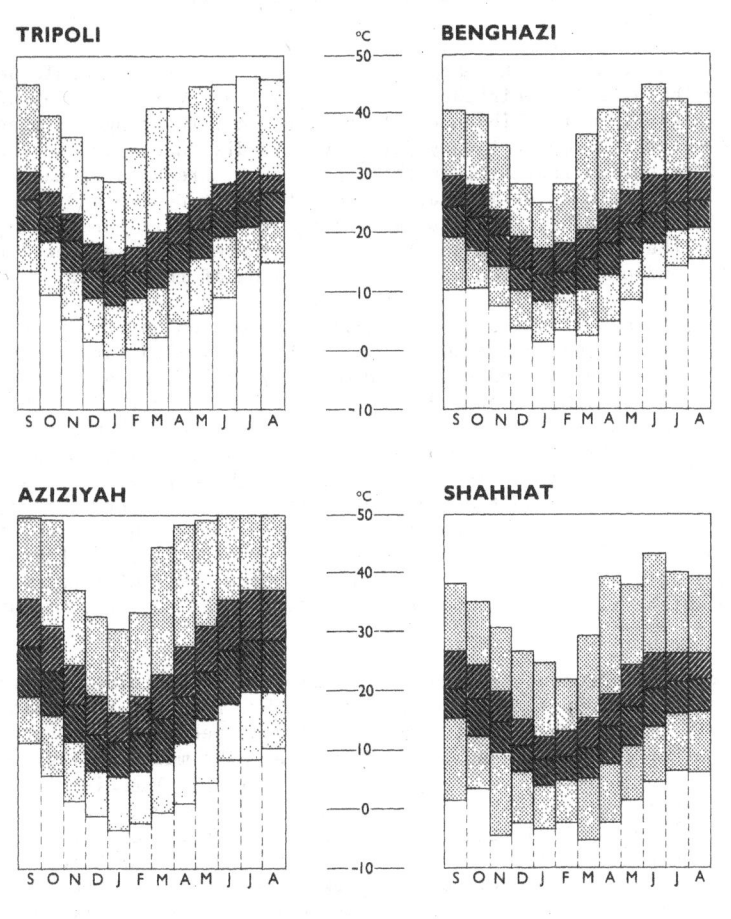
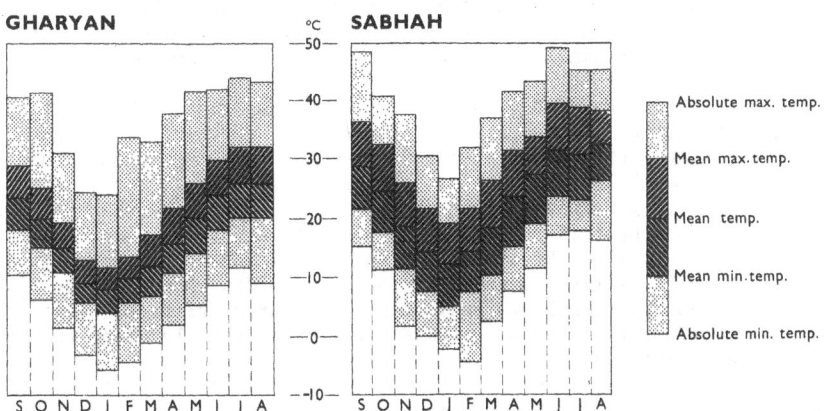

west facing coast, receives a mean annual precipitation of 362 mm. Sabratah and Suq al Khamis, to the west and east of Tripoli, respectively, and on the north-east facing coasts, receive only 216 mm. and 181 mm., respectively, in an average year. Precisely comparable effects are experienced on the coast of Eastern Libya, and the influence of topography on precipitation in the Jabal Akhdar is also closely comparable to that experienced in the Jabal Nafusah.

It might be expected that the ameliorating effect of altitude would be overshadowed by the effect of distance from the sea. However, a series of traverses inland from the Libyan coast indicate that the range of mean monthly temperatures does not vary directly with distance from the sea. What the traverses do indicate, is that there is a threshold distance from the sea, some 40 kilometres inland, at a greater distance inland than which the range of mean monthly temperatures exceeds 17°C. This threshold defines the limit of the Mediterranean zone, which is, therefore, restricted to a very narrow band on the margin of the vast 'region of the desert'.

Nine-tenths of Libya lies south of the Oasis Depression and the Surt coast. However, Kanter's isohyets are not drawn south of the 27th parallel for half the year, and in the seasons for which they are drawn so far south, the highest value south of latitude 30° north is 10 mm. a year.[14] Similarly, the data on temperatures experienced in southern and central Libya are derived from few stations, all in such contrasting topographic positions and conditions of local climate as to have little value in the derivation of a broad picture of temperature conditions for this part of the country. Thus, there appears to be neither the need for nor the grounds on which to subdivide southern and central Libya into more than one climatic region. Furthermore, any future subdivision would have to be made on the basis of local variations in climate which will probably be very closely related to local variations in topography.

If the subdivision of southern and central Libya on climatological grounds is unnecessary, the opposite must be true of Libya north of the Oasis Depression. In this northern region we have already recognised two sub-regions, that of the desert and that of the sea. The maritime region may be subdivided again into a wetter and a drier section. The distribution of units of the sub-regions, which are by no means continuous, seems very largely to reflect coastal alignments. The drier sub-region generally coincides with north-east facing coasts. On the ground, characteristics of the drier sub-region are clump grass vegetation of the steppe type, or bare, active dunes. Characteristic of the wetter sub-region are intensively worked farms. The villages of the wetter sub-region tend to be varied in size and extent. Those of the drier sub-region, like the vegetation pattern, seem to form isolated nuclei bounded by the sand around them.

In the continental subdivision of Northern Libya - the region of desert - two sub-regions are again recognisable, the steppe and the farmed sub-regions. The steppe sub-region is characterised by bare reg surfaces and dunes, with occasional sown patches of cereals in wadi beds. The farmed sub-region occurs at generally higher altitude than the steppe, but it would be misleading to define this sub-region on altimetric grounds alone. Nor is it possible to classify the sub-region as 'jaballian' or plateau, although it is there where its farms are commonly found. The dip slopes of the jabals in both Eastern and Western Libya exhibit steppe characteristics, and there is a transition from arable to pastoral sub-regions laterally along the Jabal Nafusah westwards from Yafran.

2.2.5 Seasonal characteristics

The climatic year in Libya is divisible into a warm season, June through September, and a cool season, October through May. The first and last month of each season is transitional. It is during these months that the development of the pressure cells, and their break-down, is most active and significant.

1. Summer

"Fine weather" is most typical of the warm season. One type involves high pressure over the southern Mediterranean and northern Libya, commonly as a ridge from the 'Mid-Atlantic High'; the gently moving air and clear daytime and night-time skies give rise to prolonged fine weather with a very great diurnal temperature range. The second common summer type involves the ridge from the 'Mid-Atlantic High" being positioned over Europe, and low pressure dominating the Mediterranean Basin. The Polar continental air moving west around the nose of the ridge is generally as hot and dry and stable after its passage from central Eurasia as air from the central Sahara Desert, and conditions comparable to those of the first type prevail.

2. Winter

Winters in Libya are of three types. The general pressure distribution of winter involves a ridge of high pressure from the 'Mid-Atlantic High' extending east over northern North Africa, with troughs occupying the Mediterranean Basin and the southern Sahara and Tibesti-Tassili regions. Within this context, weather types including cyclogenesis are common, due to the strong contrast between the cold dry air of continental Eurasia and the warm dry air of the Sahara Desert region. The Mediterranean is the principal zone of convergence, and the effect of the sea in rendering unstable the Polar airstreams, and in acting as a moisture-source, is extreme at this season.

A common situation involves a slowly-moving, deep depression passing east through the Mediterranean Basin. The Polar maritime air in the wake of the depression is rendered intensely instable by the warming effect of the sea-surface, and the orographic lift at the jabal faces in Northern Libya commonly gives rise to intense and prolonged precipitation.

The contrast between the air of Saharan and of Eurasian origin commonly leads to the cyclogenesis in the region inland from the Surt coast. Again, northerly cool moist air is rendered unstable in its traverse across the Mediterranean Sea. The intense rain which occurs at the frontal surfaces associated with these depressions contributes significantly to the annual precipitation of the Jabal Akhdar. The situation may develop into a less extreme weather type, however. If the 'Eurasian High' extends unusually far south, cyclogenesis will take place only in the deep south of Libya, by which time the northerly air will be extensively modified by its passage across the hot land, and contrast only weakly with the Saharan air. This situation commonly leads to the generation of very deep depressions in the region between Tunisia and Italy, and gale force winds, including ghiblis, in Libya.

2.2.6 Climate and Water Resources

The factors of greatest importance to crop-growers are precipitation, temperature, relative humidity, wind speed and soils. Stewart has observed that a definition and description of the agricultural zone of Western Libya cannot be undertaken except by relating it to rainfall, the most significant single factor that limits overall production. He goes on to say that a study of the distribution of population in each of the rainfall zones (of Western Libya) provides continuing evidence that production is rigorously controlled by the quantity of the rainfall.

However, in Libya, only something like one-fifth of total precipitation is available for use by plants. It is estimated that the other four-fifths is lost through evaporation, or runoff and deep percolation into bedrock aquifers. It seems likely that the minimum annual precipitation required for the support of cereal crops grown by substistence farmers is 200 mm. per annum, which is far more than is received on average by most of Libya. Furthermore, climatic variability is high, particularly precipitation. A 20% variation from the average is significantly harmful to grain-crops, and a variation of 20% or more in the annual precipitation has occured in 22 of the 40 years for which adequate records exist in the agricultural zone of Libya. In any twenty-year period, seven years can be expected to be drought years, in which crops will be severely damaged or lost.

The measurement of evaporation losses is complex and few data on this factor are available for Libya. Much the same can be said of the loss through runoff, which is the other principal source of loss of precipitated water for the farmer. An estimate that 4% of the total precipitation received by the agricultural zone of Western Libya is lost by surface runoff should be balanced against the estimate, by the same authority, that only 1% of the land surface of the zone affords runoff to the sea.[14] On the assumption that all water which neither evaporates nor flows into the sea nor percolates deeply into the ground is left for the farmer's use, the farmers in the best-watered parts of Western Libya have available some 55 mm. of water precipitated each year.

However, as more and more wells come into use, water which has percolated into the ground need no longer be considered totally lost. But much more needs to be known about the rate of percolation through the soils and rocks of Libya, and conservation measures are urgently needed to ensure that the use of water does not continue to exceed dangerously the low rate of recharge of the aquifers.

2.3 Water Resources

" We should look upon water with the eye of a Bedouin; cherish it like a Treasure, remembering that even to have it in limited quantities is a privilege which is not given to all." (Ardito Desio.)

"The development of the water resources of Libya is the basis for all activities in the Kingdom. The importance of water has been expressed in the agricultural development of the country to the extent that, without additional sources of water and more efficient use of water, agricultural development will not take place and, in some coastal areas, agriculture will cease to exist." (M.F. Rupp)

"In no area of Libya do we have all the information that should be collected." (J.R. Jones)

These quotations from the writings of three of the world authorities on Libyan hydrology are pessimistic. There is little point in pretending that Libya does not have a problem of water supply, or that this problem will not become aggravated as increased domestic and industrial demands for water are added to those of a new-technology agriculture. Increased efficiency in the search for water by government agencies and as a by-product of the activities of the oil companies must improve the chances of finding what water resources are available. Furthermore, increased education of those involved in agriculture in the sciences of soil and water conservation will enhance the value of the water found. This education is particularly important in an environment where water losses by evaporation and infiltration are heavy, and in an agriculture which offers only the most limited opportunity for the application of techniques to re-use water.

In the following discussion, it is assumed that agriculture will continue to be the predominant user of water in Libya. At present, with the exception of the demands of the five principal centres of administration (Al Baydah, Benghazi, Tripoli, Darnah and Tobruq), this assumption is largely valid. Manufacturing industry as a heavy user of water has yet to materialise in Libya. Water is taken from a variety of sources on and below the surface, but only limited use is made of surface sources. Wadi discharge is characteristically of poor chemical quality. Most significant of all surface sources are the springs which tap subterranean sources in the scarps of the Jabal Akhdar and the Jabal Nafusah, and those which feed the major lakes of Southern Libya. Libya's largest and most reliable water supplies come from underground storage, from perched aquifers, artesian aquifers and from below the general water table.

Very little is known of the availability of these resources, and where water has been found and tapped, dangerously little is known of the effects of drawdown, transmission within the aquifer or recharge. Moreover, the problem of ignorance of the resource base is complicated by rapid changes in the patterns of population distribution and water-use, which are occurring more rapidly than the resource-base can be explored. As a result most reports are out of date before they can be presented.

2.3.1 Surface water

Quantitative data on wadi discharge are sparse. In Eastern Libya only the Wadis Darnah, al Kuf and Latrun flow annually.[15] In Western Libya, less than 1% of the surface yields runoff in the form of flow to the sea. Each year, on average, (a notoriously misleading measure for Libyan climate and hydrology,) the Wadis Ki'am, Hasnun-Gau and Ruml-Labdah, yield some 84 million cubic metres of potentially useful water in the form of runoff.[16]

Though their surface discharge is small and irregular, the courses of the Wadis Sawfajjin, Zam Zam and Bay al Kebir, in the north-western part of Western Libya, are followed by subterranean rivers of potential if limited value. Furthermore, the course of the underground River Lete, east of Benghazi, can be traced at the surface by reference to associated collapse features in the surface of the limestone bedrock through which it flows. One hypothesis is that the River Lete is one of three branches of a huge underground drainage system which traverses Eastern Libya from the Nile valley. This hypothesis has received no support from the work of drilling companies and water engineers.[17,18]

The springs best sited for future developments are found along the scarp faces of the Jabal Akhdar and the Jabal Nafusah, within reach of the greater part of the agricultural zone of northern Libya. In Western Libya, the spring line extends some 200 kilometres between Josh and Tarhunah, but only some twenty-five noteworthy springs can be counted. The most significant of these feed the discharge of the Wadi Ki'am. Even here, however, there is little quantitative knowledge of the nature of the discharge, or whether the water comes from storage or from direct discharge of infiltrated precipitation.

Forty significant springs are listed for Eastern Libya by Ghiblawy,[19] only a few of which are within reach of the agriculturalists who form the most important potential users of the discharge from the springs. The springs with the most regular discharge are on the scarp face of the Jabal Akhdar and flow from karstic fissures in the limestone bedrock of the Jabal. Most feed brackish or salt water into small lakes on the stranded marine platforms of the Sahal. Examples are the Blue Lagoon, near al Kuefia, and Rommel's Pool, north-east of Benghazi. The chemical quality of these waters generally inhibits their use for domestic or agricultural purposes.

Of Libya's twenty or so large perennial lakes, none contains fresh water and few are sufficiently close to agricultural land or settlements to form a useful water supply. More useful are the ephemeral lakes which form at the confluences in the Wadis al Ajal, ash Shatti, Zallaf, Barjash, Andjarran and Nashaua, in Southern Libya. These lakes form as a direct result of precipitation, and provide an occasional small source of water for domestic animals.

2.3.2 Underground water

Subterranean water is tapped from artesian and perched aquifers as well as from the general water-table, but most wells in Libya tap the latter source. The most useful maps of the generalised water table in Libya are those of Jones (1964).[20] (See map facing page 36). The surface he describes was drawn by isolining the depths to potentially useful water for agricultural use. However, the net of detailed observations has so large a mesh in Libya that such small scale maps as these of the whole country are of limited practical use. More useful are the reports which resulted from the U.S. Technical Aid Programme in Libya. These deal with the most heavily populated parts of the country, but the areas with which each report deals are too small to use in drawing general conclusions about Libya as a whole. We have tried to combine the two sources - the maps and the reports - to present a meaningful impression of the water resources for the country as a whole.

The generalised ground water table decreases in elevation north-eastwards from a ground water divide somewhere between Lake Chad and the south-western border of Libya. Until very recently, useful aquifers were seldom recognised more than 50 metres below the ground surface, except below the northern Jabals, where aquifers more than 100 metres below the surface are used. Surface discharge of springs has reduced the number of deep wells which have been dug here in the past. However, many of the principal population nodes are situated in these regions. The L.A.J.S. report that Al Marj region is bereft of supplies of water sufficient for more than domestic use and the support of livestock above depths of 187 metres, is disquieting in this context.

Perched aquifers are, by definition, sources of only limited quantities of water. However, perched aquifers are commonly of great importance because of the generally limited water supply available to some Libyan settlements and projects. Sixteen significant perched aquifers are mapped by Jones, three are located where they are of little use, and ten in the Jabal Akhdar. It is probable that this geographical imbalance is a function of the inadequate

LIBYA-WATER RESOURCES

LIBYA - APPROX. DEPTH TO USABLE GROUND WATER

- —20— Contours of depths in metres
- — — — Boundary of zone for which data is available
- ▲ Perched aquifers
- ■ Flowing wells
- .... Major spring lines

INTERNATIONAL BOUNDARIES NOT AUTHENTICATED

hydrological data. In Western Libya, the most valuable perched aquifers are those near Mizdah and near al Qassabat. Many of the perched aquifers of the Jabal Akhdar lie near the main roads. For example, two occur near Martubah, on the Darnah-Tobruq road, and six more along the Darnah-al Baydah-al Marj routeway, one of them at al Baydah itself. The well-logs associated with work by Newport and Haddor in the al Marj district indicate that the perched aquifers of the Jabal Akhdar are often supported by shaly partings within the Eocene limestone bedrock.[21]

2.3.3 Artesian aquifers

The distribution of usable artesian aquifers in Libya is better known than that of perched aquifers. The Surt Basin has been a zone of crustal downwarping and sedimentation since late Paleozoic times, and its overall basinal structure makes it a natural focus for artesian waters collected from a very wide area indeed. Some 20 kilometres south-east of Surt good quality water under artesian head was tapped in a Tertiary limestone. The water circulates in the solution-enlarged fissures of the limestone.

Limestones of comparable age contain artesian water beneath the dip slope of the Jabal Akhdar, the water presumably migrating southwards down the structural dip from the groundwater divide beneath the jabal crest. Around Benghazi, artesian water of another source has been tapped at a variety of depths to some 200 metres below the surface. The water in these aquifers varies in quality from good in the upper parts to brackish in the lower parts of each aquifer, and the rate of transmission of the water varies with the degree of fissuring of the rock.

North of the Jabal in the northern part of Western Libya, artesian water is obtained from aquifers in a variety of rocks at a variety of depths. At the coast, generally poor quality water is obtained from the Tertiary Gefara sediments. Mesozoic rocks contain water under artesian head which is usefully tapped in the Tripoli district, although water from the Triassic rocks in the same district is heavily mineralised. Triassic rocks are believed to form the aquifer tapped by deep drilling near al Aziziyah, the water from which is similarly mineralised, probably through contact with and solution of the evaporites which form a significant part of this geologic series.

In central and southern Libya, demand for water is more local than in the north, and exploration and drilling have been less widespread. Artesian water makes its presence abundantly obvious, however, for a distance of some 150 kilometres along the Wadi ash Shatti, in Fezzan, where agriculturally useful water flows unchecked from springs under artesian head. Perhaps Libya's best artesian water, with regard to quality and quantity, is that to be found in the Nubian Sandstone series of Southern Libya. Large quantities of good water are taken from these rocks in the Sabhah-Awbari region. The greatest limitation on the use of these aquifers is the depth at which they lie. However, recent finds in the overlying tertiaries of the Kufrah region indicate that there may well be large quantities of untapped water in certain restricted parts of Libya.

Other parts of Libya are less fortunate. Beneath the Hun-Waddan region, the artesian aquifer is isolated by large displacement faults, and could not support extended withdrawals. Beneath Hun, the water is hot and heavily mineralised, and unsuitable for use on the local soils.

2.3.4 Quality of ground-water

The quality is judged against the use to which it is to be put. Furthermore, water which can be used with impunity on quickly-draining soil may not be suitable for use on a heavier soil for fear of salination. Thus, to assist interpretation of our discussion of ground water qualities the rating formulated by Newport and Haddor[21] are noted below:-

Rating	Approx. Dissolved Solids parts per million
Good quality	Up to 1500
Fair quality	1500-3000
Poor quality	More than 3000
Fresh water	Up to 3000
Brackish - moderately mineralised	3000-6000
Salty - highly mineralised	More than 6000

The introduction of seawater into an aquifer leads to the salinization of the lower part of the aquifer. Since seawater tends to be introduced into an aquifer laterally, and freshwater vertically down from the surface in the first instance, and since salt water is more dense than fresh, little mixing of the two takes place. The freshwater tends to float on the saline. Man has damaged ground water resources in at least two ways in Libya. One is by careless withdrawals of water from the aquifers. Beneath the coast of any landmass is a zone of junction between infusing seawater and the freshwater of the aquifers migrating coastwards under hydrostatic head. It is recognised by hydrologists that an increase in the water-table depth by one metre will lead to a rise in the level of the zone of junction between salt and fresh water of forty metres. Clearly, near the coast, where the potential hydrostatic head is limited by the limited elevation of the land surface, lowering of the water table by excessive and unco-ordinated demands by individual well-operators may lead to disasterous salinization of the aquifers. From this point of view, it is particularly unfortunate that Libya's best agricultural land and her largest cities occupy a narrow coastal strip, thus concentrating the demand for water where it can do most harm.

The second important detrimental influence commonly exerted by man on his ground water concerns aquifers at shallow depths. The ready availability of these aquifers commonly encourages their use. However, evaporation from the surface may lead to the capillary lift of water from the aquifer into the soil and to the deposition of salts in the soil as a result of continued evaporation. These salts may well be flushed down into the aquifer again under the influence of irrigation, or the next rainstorm, in much greater concentrations than existed before. The misuse of irrigation water aggravates this process to a certain extent. Water left on the soil surface to evaporate will deposit its contained salts and salinize the soil. The next rainstorm will flush these salts into the shallow aquifers. Since the shallowest aquifers tend to occur near the coast, as does the agricultural zone in Libya, the coastal aquifers are being salinized from above and below.

Away from the coastal districts, we have little detailed knowledge of the quality of ground water. Good water has been found beneath the surface of the Jabal Akhdar, and beneath the sand seas of Eastern Libya. Most of Southern Libya is underlain by good water, it seems, with the exception of the Awbari Sandsea, where the water tends to be brackish. Good water has been found beneath the western part of the Hamada al Hamra, and beneath the eastern part of the Jabal Nafusah. Elsewhere in Libya north of the 26th parallel, there are inadequate data for even broad generalisations, and the aquifers tend to contain only poor to brackish water, in large parts of Marmorica, declining to salty (see maps facing pages 24 and 36).

2.3.5 Decline in ground-water levels

Even in 1962, Ghiblawy could see that over-exploitation of the ground water around Tripoli was so rapidly lowering the static water level in many aquifers that a time could be foreseen in the not very distant future when the cost of irrigation would exceed the economic limit.[19] The economic break-even point for farmers using irrigation in Libya is rising rapidly. The cost of employing well diggers is rising with the increasing scarcity of the diggers, and with the increasing depth of the aquifers as the use of water leads to a decline in the water level. This decline is aggravated by the unco-ordinated use of motor pumps, and the pumps themselves cost the farmer far more than did the use of the donkey-operated dalu.

The rate of drawdown in an aquifer is primarily a function of the volume of water in the aquifer and the rate of transmission of water through the aquifer. Drawdown on one isolated well can be controlled by controlling the rate of withdrawal from that well. Drawdown that goes on unchecked on a number of wells in one locality may lead to widespread permanent lowering of the static water level, possibly accompanied by salinization in coastal districts.

Rates of lowering the ground water are rapid in the agricultural zone of Libya. In Western Libya, the ground water level around al Qarahbulli and az Zawiyah declined at rates between 0.14 - 0.16 metres per annum between 1930 and 1960. The average rate for the period 1958-62 was about 0.25 metres per annum, however, and in the year 1961-2 alone rates between 0.5 and 0.7 metres were recorded.[22,23] Between the 1920s and the 1960s, declines of the static water level by one metre occurred around Tripoli and Suq al Jumah, up to five metres some six kilometres to the south and up to 12 metres around Suwani bin Yadim and Bin Gashir, which are situated 20 kilometres from the coast. Details of the very high rates of decline of one metre per year since 1960 at Suwani bin Yadim and Bin Gashir are shown on the diagram facing page 40; a much smaller, but significant decline is evident at the coastal observation well at Mellahah. The danger of declines near the coast with reference to sea water intrusion is explained in paragraph 2.3.4. Furthermore, recharge is negligible throughout the country. In one of the few existing analyses of the origin of ground water, Stuart estimated that 60% of the water pumped from the Gefaran aquifers in Western Libya comes from gross annual recharge, 25% from storage and 15% from water which would have served to assist in the recharge of the aquifer had it not been withdrawn on its way down through the overlying rock.[24]

WATER LEVELS IN WELLS
IN THE WESTERN PROVINCE

MELLAHAH, BIN GASHIR, SUWANI BIN YADIM

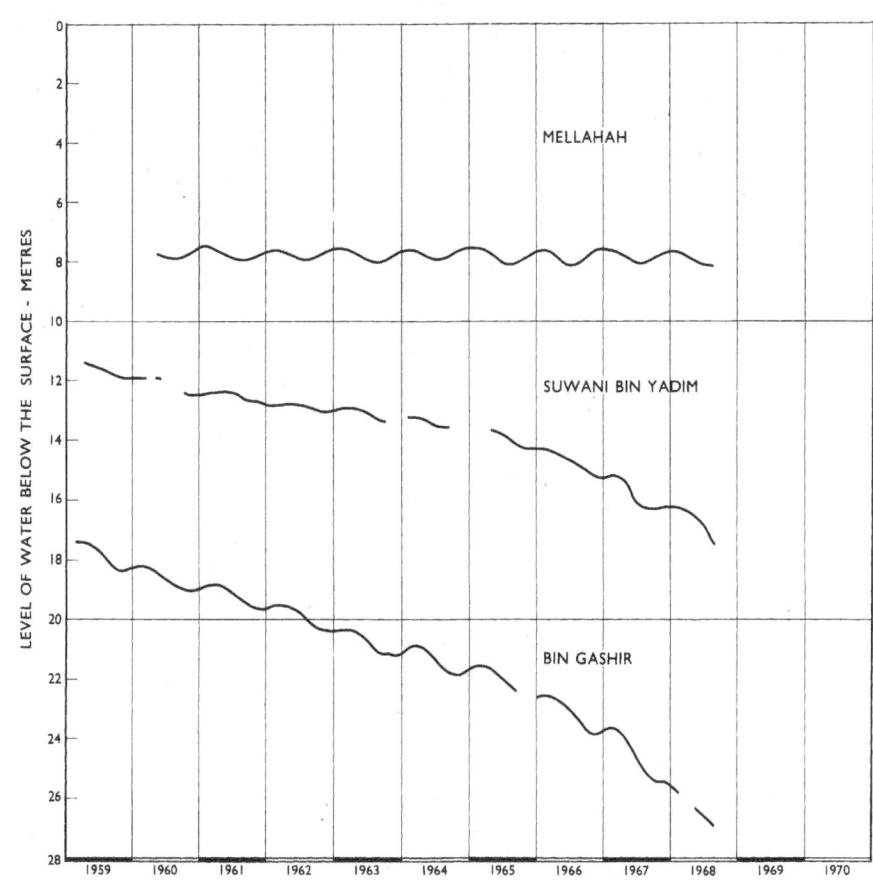

SOURCE :- Ministry of Agriculture, Soil & Water Conservation Department.

Stevens water level recorder in all three wells providing almost continuous records.

2.3.6 Water conservation

Conservation of water resources is clearly very important for Libyan agriculture, and may be considered under three headings: salvage, control and education. The salvage of potentially wasted water is technically relatively simple, but is expensive. The control of the surface runoff by dams and diversion weirs will contribute to soil conservation as well as reducing water wastage. The tapping of subterranean water currently lost from aquifers outcropping below sea-level at the coast is another possible measure of conservation. Reduction of water-loss in irrigation by the use of impervious concrete, metal or plastic lined pipes is a third possibility, and the re-use of water, as for example in sewage processing, is a fourth. While there is an increasing consciousness of the need for greater economy in water use, and techniques are gradually improving, a considerable volume of water is still lost, and conservation has yet to make an appreciable impact on slowing down the rate of fall in the aquifers in the coastal regions of the country.

In all, Libya is relatively poorly endowed with land and water resources and, even given optimal economic conditions, farming would remain strongly inhibited by natural conditions. Scanty rainfall may be partly compensated by drawing upon underground water reserves, though in most areas this represents the mining of a non-replenishing or an only slowly replenishing resource. New water reserves are being located, though probably not at a rate equal to that of withdrawal, while many of the largest of recent finds lie far from the present agricultural areas.

References

CHAPTER 2

Geology and Surface Form.

1. Klitzch, E., 'Comments on the Geology of the Central Parts of Southern Libya and Northern Chad' in South-Central Libya and Northern Chad, (Petroleum Exploration Society of Libya), p.1-18, Tripoli 1966.

2. Klitzch, E., 'Geology of the North-East Flank of the Murzuq Basin' First Saharan Symposium, Petroleum Exploration Society of Libya, p.97-113, Tripoli 1963.

3. Fürst, M., 'The Serir Tibesti, its Form, Material and Development' South-Central Libya and Northern Chad, (Petroleum Exploration Society of Libya), p.43-6, Tripoli 1966.

4. McKee, E.D. 'Origin of the Nubian and Similar Sandstones.' Sond. aus der Geol. Rund., Band 52, p.551-587, 1962.

5. Desio, A., 'Breve Synthese de l'Evolution Morphologique du Territoire de la Lybie.' Bull. Soc. R.G.S. d'Egypte, v.25, p.9 et seq., 1953.

6. Pesce, A., 'Uau en Namus', in South-Central Libya and Northern Chad, (Petroleum Exploration Society of Libya), p.47-52, 1966.

7. Ziegert, H., 'Climatic Changes and Paleolithic Industries in Eastern Fezzan', in South-Central Libya and Northern Chad, (Petroleum Exploration Society of Libya), p.65-8, 1966

8. Butzer, K.W., Quaternary Stratigraphy and Climate in the Near East, Bonn, 1958.

9. Di Cesare, F., Franchino, A. and Sommaruga, C., 'The Pliocene-Quaternary of the Giarabub Erg Region.' First Saharan Symposium, Petroleum Exploration Society of Libya, p. 30-48, 1963.

10. McBurney, C.B.M. and Hey, R.W., Pre-history and Pleistocene Geology in Cyrenaica, Libya, Cambridge, 1955.

11. Hey, R.W. 'The Quaternary Geology and Paleolithic Archeology of Libya', in Quaternaria, v.6, p.435-449, 1961.

12. Ministry of Communications Meteorological Service, Monthly and Annual Climatic Data for Libya, typescript.

13. Stewart, J.H., Land and Water Resources of Tripolitania; a measurement of the land and its potential, USOM to Libya, report, 1960.

14. Kanter, H., Libyen (Libya), Berlin, 1967.

15. Kanter, H. *Libyen (Libya)*, Berlin, 1967.

16. Stewart, J.H., *Land and Water Resources of Tripolitania; a measurement of the land and its potential*, USOM to Libya, report, 1960.

17. Zinevrakis, M., *The River Lethon Dam*. Memo to the National Bank of Libya, Tripoli.

18. Messrs. A.P.I. Cotterell carried out ground water investigations for the British Administration in the Benghazi District in 1950.

19. Ghiblawy, I.R., *Agricultural Development in Libya*. Typescript report in the Bank of Libya, Tripoli, March, 1962.

20. Jones, J.R., *'Ground-Water Maps of the Kingdom of Libya'*. Open file report, USGS, 1964.

21. *'Ground Water Explorations in al Marj Area, Cyrenaica'*, USGS W.S.P. 1757-A.

22. Ogilbee, W. and Tarhuni, H.A., *'Ground Water Resources of the Qarabulli Area, Tripolitania'*, USGS/USOM/Govt. of Libya Open File Report, 1962.

23. *'Ground Water Resources of the Az Zawiah Area, Tripolitania,'* USOM/Govt. of Libya Open File Report, 1962.

24. Stuart, W.T., *'Significance of the Decline in Ground Water Levels in Tripolitania, Libya, as Determined by Pumping Tests,'* USGS/USOM/Govt. of Libya typescript report, 1960.

Chapter Three

AGRICULTURAL LAND USE AND CROP PATTERNS 1911-1960

3.1 Agricultural Land Use

Although settled agriculture was developed in the coastal and Jabal regions of northern Libya[1] and in small oasis pockets in southern Libya[2] at an early date, the scale of arable and orchard cultivations is thought to have been limited to small areas around coastal towns, to the better-watered hill lands such as the eastern Jabal Nafusah and the Shahhat region of the Jabal al Akhdar, and to the major wadis and semi-artesian basins of the south, such as the Jarmah area of Wadi al Ajal. Possibly the most extensive developments were carried out in the Roman period (approx. 145-450 AD) when olive plantations were established and cereals grown, partly for export. Later incursions by the Berbers and Vandals in the fifth century brought about a rapid decline in agriculture and, despite a brief revival under Byzantine control affecting mainly the Leptis Magna area, agriculture had scarcely recovered before the advent of the Arab conquests beginning in the years 641-643 AD.

The Arab invaders, with a few notable exceptions, were nomadic and semi-nomadic pastoralists with little interest in sedentary agriculture. Orchards, farms, water-lifting and wadi control works fell into ruin or, in some cases, were destroyed. Land use during the closing years of the Ottoman period, which ended in 1912, was dominated by the grazing needs of the flocks and the associated shifting cereal cultivation in rainfed areas. Small orchards of olive and date palm trees survived in Western Libya where rainfall and political conditions permitted, although it appears, from early Italian maps, that such areas were considerably more restricted than the traditional garden areas indicated on Land Use Map 8. In Eastern Libya nomadic society was the rule except for a few alien urban settlements along the littoral, and no orcharding was practised.

In the closing years of the Turkish administration efforts were made to develop agriculture as a means of implementing the Ottoman land codes and raising the ability of the country to pay higher taxes. At the same time, the relative peace imposed on the area during the nineteenth century encouraged the growth of sedentary agriculture, and, in Western Libya, which was the area principally affected by the trend, some 357,000 persons were reported as sedentary in 1917, against 128,000 semi-nomads and 85,000 purely nomadic.[3] Land use in the same period (1931 estimates) was reported as 17,000 ha. of traditional gardens (suani), 6,000 ha. of rainfed orchards (ginan) (suani and ginan together 23,000 ha.), and 9,000 ha. of jabaline gardens, while lands under grazing and shifting cultivation are assessed at more than one million hectares (see Table 3.1). The situation in Eastern Libya was somewhat different. The reported population was small, totalling only 185,000, of which the majority were reported as sedentary (73%), though these figures are distorted somewhat by the retreat of nomadic groups following the Italian military offensive on the area (see Table 3.2).

Table 3.1 Estimates of Areas of Land Use 1933-1960

Hectares

Census/Estimate Source	Date	Total Land	Irrigated		Non-Irrigated		Forest and Woodland	Pasture & Rough Grazing
			Trad'l Gardens	Modern Sector	Trad'l Gardens	Modern Sector		
WESTERN LIBYA								
Gov. of Tripoli	1933[1]	53,934	–	2,155	–	49,821	1,968	–
Agricultural Census	1937	76,334[2&3]	–	9,934	–	63,439	2,961	–
Rowland & Robb (B.M.A.)	1945*	8,404,050	50,000	59,000	127,000[4]	165,000[5]	3,050	8,000,000
Agricultural Census	1960	2,879,377[6]	167,069[7]		672,327[8]		34,365	1,120,766
			1,724,246[9]					
EASTERN LIBYA								
Statistiche sulla col'e d.Libia 1937	1933	–	–	–	–	24,485[10]	–	–
Agricultural Census	1937	31,645[11]	–	816	–	22,822	8,007[12]	–
B.M.A. Estimates	1945*	187,250[13]	15,000	1,000	141,900[14]	29,350	–	–
Agricultural Census	1960	835,975	17,091[15]		303,668[16]		28,901[18]	
					795,997[17]			

* Estimates   See additional notes on the next page   '–' = not recorded

Notes on Table 3.1

It should be noted that the 1945 figures are estimates only.

1. *Italian only*
2. *Net productive land*
4. *Dryland traditional excludes shifting cultivation area estimated at 200,000 ha. in 1945*
5. *Dryland modern includes areas of newly developed ENTE and INPS estates not provided with irrigation water estimated at 60,000 ha.*
6. *Total excludes 145,052 ha. 'other land'*
7. *Including fallow*
8. *Excluding fallow*
9. *For total arable and permanent crops including shifting cultivation and fallow*
10. *Total land reported in concessions - Italian only*
11. *Net productive land - Italian only*
12. *Plantations only*
13. *Excluding associated forest and woodland*
14. *Excluding production by nomadic groups*
15. *Including fallow*
16. *Excluding fallow*
17. *Including fallow*
18. *Woodland only*

Table 3.2 Population by Status, 1917

	WESTERN LIBYA		EASTERN LIBYA	
SEDENTARY	357,000	63%	134,000	73%
SEMI-NOMADIC	128,000	22%	16,000	9%
NOMADIC	85,000	15%	35,000	18%
TOTAL	570,000	100%	185,000	100%

Source: D'Agostini[3]

Land use at the time of the Italian occupation was orientated largely towards pasture and shifting cultivation of grain, with very small pockets of permanent cultivation near the main towns, particularly Benghazi and Darnah. Italian writers at the time describe the area as appearing abandoned, with most people tent-dwellers, often prone to move following the rain.[4]

3.1.1 The Italian Colonial Period, 1911-1942

The impact of Italian colonialism on the use of land for agriculture began on a small scale but gradually increased in intensity over the period, reaching its climax in the late 1930s. In the period 1911-22, the Italians were concerned mainly with consolidating their military position in Libya. More or less continuous warfare in Eastern Libya, and sporadic, but highly disruptive fighting between Italians and Arabs in Western Libya, had an adverse effect upon agricultural prosperity. Many farmers gave up cultivating the oasis areas and took once again to the nomadic life, or moved to the interior where Italian forces were not in control. In Eastern Libya, population was reduced by deaths in battle and by the wholesale movement of tribal groups either to the interior or into the adjacent areas of Egypt. The Italian approach to their acquisition of Libya was at the same time strategic and paternalistic, and it was expected that social and economic life would continue unchanged. In consequence, only small areas of mainly urban land were alienated from indigenous holdings, and no positive steps were taken to alter the pattern of rural land use.

Following the bitter fighting between the Italians and Arabs, which persisted until 1922 in Western Libya and until 1930-31 in Eastern Libya, Italian policy changed considerably, accelerated by the rise of fascist government in the metropolitan country. The colonial authority pursued political pacification of the country more energetically and consolidated its position by opening up opportunities for Italian agricultural developments in both northern provinces. Although Italian land acquisitions totalled some 9,613 ha. by end 1923 and rose to 204,417 ha. by end 1928, only 113,209 ha. had been granted in concessions and only limited areas had actually been reclaimed and planted. Even at this late date, therefore, the Italian impact on rural use was confined to the development of a few concessions concentrated around the major settlements. Economic disruption of the eastern province continued to exert a negative influence on the use of the coastal and jabaline pastures, with the tribes moving south outside the range of Italian control or leaving the country

WESTERN AND EASTERN LIBYA

Lands scheduled for Agricultural Development by the Italian Administration, State Agencies, Companies and Private individuals.

Maps after Servizio Cartografico Min. Afr. Ital.

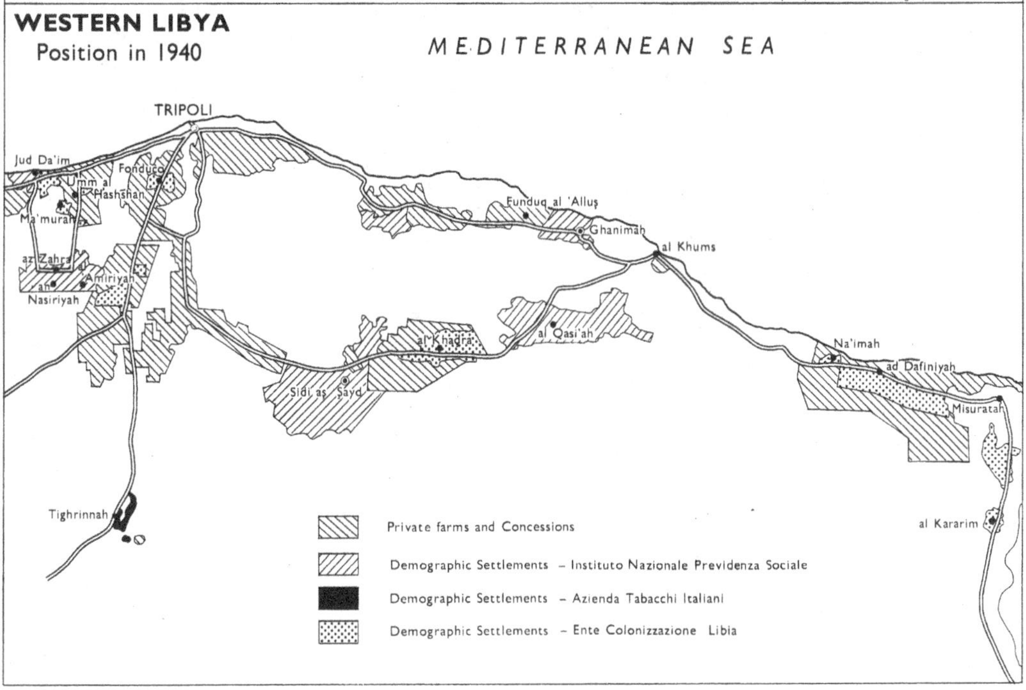

WESTERN LIBYA
Position in 1940
MEDITERRANEAN SEA
TRIPOLI
Jud Da'im
Fonduco
Umm al Hashshan
Ma'murah
az Zahra
al Amiriyah
an Nasiriyah
Funduq al 'Allus
Ghanimah
al Khums
al Khadra
al Qasi'ah
Sidi as Sayd
Na'imah
ad Dafiniyah
Misuratah
al Kararim
Tighrinnah
Private farms and Concessions
Demographic Settlements – Instituto Nazionale Previdenza Sociale
Demographic Settlements – Azienda Tabacchi Italiani
Demographic Settlements – Ente Colonizzazione Libia

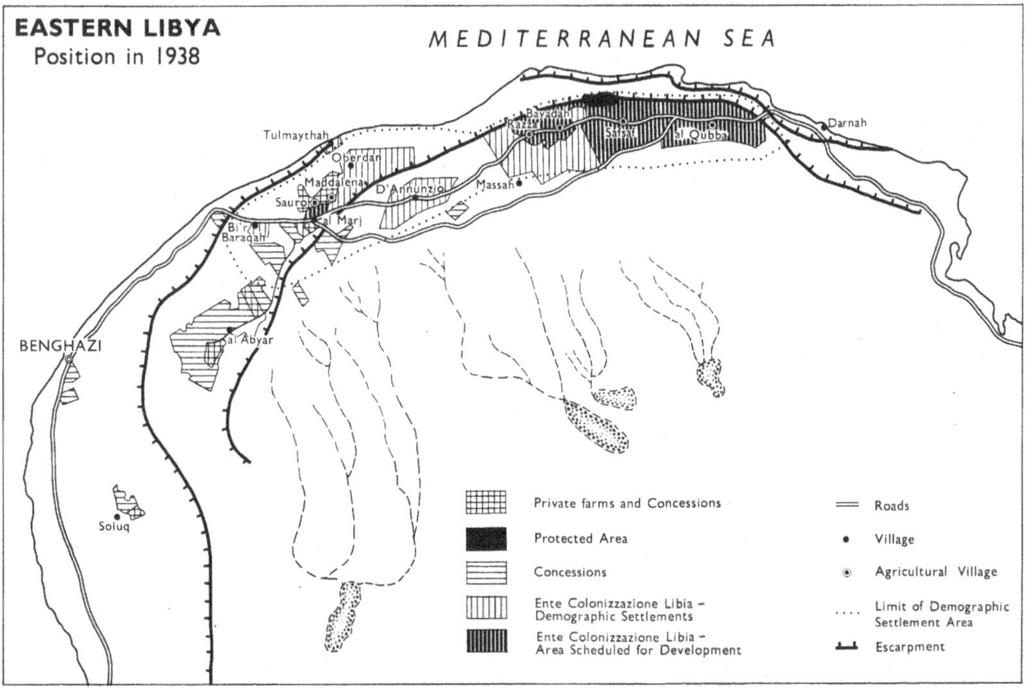

EASTERN LIBYA
Position in 1938
MEDITERRANEAN SEA
Tulmaythah
Oberdan
Maddalena
Sauro
D'Annunzio
Massah
Razza
Bayadah
Safsaf
al Qubba
Darnah
al Marj
Bi'r Baraqah
al Abyar
BENGHAZI
Soluq
Private farms and Concessions
Protected Area
Concessions
Ente Colonizzazione Libia – Demographic Settlements
Ente Colonizzazione Libia – Area Scheduled for Development
Roads
Village
Agricultural Village
Limit of Demographic Settlement Area
Escarpment

altogether. In Western Libya, firm military and political administration fostered the growth of sedentary agriculture in the traditional areas and there is evidence that security and increasing urban demand for food crops led to greater concentration by indigenous producers on arable farming at the expense of animal husbandry.[5] Newly-founded agricultural estates were modelled on French colonial developments in Tunisia and most units were large with an estimated two-thirds of all farms occupying more than 1,000 ha. Land use systems adopted in the period were mainly orchard/grain based, utilising crop associations including olive, almond, vine and wheat and barley. While some full irrigation of crops was undertaken in the Tripoli region, most land was cultivated by dry land or semi-irrigation techniques, with a relatively extensive use of land, especially in eastern Libya.

From the late 1920s, and with increasing effect from 1931, the Italian government demanded the settlement of Italian peasant farmers and a more rapid rate of agricultural development in the colony. Private concessions remained a vehicle for this new policy, more lots being allocated than formerly, subject to the condition that all or part of the estates be made over to share-cropping peasants. At the same time, increased activity by the colonisation agencies led to a more rapid reclamation of land for purely peasant settlement. By the end of 1936 the Italian administration reported that a total area of 150,530 ha. had been granted in concessions, of which 75,504 ha. were developed for agriculture and forestry, including 64,682 ha. of orchard, 1,423 ha. of woodland, 8,093 ha. of dunes stabilised by wood land and 2,307 ha. of irrigated arable land.[6]

In the late 1930s, efforts were made to increase peasant settlements through the colonisation agencies, intensifying agricultural land use, since all peasant farms, whether worked as share-cropping plots on a private concession as at La Valdagno (al Khums) or as peasant proprietor units, tended to have higher percentages of land under irrigation and to include a relatively larger area of intercropped land than the large private farms. In contrast to the mainly dry land or at best semi-irrigated orchard plantations of the large farms, peasant farms on 'Ente per il Colonizzazione della Libia' (ENTE) estates in Western Libya followed a more or less standard pattern in which 25 ha. plots, making up the individual farms, were utilised for dry land olives (10 ha.), dry land almonds (5 ha.), dry land vines (3-4 ha.), and irrigated cereals, vegetables and flowers (4-5 ha.). In Eastern Libya, the characteristic land use pattern adopted by the land settlement agencies comprised a 25 ha. dry land plot given over to vines (2 ha.), almonds (4 ha.), olives (5 ha.), other fruits (0.25 ha.), cereals (10.75 ha.) and non-agricultural land (1 ha.).[7]

Official concern with colonising activities was exclusively directed at the Italian farmed area until 1938, when it was decreed that suitable Arab farmers would be settled on special estates at al Ma'murah (500 ha. developed) and Na'imah (500 ha. allocated). The Arab sector undoubtedly derived some benefit from the Italian extension services and technical agencies, and to a very limited extent from the demonstration effect of the modern Italian units, on which many Arab farmers worked as labourers. In other ways Arab areas suffered from Italian settlement activities, with the loss of better-watered pasture and shifting cultivation areas in the steppe lands adjacent to the oases of Western Libya, where small garden areas, especially in Tripoli and Tajura oases were bought by colonists for re-development. In Eastern Libya, concentration of dissident tribal groups in army-controlled areas and considerable alienation of the best-watered areas of the Jabal al Akhdar reduced the area utilised by the Arab sector, especially for shifting cereal growing.

Small scale irrigation developments in Southern Libya, where government farms were constructed in the main oases, and new gardens handed over to Arab farmers in Ghudamis, generally assisted sedentary farming, though Italian interest in this area was more strategic than economic.

By 1940, the land use pattern of Libya had been altered radically by Italian colonising efforts. Quite apart from the orchard plantations in the coastal plains and northern hill lands of Western Libya, the application of modern methods of water-lifting had made possible intensive use of land for irrigated arable crops in a broad belt of the province lying in the steppe to the south of the Arab oases from Zuwarah to Misuratah. Developments in Eastern Libya, although less impressive, since many settlement estates were only in the first stages of reclamation to crop use when the Second World War curtailed the programme, had succeeded in raising the level of land use from grazing and shifting cultivation to organised orcharding and relatively sophisticated mechanised cereal cultivation.

Table 3.1 indicates the probable development in the areas given over to various farming and land use types after 1931. The most meaningful assessment of the Italian contribution to modern irrigated and modern dry land use is that for the year 1945, when in Western Libya 14.6 per cent of total land and 54.1 per cent of all irrigated land was accounted for by Italian modern-sector irrigated farms, and 40.8 per cent of total land and 56.5 of dryland was held by Italian farmers under modern dryland farms. Virtually all plantation woodland was Italian sponsored, the 3,050 ha. reported in Table 3.1 represents only woodland outside agricultural estates. Estimates of land area under irrigated and dryland management for the indigenous and Italian sectors contained in Table 5.1 for the year 1945 are less reliable than those for Western Libya, but they indicate the approximate importance of the respective farm and land use types. In Eastern Libya, some 0.5 per cent of total land was Italian developed (but by 1945 not under Italian control). At the same time, 15.7 per cent of total land was held in dryland Italian-developed estates, which accounted for 17.1 per cent of all dry land farms. All 8,007 ha. of woodland plantations were laid out by the Italian administration. In all, Italian developments more than doubled the land area under active use for arable, orchard and woodland and converted the farmland in Italian hands to more valuable and productive cropping patterns, especially in Western Libya. This was achieved without major dislocation of the indigenous land use pattern in most areas.

3.1.2 The Post-colonial Period 1942-1951

Expulsion of Italian authority following the military advance of Allied forces was the culmination of two year's bitter fighting, devastation of agricultural areas and depopulation in Eastern Libya. Virtually all of the Italian agricultural settlers left the land in Eastern Libya and much of their former lands, only recently reclaimed, relapsed from orchard and cereal cropping to grazing and occasional shifting cultivation by indigenous groups. Western Libya, by contrast, suffered no such decline in either the area of the intensity of land use. Italian farmers were encouraged to stay on their farms and the extremely high prices offered for food crops stimulated continued cultivation, at least until 1944,[8] as did exceptionally favourable weather conditions during 1944, 1945 and 1946. Despite active aid to agriculture under the care-and-maintenance policy of the British Military Administration, prosperity declined somewhat in the late 1940s as military expenditures dropped and Libya was isolated from former markets in metropolitan Italy, although the worst effects of this, and drought, were off-set in part by the maturing of the olive trees planted in the pre-war era, production from which became available for domestic consumption and export in increasing quantities.

Attempts were made by the British Administration in Eastern Libya to re-invigorate indigenous agriculture through the institution of a hill farm scheme on the former Italian estate of al Qubbah (Giovani Berta), where 65 farms were maintained under intensive crop management on the former Italian model. Meanwhile, the al Marj plain was taken over by the administration for use as a wheat growing area within the framework of the Middle East Supply Centre. In 1950 it was officially reported that 4,787 ha. were sown with wheat and 165 ha. with barley by the al Marj organisation, while a further 781 ha. were under contract cultivation by Arab farmers. Vegetable cultivation was also encouraged both at al Gharig, adjacent to al Marj, and in several of the southern oases including Jalu. Importantly, pasture land use regained the levels prevailing before the Italian wars with a rapid build-up of herds.

Table 3.3 Numbers of Animals, 1926, 1933 and 1946

YEAR	SHEEP	GOATS	CATTLE	CAMELS	HORSES	MULES DONKEYS
1926	800,000	70,000	10,000	75,000	14,000	9,000
1933	98,000	25,000	8,700	2,600	10,000	5,000
1946	662,000	528,000	35,000	35,000	7,000	15,400

Source: British Military Administration Handbook on Cyrenaica, Vol VII & VIII.

3.1.3 Period of Independence Before Oil Revenues, 1951-1961

The decade following the grant of independence in 1951, though apparently a period of economic stagnation, saw several important changes in the cropping pattern. Government policy towards agriculture retained a strand of continuity in the period of the British Military Administration, with British and Italian staff remaining in their posts. Generous and careful treatment of the Italian farming community was designed where possible to keep Italian farmers on the land, and development of new agricultural areas was extremely limited and cautious in line with a policy of keeping small-scale intensive farming and extensive cereal growing and herding as the basis of the nation's economy. Purely indigenous development was inhibited by the poverty of people and government, and most central services provided for the sector were foreign-financed and run through Point Four, and British, French, Italian and Egyptian aid.

Many Italian farmers stayed on the land in the years after independence, but farmers who had not completed the terms of their original agreements with the Italian colonising agencies, or who were on farms without fertile soils or adequate water supply and were isolated from urban life and markets, gave up or, more commonly, sold out, their holdings. In this way an entire estate at al Kararim, relapsed from intensive cropping under irrigation to dry land orcharding of a primitive kind. On private estates too, many 'messadria' tenants left the land, for example at La Valdagno, near al Khums. Generally, however, neglect of formerly productive holdings by abandonment, part-time farming (where operators took jobs in the towns) or reversion to self-sufficient production under indigenous operators affected only a minority of holdings.

The few Arab farmers able to afford the purchase of Italian farms maintained their output, while the peasant farms established during the era of intensive demographic settlement in the 1930s, and especially the middle and late 1930s, reached high yields as the major olive plantations on them matured in the years 1951-54. In Eastern Libya, land use deteriorated somewhat after independence. The al Marj wheat scheme and the organised hill farm scheme collapsed; and the total areas tilled and the standards of cultivation fell. Insecurity of tenure of the Arab farmers occupying former Italian estates, which were let on annual leases, discouraged farmers from planting anything but temporary crops by traditional methods. Only private estates developed by the Italians retained significant areas under orchards, and the predominant use of land throughout the province was livestock grazing with associated shifting cultivation.

Cropping in the traditional gardens of Western Libya retained considerable importance, aided by the greater use of irrigation water as diesel and electric pumps replaced 'dalu' water lifting on the larger and more prosperous farms. Apart from the rapid (though fluctuating) increase in olive oil output, changes were wrought in crop production by the groundnut boom of the mid-1950s and the increasing acreage under tomato crops, average production of these two crops rising by some 600% and 400%, respectively, between 1945/50.[9] Although intercultivation of the date palm remained a feature of the traditional oases, the falling value of low quality dates adversely affected the coastal palmeries and the average annual harvest dropped for the country as a whole by some 35% between 1945/50 and 1954/60.[10]

Table 3.4 Land use 1960

Hectares

AREA	ARABLE LAND	ORCHARDS AND FRUIT PLANTATIONS	PERMANENT MEADOW AND PASTURE	WOODLAND AND FOREST	OTHER LAND
WESTERN LIBYA	1,604,988	119,258	1,120,766	34,365	145,052
EASTERN LIBYA	741,763	8,346	14,766	28,901	13,299
SOUTHERN LIBYA	28,324	6,753	218	7	1,921
LIBYA TOTAL *	2,375,074	134,357	1,135,750	63,274	160,273

* *Discrepancies due to rounding*

Source: Agricultural Census, 1960.

In general, Libyan farming did not develop rapidly in the 1950s. The British Military Administration, which followed the Italian administration in 1942 in Eastern Libya and in 1943 in the West, did not allocate resources for agriculture to the same extent as had its predecessor. The international assistance which increased after independence in 1951, did not bring about remarkable changes in the landscape, except at Wadi Ki'am in Western Libya. Even this scheme, however, covered less than two square kilometres. In the 1950s Libyan agriculture was not only changing slowly, but land which had been developed before 1940 was being farmed at a lower level of efficiency than twenty years before.

3.2 Crop Patterns by Farm type. 1912 - 1960

In considering crop patterns on settled farms it has been found convenient to group farms according to a farm type classification, as follows:-

Irrigated & semi-irrigated	a. Traditional	Type 1
	b. Modern	Type 2
Non-irrigated (dry farms)	a. Traditional	Type 3
	b. Modern	Type 4

As the organisation of this section is historical it is natural to discuss first the traditional farms, both irrigated and dry, and to follow with a treatment of modern farms of both types.

Traditional farms are those irrigated and dry farms which are Libyan owned and run and which date generally from before 1911. The irrigated farms are located on the coast of Eastern and Western Libya, (see map 8, lower part - Appendix 8) and occur as isolated oases in Southern Libya. In Western Libya, non-irrigated traditional farms are a feature of the Jabal Nafusah and the area around Al Qassabat (between Tarhunah and al Khums - Map 8 lower part - Appendix 8). See also Map of Sample Points for the 1968 Survey facing page 74. In Eastern Libya traditional dry farming is carried out in the Jabal Akhdar, but to a limited extent.

In this chapter we have identified modern farms as those set up between 1911 and 1939. They can be Libyan or Italian owned, and can be run by an Italian or Libyan owner or manager. Modern farms have in turn been classified as irrigated, (including semi-irrigated), and dry farms. The distribution of these farms in Eastern and Western Libya can be seen on Map 8, lower part.

3.2.1 Traditional Gardens

Cereals

Some 20,000 metric tons of barley, the main grain crop, was produced on average each year on traditional farms in Western Libya in the Ottoman period according to Turkish estimates of crop production. These estimates were made for taxation purposes and represent rough assessments of the output of the major traditional crop, cereals. This level was maintained during the early years of the Italian period and rose only after the military pacification of the area. Cereal production by Arab farmers, including oasis garden and steppe areas, rose steadily (Table 3.5), with the dryland areas remaining of greatest importance. The bulk of such cultivation took place in the steppe.

Table 3.5 Arab Wheat and Barley Production in
Western Libya 1931 - 36
Metric tons

Barley	1931	1932	1933	1934	1935	1936
Dryland traditional gardens	20,000	30,000	60,000	28,000	40,000	3,000
Traditional irrigated gardens	1,500	1,500	2,000	1,500	750	-
Wheat						
Dryland traditional gardens	3,000	2,000	3,680	6,000	7,500	-
Traditional irrigated gardens	-	-	-	-	-	

Source: Rowland & Robb, Land Resources in Tripolitania, 1945.

Barley production in the years 1931-35 averaged 35,000 tons, a level maintained until the early years of World War II, when failure of rainfall and economic disruption caused a sharp decline in production. From 1942/43, improved weather conditions and a rise in the price of cereals led to increased output until the early 1950s (except for 1947 when there was a severe drought). Output of barley fell gradually during the 1950s, though levels of production from traditional units remained higher on average than in the pre-war years. Even in the poor rainfall year 1954/5 barley production totalled 32,500 tons from dry land steppe holdings and 2,500 tons from oasis land, while wheat production ran to 4,350 and 2,000 tons for the same two areas, respectively. Good conditions in 1955/56 sustained steppe and oasis barley output at 74,000 and 2,600 tons respectively, and wheat production at 10,650 and 4,000 tons, a considerable improvement over similar rainfall years in the pre-war period.

The acreage of barley sown and harvested has fluctuated erratically, though with a tendency to increase over the review period. Barley acreages in Western Libya are estimated to have averaged 10,000 ha. in 1931-36, ranging from a minimum of 5,800 ha. in 1931 to a maximum of 17,150 ha. in 1933. A rapid expansion of the acreage took place after 1943, reaching a high point in 1946 at 316,000 ha.[11] In 1955, some 250 ha. of oasis land and 211,500 ha. of steppe land in Western Libya was under barley, respectively being, 92.5% and 2.5% of the value of the total output of barley for Western Libya.

Trends in the area under cultivation and output of barley in Eastern Libya are less well documented than those for the west of the country, but from evidence available, it would seem that traditional cultivation was limited to dry land barley at a subsistence level[12] and was depressed below levels prevailing in the Turkish period by the adverse effects of the Italo-Sanussi Wars. The area of barley on traditional dry land holdings is estimated at 59,643 ha. for 1945, when output was some 7,897 metric tons. Official estimates are not reliable but are shown in Table 3.6 for 1955, 1960 and 1965.

Whereas rainfall variations have a marked effect on the area cultivated and yield obtained in the almost exclusively dryland grain areas of Eastern Libya, and obscure any trends in the barley acreage, it is clear that wheat cultivation increased rapidly in relation to barley throughout the 1950s, and both area and output were greater than for barley. Distribution of improved seeds, and changing consumer demand both in rural areas and in the towns aided the change in cropping pattern. A less marked but similar trend is discernible in Western Libya. Trends in output of cereals in Southern Libya (for which statistics are most unreliable) are not known with certainty, though official returns indicate a constant acreage of some 400 ha. of wheat and 1,000 ha. of barley during the 1950s, all irrigated.

Table 3.6 Estimates of Barley and Wheat Acreage and Output: Eastern Libya
(metric tons and hectares)

Year	Barley		Wheat	
	output (mt.)*	area (ha.)	output (mt.)*	area (ha.)
1945	7,897	147,378	4,979	85,518
1955	18,200	112,840	10,700	-
1960	31,517	197,496	12,701	88,948
1965	34,164	105,660	43,718	129,419

Source: BMA and Government of Libya *Metric tons.*

Although cereal production remained second to livestock by value in the traditional sectors, the gradual improvement in the output of cereals had an important effect in raising living standards of the Arab population. At the same time, changes in both the area and the productivity of other types of land use also took place after 1911, especially in Western Libya.

Tree crops

Tree crops in Western Libya have for many years represented an important element in output from traditional farms. In oasis gardens the date palm occupied more land than all other fruit trees, with an estimated 30,000 ha. in 1960. Available estimates suggest a gradual decline in the number of trees in Western Libya from 1,768,084 in 1945 to 1,614,800 in 1960, and to 1,271,979 in 1965, with a corresponding but less well documented fall in output. The quality of dates produced in the littoral oases is poor and their main value is as animal feed. At the same time, the many products of the date palm from timber and fronds to laghbe (beer) and date-stone coffee lost importance as better alternatives became available to farmers. Although newly reclaimed farms tend to have only a scattering of date palms, the traditional oases retained their characteristic palm plantations reflecting both conservatism on the part of the owners and the continuing value of the palm as an insulation cover for irrigated crops in the suani.

Eastern Libya, never an important date growing region, also saw a fall in the number of palms. This continuing trend is reflected in recent figures which show a decline from 250,000 acres in 1960 to 150,000 in 1965. The position of the date palm in Southern Libya has remained more or less stable, and has been further supported by the activities of the date factory at Jufrah. Some 1,350,000 trees covering 50,000 ha. were reported in the area in 1960 while annual output ranges between 7,000-9,000 tons. Whereas the main date areas in Western Libya are associated almost exclusively with the traditional irrigated sector, those in Southern Libya are not irrigated except incidentally in the small areas under cultivation for field crops.

The olive tree is second to the date palm in traditional irrigated gardens but in the traditional dryland sector olive culture is paramount, having been wide-spread in Western Libya before the growth of modern Italian plantations after 1911. Major traditional olive areas include the jabal front around Gharyan, Tarhunah and Qassabat with large numbers of scattered trees and small gardens in the jabal and steppe. It is estimated that the number of olives in the traditional sector has risen from 450,000 in 1910 to 828,624 in 1935 and 970,000 in 1945 though falling to 827,928 by the mid-1950s, a growth fostered by the introduction of improved varieties and techniques of cultivation, more modern means of processing and access to the Italian market. Although output from traditional olive cultivation does not rival output of the modern sector, yields under the former tend to be more stable from year to year, partly because traditional jabal gardens occupy the more favoured climatic regions, particularly around al Qassabat, and partly because more individual attention is devoted to the trees and gardens to secure water supply (including ditches to catch rain water run-off and a mud retaining wall around each tree). Olive growing played only a small role in the traditional land use pattern of Eastern and Southern Libya, and the 1,600 ha. reported under olives in the Jabal Akhdar region in 1960 represents Italian plantings, only a small proportion remaining associated with the traditional sector.

Vegetables

Cultivation of vegetables in the traditional farming areas is restricted to the irrigated oases or to a few areas of annual inundation such as al Gharig (al Marj Plain). Before 1950 and the introduction of the mechanical pump in traditional areas, the acreage of vegetable and fodder crops was limited by access to irrigation water raised by the dalu lift, which it is calculated,[14] permitted some 57% of oasis land to be irrigated in Western Libya, of which some 52% was available for field crops. In any one year, only a fraction of crop land was irrigated, varying from 6.7% in Zawiyah oasis to 30.3% in Surman.[13] Lucerne, for fodder, accounted for an average of 10% of cultivated land, with the remaining irrigated acreage given over to potato, onion, tomato, water melon, broad beans, millet, barley and occasional crops of tobacco and henna.[13] Demand for self-sufficiency in vegetables and fodder, together with the restricted volume of irrigation water available, led to conservative attitudes towards field crops. Even during the groundnut boom of the 1950s, the oasis areas played only a minor role, accounting for less than 2.3% of production in the Zawiyah area in 1952, including modern irrigated Libyan farms.[15]

3.2.2 The Modern Sector

Until the decrees in 1928 calling for the establishment of Italian peasant settlement in Libya, modern farming was in the hands of capitalist farmers and was predominantly dry land orcharding of olive, almond and vine (see Table 3.1). Although the area devoted to irrigated cropping grew in importance from 1933, dry land farming dominated the modern sector. Cropping in the modern sector was almost entirely market oriented and much of it was for export until World War II. The major permanent development of the modern sector was concentrated in Western Libya, which was the exclusive domain of modern irrigated agriculture until very recent times.

Barley production never occupied a significant part in the cropping pattern on modern farms. Even as late as 1936, Italian 'aziendas' contributed less than one million tons to total output and in 1956 it was reported that only 5% of output was derived from the modern sector, with 3.2% produced on dry land or semi-irrigated land. Interest in wheat growing on modern farms has been greater.

The basic cropping pattern on modern farms was set in the early period of colonisation and in large part followed the model laid down by the French in Tunisia, with olive, almond and vine grown either in single plantations, or, more often, associated together, the earlier yielding vine and almond giving cash income to the farmer before the major olive plantings became fully productive as late as fifteen years after planting. The olive was laid out on a 20 x 20 metre, almond 10 x 10 metre, and vine 2 x 2 metre regular grid in dry land and semi-irrigated plantations, which by 1937 accounted for 93% of all olives in the country, 97.7 per cent of all almonds and 98.6% of all vines (see Table 3.8).

Fruit trees other than the olive and date have a long-established importance in traditional farming in Western and Southern Libya, though only in limited coastal and inland oases in Eastern Libya. As early as 1926 it was reported that traditional oasis gardens in Western Libya carried fruit trees at between 5.5 to 5.8 trees per cultivated hectare against 73 to 96 palms per hectare and 14.2 to 18.6 olives per hectare. The relative importance of date, olive and other fruit trees and trees grown for shade, timber and hedging was reported at 77.9, 15.2, 6.9 and 0.005 per cent respectively (figures for Zawiyah Oasis).[13] By 1952 the situation in the same area had changed, with date, olive and other fruit trees accounting for 47, 42 and 11 per cent respectively.[14]

Most fruit trees in the traditional gardens are part of the kitchen garden and despite the large variety of production, including almond, vine, plum, pomegranate, apricot, peach, apple, pear, fig and prickly pear, few occur as orchards. Palm and olive apart, almond and vine have been the most common fruit trees in the oases until recent years, though citrus has increased in importance since 1950, citrus trees being twice as frequent as almond though still accounting for only 2% of total trees planted. By 1958, it was reported that production of citrus fruits from traditional irrigated areas accounted for some 18% of total output in Western Libya, though much of such output was consumed on the farm, and the oasis areas did not participate as much as modern irrigated farms in the rapid expansion of citrus acreage, which rose by more than 300% between 1938 and 1959. The cropping pattern in traditional dryland gardens has altered little in the last half century and apart from the continued spread of the olive noted above, the basis of the jabal orchards - fig, peach and almond, - has remained unchanged. The acreage of orchards in the Jabal Nafusah (excluding the Jabal Tarhunah and Jabal Qassabat) is shown in Table 3.7. This same table also shows that there is considerable variety in land use for fruit tree cultivation from crop to crop and area to area, though through the Jabal Nafusah a high proportion of trees are scattered, and become more scattered with declining rainfall from Gharyan to Nalut.

Table 3.7 Distribution of Traditional Fruit Orchards -
Jabal Nafusah 1960 and Showing the Percentage
of Traditional as Opposed to Other Plantings

	Olives		Almonds		Dates	
	Orchards ha.	% of all olives	Orchards ha.	% of all almonds	Orchards ha.	% of all date palm
Gharyan	4,324	37.7	1,231	72.5	046	37.6
Yafran	5,383	22.5	368	71.6	692	11.6
Nalut	1,490	59.3	-	25.0	917	17.1

	Figs		Peaches	
	Orchards ha.	% of all figs	Orchards ha.	% of all peaches
Gharyan	3,517	79.3	221	54.5
Yafran	6,707	68.2	43	16.4
Nalut	1,699	55.6	1	...

Source: 1960 Census of Agriculture.

Table 3.8 Italian Plantations of Olive,
Almond and Vine, 1937.

Number of trees

	OLIVE		ALMOND		VINE	
	Dry/semi irrigated	Irrigated	Dry/semi irrigated	Irrigated	Dry/semi irrigated	Irrigated
Western Libya	1,644,458	105,585	1,317,459	34,226	28,546,825	514,203
Eastern Libya	147,638	2,344	189,233	1,605	1,887,073	30,972
Libya Total	1,792,096	107,929	1,506,692	35,831	30,433,898	545,175

Source: Primo Censimento Generale delle Aziende Agrarie Metropolitane della Libia al 21 Aprile 1937.

Italian contributions to olive oil output were initially modest and began to rival output from the traditional sectors only after the major plantations laid out in the mid-1930s came into production in the period 1950-53. Output of almonds and grapes by the modern sector was important in the pre-war period; Italian almonds reaching the Tripoli market exceeded indigenous sales by 1936, and Italian grapes did so by the early 1930s. From 1950, the mixed olive/almond/vine plantations in the modern sector were converted to purely olive culture in areas where Italian farmers had the confidence to continue their farm development programmes. At the same time, there was a marked growth in citrus plantings, fostered by disappointing yields from the olive and fears concerning the competitiveness of Libyan produce in a hardening international market for the commodity. Total output of citrus fruits rose from 2,285 metric tons in 1937 to more than 8,000 metric tons in 1957 the majority being accounted for by the modern sector, where the acreage had grown from 132 ha. in 1937 to 1,040 ha. in 1960, all irrigated.

Although orcharding was the base on which most modern developments took place, irrigated field crops were important in Western Libya, especially in Italian share-cropping and demographic settlements. Returns for the Tripoli market in 1938 show that Italian produce rivalled that of indigenous farms even in traditional crops, with 50.5% of broad beans, 68.6% of tomatoes, 53.6% of pepper and 11.6% of potatoes. The modern sector has maintained a clear predominance in new or export crops, with 90 per cent of groundnuts grown on irrigated modern farms, accounting at its peak for some 4,500 ha. of the crop.

By 1960, the modern sector was responsible for an average of 5% of total barley, 50% of total olive, 80% of all citrus and 90% of groundnut output and also made substantial contributions to the production of other crops, especially tomato and melon.

3.2.3 Grazing and Livestock

Under traditional nomadic and semi-nomadic systems, grazing land includes all areas where cultivation, usually shifting cultivation, does not exist. Pastoral communities distinguish the utility of different areas only as they bear upon the need for seasonal movement of the flocks. With the spread of sedentary agriculture within the last century, the livestock economy has become more transhumant than nomadic, and the need to pasture the herds has been met by more restricted movement, leading to a concentration of grazing activity on the margins of the cropped areas. In Eastern Libya, the growth of static farming occurred much later and is less universal than in the west. Much of the area remains in pasture with a mainly transhumant economy. Until 1960, modern sector farming had no interest in the Libyan steppe ranges and the grazing areas defined on Map 8 Appendix 8 were exclusively associated with the traditional sectors. Since that time the take-over of ex-Italian farms by indigenous farmers with rights to grazing in the tribal pastures has modified the position slightly.

The grazing lands associated with the traditional irrigated farms of Western Libya include both the Gefaran ranges and the fallow and uncultivated areas within the oases, which are used for scavenging by livestock kept on the farm. Livestock on modern farms held by Italians are grazed on-farm, and stall-feeding is also practised. The most used areas of the Gefara are those receiving rainfall of more than 200 mm. on the undulating littoral steppe south of the Italian developed modern farms, but rarely more than 50 kilometres from the oasis lands. Parts of the Gefara Plain with a lower rainfall and lying more distant from the oases, are also used for grazing occasionally.

The large areas of the inner steppe, including the western Gefara, the wadi systems south of the Jabal Nafusah, the better watered enclave along the Gulf of Surt and the pasturelands in and around the Jabal Akhdar have sustained nomadic and semi-nomadic society and have only a tenuous relationship with the areas of traditional irrigated farming, although they were often closely related to the traditional dry land gardens in Western Libya and in recent years to the modern dry land sector in Eastern Libya. In years of good rainfall, these areas sustain a lush spontaneous vegetation, while at other times, the underground water in the wadi basins permits the growth of drought resistant plant associations capable of grazing small herds. With the very large areas at the disposal of herdsmen, it is unusual for pasture to fail throughout the tribal territory. The extreme southern steppes of the Ghibla and Dahar are utilised by small groups of nomads, often for camel herding. In general, however, the distant steppe lands have been losing importance as Libyan farmers take an increasing interest in modern farming in the northern coastlands and as the herding communities are attracted to urban areas and into work with the oil companies exploring and developing oil fields in the south.

Assessments of the areas of grazing land vary substantially from the estimate in the 1960 Census of Agriculture of 1,135,750 ha. of permanent meadows and pasture to the BMA estimate of 8,000,000 ha. for Western Libya alone. (Table 3.1) The census estimate excludes tribal grazing lands not associated with agricultural holdings, effectively omitting the pasture lands of much of Eastern Libya. Taking into account all grazing areas in Libya, the Ministry of Agriculture estimated in 1960 that there were some 8,000,000 ha. of pasture, of which 7,500,000 ha. were in Western Libya including the Gulf of Surt enclave. Estimates of livestock numbers indicate that the flocks declined during the Italian period, especially in Eastern Libya, and recovered rapidly after World War II. Since then fluctuations in holdings have been related to periods of good and poor rainfall. Sheep and goats represent the major herds, though cattle are important on modern and large traditional farms and camels are kept in large numbers, generally associated with traditional farming (see Table 3.9). Output of the livestock sector varies with climatic conditions and is in any case difficult to quantify in view of the distant location of, and transhumant regime followed by, the flocks. Estimates in Table 3.10 are only approximate.

Table 3.9 Livestock in Libya

a. Libya

Year	Sheep	Goats	Cattle	Camels	Horses	Donkeys
1945	79,387	570,494	38,717	130,791	18,276	35,978
1955	1,471,000	1,142,000	135,000	152,000	...	...
1960	860,000	950,000	80,000	153,000	...	...
1965	1,461,221	1,338,726	108,634	286,427	34,452	132,637

b. Western Libya

Year	Sheep	Goats	Cattle	Camels	Horses	Donkeys
1945	379,387	500,494	28,717	55,791	4,276	26,978
1955	429,000	436,000	49,000	70,000	...	...
1960	500,000	600,000	50,000	80,000	...	...
1965	284,283	829,061	73,899	196,097	15,099	87,399

c. Eastern Libya

Year	Sheep	Goats	Cattle	Camels	Horses	Donkeys
1925	800,000	70,000	10,000	75,000	14,000	9,000
1945	413,000	445,000	21,000	32,000	6,000	14,070
1955	1,032,000	691,000	86,000	76,000	...	...
1960	350,000	335,000	30,000	67,000	...	...
1965	578,510	464,606	34,631	58,163	19,251	34,168

Sources: BMA Handbooks, Rowland and Robb, op.cit., Ministry of Agriculture statistical bulletins.

Table 3.10 Livestock Products in Libya
1959

	Western Libya	Eastern Libya	Southern Libya	Libya
Milk production in 1000 litres				
Cow milk	8,250	3,600	-	11,850
Goat milk	8,360	5,900	200	14,460
Sheep milk	8,400	-	-	8,400
Camel milk	-	19,900	2,000	21,900
Total	25,010	29,400	2,200	56,610
Other products				
Wool (quintals) (100 kgs)	14,000	10,200	200	24,400
Hair "	3,600	3,150	120	6,870
Eggs (million)	45	13	3	61
Number of animals slaughtered				
Cattle and calves	13,670	6,466	-	20,136
Sheep and lambs	215,600	105,270	4,000	324,870
Goats and kids	178,600	60,511	5,000	244,111
Camels	8,000	1,693	-	9,693
Pigs	1,450	-	-	1,450
Meat production in quintals (=100 kgs)				
Beef and veal	12,300	4,600	-	16,900
Mutton and lambs	30,180	13,260	560	44,000
Goat meat	23,220	7,360	500	31,080
Camel meat	1,440	3,570	-	5,010
Pork	1,390	-	-	1,390
Chickens	500	200	50	750
Total	69,030	28,990	1,110	99,130

Source: Ministry of Agriculture statistics 1954-1960

References Chapter 3

1. Herodotus, *Africum Bellum*.

2. Ibn Khaldrun, *Kitib-al-Ibar*, Bulak Edt. 1284. A.M.

3. Agostini, E. di, *Le popolazioni della Tripolitania Notizie ethniche e storiche*, Governo della Tripolitania, Ufficio politico-militare. Parte I (Testo), Parte II (Tavole). 2 Vols. Tripoli 1917. Also *Le popolazioni della Cirenaica*, companion volume.

4. Maugini, A., *Flora ed economica agraria degli indigeni*. 1931.

5. McLachlan, K.S., *A geographical study of the coastal zone between Homs and Misurata, Tripolitania.* 1961.

6. Palloni, G., *Statistiche sulle colonizzazione della Libia*. R. Ufficio Centrale per i servizi agrari della Libia.

7. Palloni, G., *I contratti agrari degli Enti di Colonizzazione in Libia.* 1945.

8. British Military Administration. *Handbook on Tripolitania.* 1947.

9. Ghiblawy, I.R., *Agricultural development in Libya,* 1962.

10. *Census of Agriculture,* 1960.

11. Rowland and Robb, *Survey of land resources in Tripolitania*, British Military Administration, 1945.

12. Evans-Pritchard, E., *The Sanussi of Cyrenaica,* 1969.

13. Leone, G., Miele, A.C., Tappi, M., *Nuovo contributo al censimento agrario delle oasi della Tripolitania,* 1926.

14. De Cillis, E., *L'Oasi di Tripoli*, Bollettino di Informazioni Economiche del Ministero delle Colonie, 1920.

15. Theodorou, N.T., *Indigenous and Italian farm enterprises in the Zawia area,* FAO, 1954.

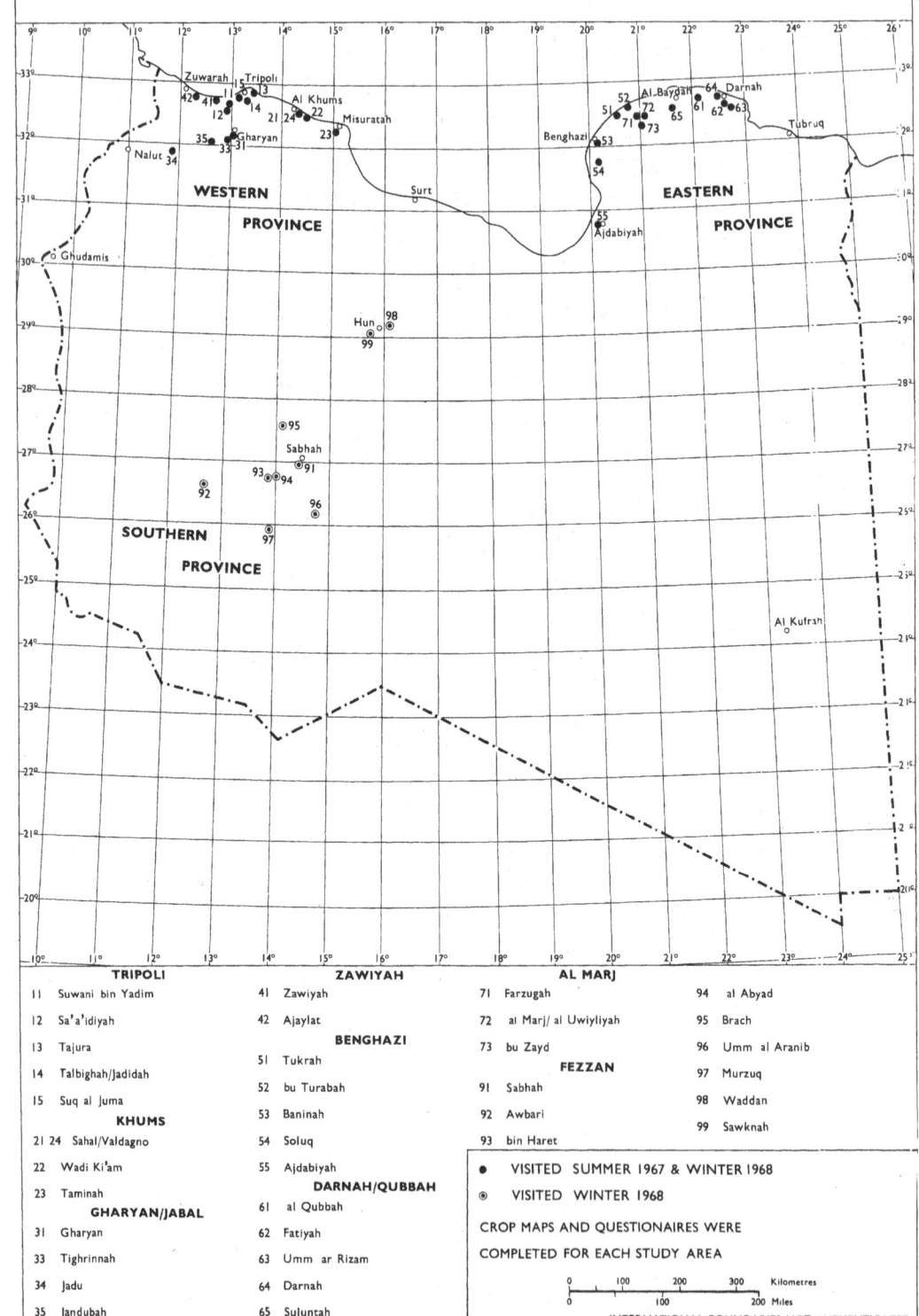

Chapter Four

LAND USE AND CROPPING PATTERNS: PRESENT POSITION AND RECENT CHANGES

4.1 <u>General statement regarding the survey and the air photo coverage</u>

The joint universities survey was undertaken to establish the character of Libyan agriculture and to identify the changes in farming consequent upon the increase in the income of the country since 1961. This was to be achieved by means of land-use and crop surveys in a number of case study areas (see crop survey maps 1 to 8). Each of the following farm types:-

Irrigated & semi-irrigated	1.	Traditional	(see photo facing page 76)
	2.	Modern	(see photo facing page 76)
	3.	Government	
Non-irrigated	4.	Traditional	(see photo facing page 110)
	5.	Modern	(see photo facing page 118)
	6.	Government	(see photo facing page 118)

has been covered, where they exist, by one or more 'purposive samples'* in Eastern, Western and Southern Libya   (see map facing page 67).

Traditional and modern farms, both irrigated and non-irrigated have been distinguished according to the estimated date of their first development. Areas in which settled agriculture commenced after 1911 are counted as modern. Older farms have been recorded as traditional. There are some exceptions, where farms using traditional methods have been extended since 1911, for example in Southern Libya since 1960. These have been enumerated as traditional farms. Government farms have all been founded since independence (1951), sometimes in previously unfarmed areas (e.g. Wadi Ki'am and Sa'a'idiyah), and elsewhere in areas developed between 1911 and 1939.

In addition questionnaire surveys were completed for the same areas as the crop mapping and these contributed data concerning farm inputs and outputs as well as establishing such important details as farm size and the number of residents per farm. Field enumeration was completed for the agricultural year Sep'67 - Aug'68.

---

* *The areas studied were selected on the basis of the authors' knowledge of agricultural Libya. Each farming type was studied. As map or air photo cover at 1:5000 to 1:20000 was necessary for the crop surveys, and as such cover is not comprehensive, some limitations were placed on the selection of case studies.*

Table 4.1 The Extent to which Libyan Farming Types have been Covered by the Detailed Examination of Air Photographs for Selected Areas

	IRRIGATED & SEMI-IRRIGATED			NON-IRRIGATED					
	Traditional farms	Modern farms (private)	Modern farms (NASA)	Traditional farms	Modern farms (private)	Modern farms (NASA)	GRAZING	OTHER (woods & waste)	TOTAL
	(square kilometres - except where percentage indicated)								
WESTERN LIBYA									
Talbighah	5	16	-	-	8	-	6	5	40
West of Ajaylat	2	11	-	-	-	-	27	-	40
Suwani bin Yadim	-	18	-	-	15	-	3	4	40
Gefara	-	-	-	4	-	-	36	-	40
Jabal Nafusah	-	-	-	4	6	-	29	1	40
Wadi Ki'am	15	-	4	-	3	-	9	9	40
Total	22	45	4	8	32	-	110	19	240
Total % of each land use for study areas	9%	19%	2%	3%	13%	-	46%	8%	100%
Estimated % of each land use for WESTERN LIBYA*	8%	18%	1%	16%	7%	-	40%	10%	100%
EASTERN LIBYA									
Al Marj	-	-	-	-	12	24	3	1	40
Farzugah	-	-	-	-	-	8	31	1	40
Al Qubbah	-	-	-	-	-	4	1	1	6
Total	-	-	-	-	12	36	35	3	86
Total % of each land use for study areas	-	-	-	-	14%	42%	41%	3%	100%
Estimated % of each land use for EASTERN LIBYA*	3%	2%	1%	4%	20%	20%	40%	10%	100%

* Such a comparison would not be relevant for the study area in Southern Libya as agriculture is so scattered

Sources for the estimates of the percentages of farming types in each province:

1. Rowland and Robb 'Land use in Tripolitania' 1945
2. U.S. A.M.S. Map Series p.761 1:50,000 1958-62
3. Agricultural Census, 1961
4. 1968 Joint Project survey of Western Libya

* *50% assumed as grazing and other use even in the areas of settled agriculture being considered.*

Another technique was used to identify changes in agriculture between the period before 1961 and the years 1966 to 1968. Air photos were available for most of agricultural Libya for the 1953 to 1954, and the 1965 to 1966 periods, and so a general comparison has been possible, summarising the changes in Eastern, Western and Southern Libya. In addition to this summary ten specific areas, generally of 40 square kilometres, have been analysed in detail. For some of these last analyses it was necessary to have photographs flown specially during 1968 (see opposite).

Table 4.1 shows that our detailed air photo examination has emphasised the irrigated farms in Western Libya and the farming of the National Agricultural Settlement Authority in Eastern Libya. These areas have been given greater attention, because in them the most important changes are taking place. The figures in the table should be used with care, as in some cases the areas classified are not perfectly homogeneous, for example rough grazing may form a minor part of an area defined as modern irrigated farming. The table shows the areas which have been examined in detail and that they reasonably represent the proportions of the various farming types found in Libya.

We have a rather more precise check upon the degree of representativeness of our work in Western Libya as a result of the survey carried out these during 1968, when farms were classified in the same way. Table 4.2 shows this comparison.

Table 4.2

Western Libya - a Comparison of the Proportions of the Farming Types Defined by the 1968 Systematic Sample, with those of the Areas Selected for Detailed Examination, Using Air Photos

	Irrigated & semi-irrigated			Non-irrigated			
	Trad'al farms	Modern farms (private)	Modern farms (NASA)	Trad'al farms	Modern farms (private)	Modern farms (NASA)	Total
Proportions defined by 1968 sample	26%	49%	under 1%	18%	7%	0%	100%
Proportions examined with air photos	25%	59%	under 1%	10%	5%	0%	100%

4.2 Agricultural Land Use in Libya Against a Background of Rising Oil Revenues 1961-1968

The broad outlines of the use of land in northern Libya in 1968 are presented in Table 4.3. Irrigated cropping was practised on 3.3% of total land, while dryland areas accounted for 3.4% and grazing lands for 89%. Of total irrigated

LIBYA

CHANGES IN AGRICULTURE

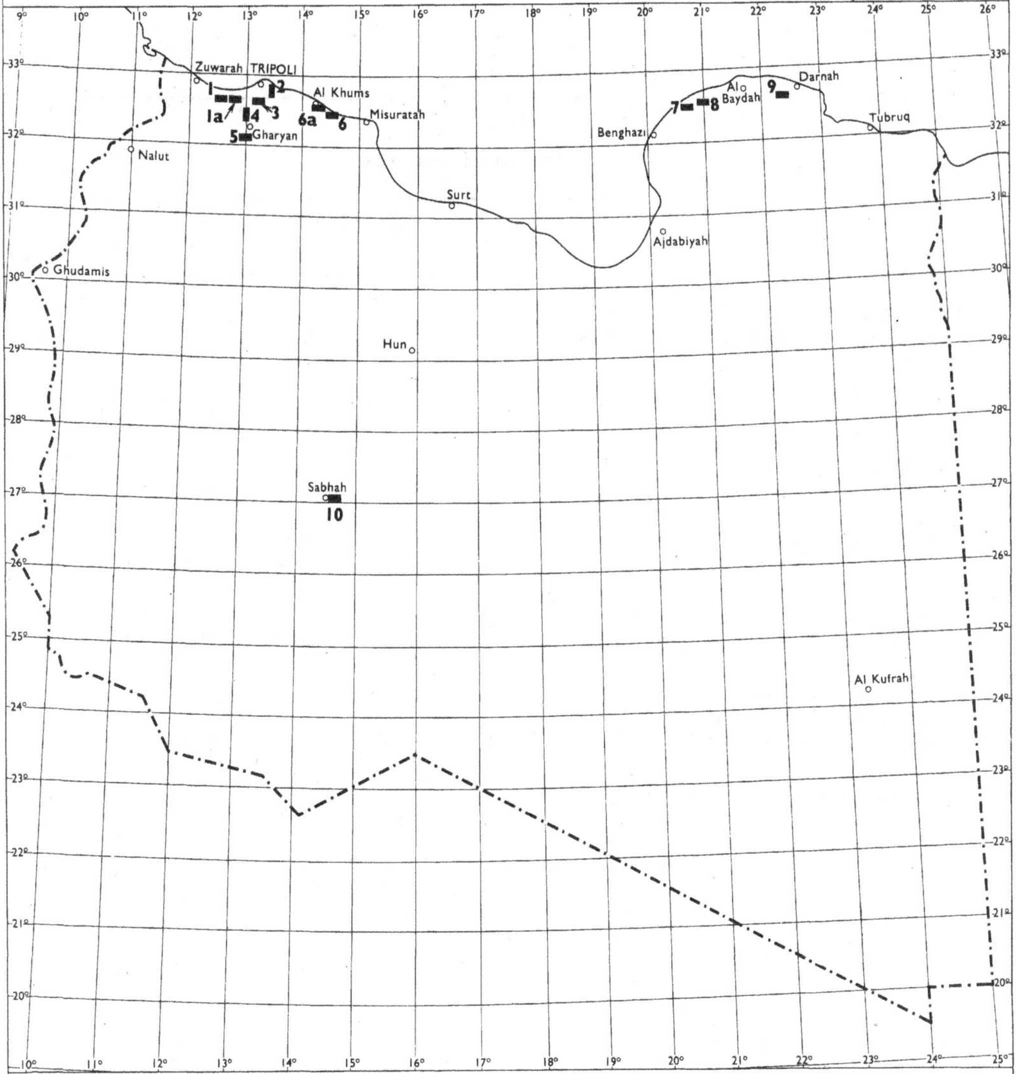

Air photographs of areas approximately 40 square kilometres have been examined and compared in great detail.

Air photographs taken at a period before 1958 and after 1965 were used.

Field work was also utilised.

1	West of Ajaylat	6	Wadi Ki'am
1a	South of Sabratah	6a	Al Khums
2	Talbighah	7	Farzugah
3	Suwani bin Yadim	8	Al Marj
4	Gefarah	9	Al Qubba
5	Jabal Nafusa	10	Sabhah

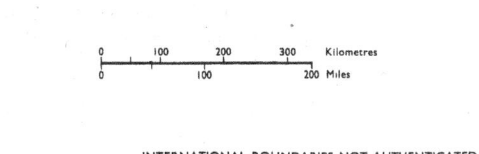

INTERNATIONAL BOUNDARIES NOT AUTHENTICATED

Table 4.3

Areas of Particular and Mixed Land Use Types

1967 - 1968

Land Use Type	Area Square kilometres					
	West Libya	%	East Libya	%	Total	%
Cropland - Irrigated traditional gardens	535	1.4	124	0.5	659	1.1
Irrigated modern sector	1389	3.6	-*	-	1389	2.2
Non-irrigated traditional gardens	1228	3.2	128	0.5	1356	2.1
Non-irrigated modern sector (and tree crops)	508	1.3	319	1.3	827	1.3
Unimproved grazing with shifting cultivation	20513	53.7	4731	18.7	25244	39.8
Unimproved grazing with shifting cultivation and unproductive land	9970	26.1	-	-	9970	15.7
Unimproved grazing with unproductive land	1804	4.8	13495	53.3	15299	24.0
Woodland	191	0.5	25	0.1	216	0.4
Woodland - Open woods and shrubs, with unimproved grazing	-	-	5971	23.6	5971	9.4
Unproductive land (including settlements)	382	1.0	278	1.1	660	1.0
Sabkhah	1680	4.4	228	0.9	1908	3.0
Total**	38200		25299		63499	

* *The irrigated modern farming in East Libya is very limited in extent and could not be shown on the map at the 1:1,000,000 scale.*
** *Discrepancies due to rounding.*
Note:- The areas listed as West and East Libya are not the same as the Western and Eastern Muhafadat.

land, 93% was in Western Libya, and all modern irrigated farming, accounting for 68% of the total, was concentrated there. From Table 4.3 it can be calculated that dryland farms in Western Libya made up 79% of the total of Libyan unirrigated holdings, and 72% of land in this grouping was associated with the traditional dryland farming against only 29% in Eastern Libya. Modern dryland farms in Western Libya covered less than half the acreage taken up by traditional units, with 23.3% of total dryland. In Eastern Libya the situation was reversed, with more than twice as much land in modern holdings as in traditional.

Shifting cultivation is practised over a relatively much larger area in Western Libya than Eastern Libya, reflecting in the main the better climate and the more commercially orientated nature of farming. Grazing areas stand out as the areally most significant zones in both provinces, underlining the continuing importance of the livestock sector. No less than 89% of land is used mainly for grazing activity, while 9.9% is used occasionally for livestock fattening, scavenging by on-farm stock and fodder growing.

Above all, the data in Table 4.3 show clearly that very little land (4.0%) in northern Libya is totally unutilised for agriculture. At the same time, it will be apparent from the foregoing outline of changing land use in Libya, that conditions are far from static and that the development of more intensive forms of land utilisation has been a persistent albeit erratic trend since the turn of the century.

Large and rising oil revenues which began after the extensive oil exploration expenditures from about 1958, resulted in the discovery of great quantities of crude oil. While oil operations have had only a minor direct effect on the agricultural area, since the major oil fields, pipelines and export terminals are located in the arid and agriculturally unimportant areas of the Gulf of Surt, the indirect impact on the agricultural sector as a whole, (see Chapter 6) and therefore on the pattern of land use, has been considerable.

Between 1960 and 1968 total arable and orchard land in Western and Eastern Libya increased by some 8.7% according to available statistics. Such a minor change could be accounted for by annual variations in dryland grain sowing. One indirect effect of the oil revenues has been the considerable expansion in irrigation by indigenous farmers, who have purchased ex-Italian estates, as well as the greater use of semi-irrigation techniques in formerly dryland orchards and the appreciable expansion of irrigated cropping on newly reclaimed lands aspects which are discussed in regional context in the following sections.

4.3 Western Libya

4.3.1 Geographical Distribution of Land Use

Cropland of all kinds has been developed in those areas receiving a rainfall of over 200 mm. each year. A small proportion of Italian-sponsored farmland south of Zawiyah and south of Misuratah and isolated gardens in the extreme west of the Jabal Nafusah have been developed in areas where rainfall is lower. The majority of traditional dryland gardens are to be found in the Jabal Nafusah in the area receiving more than 250 mm., while the greatest density of dryland orchards are located in areas receiving more than 300 mm. of relatively reliable rainfall! Modern farming has followed the same pattern, but because existing Arab gardens and scattered fruit trees already monopolised the best watered basins and valleys, the later estates have grown up in the climatically less-favoured lands further south in the 250 to 200 mm. rainfall zone. Traditional tribal cultivation in Western Libya lies in a zone extending into the undulating Gefara Plain where rainfall drops to an average of 150 mm. and less. In those areas of Western Libya south of the 32nd parallel where shifting cultivation is carried on, activity is restricted to the immediate vicinity of the wadis.

The location and extent of the traditional irrigated gardens are mainly determined by the existence of and ease of access to the upper water table. Traditional irrigated gardens have grown up in the coastal rim where the shallow water table is closest to the surface, though all the major oases are also located in areas with a rainfall averaging more than 250 mm. The coastal gardens of Western Libya have always been a very important part of Libyan agriculture. Before 1911 all the important irrigated farming of the province was concentrated in this zone, and it is likely therefore that at least 50% of crop output for the province was derived from the coastal gardens. Between 1911 and 1939 the area fully or partially irrigated was more than doubled, for areas up to 20 and sometimes 40 kilometres from the coast were developed by Italian settlers on a modern basis.[2]

Farms in the traditional sector usually include areas in more than one land use zone. Traditional oasis holdings take in at least a portion of irrigated and unirrigated garden within the area defined in Map 8 as traditionally irrigated farmland. At the same time these farms normally have ownership and usufruct rights in the Gefaran steppes for grazing and shifting cultivation. Further differentiation in land use arises in each individual land use zone, where farmers normally own more than one plot, partly because the quality of land varies, but much more as a form of insurance against crop or pasture failure due to poor rainfall in one area. Modern farms are less scattered and differences in land use derive mainly from the application or otherwise of irrigation within the farm boundary, usually encompassing one consolidated plot (86.8% of all modern farms comprised one parcel in 1968, also note Symap 1.2 - see Appendix 9). Modern farms of the steppe area draw their water from aquifers deeper than the first water table and in some cases from considerable depth.

From data collected in 1968 it has been calculated that modern dry farming on the hill areas accounted for some 15% of the cultivated area of Western Libya. The largest single area of Italian demographic development was in the Tarhunah area, where some 10,957 hectares were developed as 180 holdings. In addition there were a number of large private farms of over 1,000 hectares each, especially around Tarhunah, while south of Gharyan, around Tighrinnah, tobacco farming was set up on a modern basis.

Dry land traditional farms include fruit gardens, land for shifting cultivation and grazing areas, and tend to be more scattered geographically and fragmented than all other types of farm. Air photos show that there have been few extensions of traditional farming, and in some areas fields have been abandoned; this is true near Yafran, both on the Jabal and at its foot, and near Jadu.

4.3.2 Size of farm

Management of land use within the farm is very much influenced by the size of farm. Although rainfall amounts and periodicity are unreliable throughout the country and affect farm productivity, even within the irrigated sector, precaution against annual and regional variations in rainfall is not necessarily

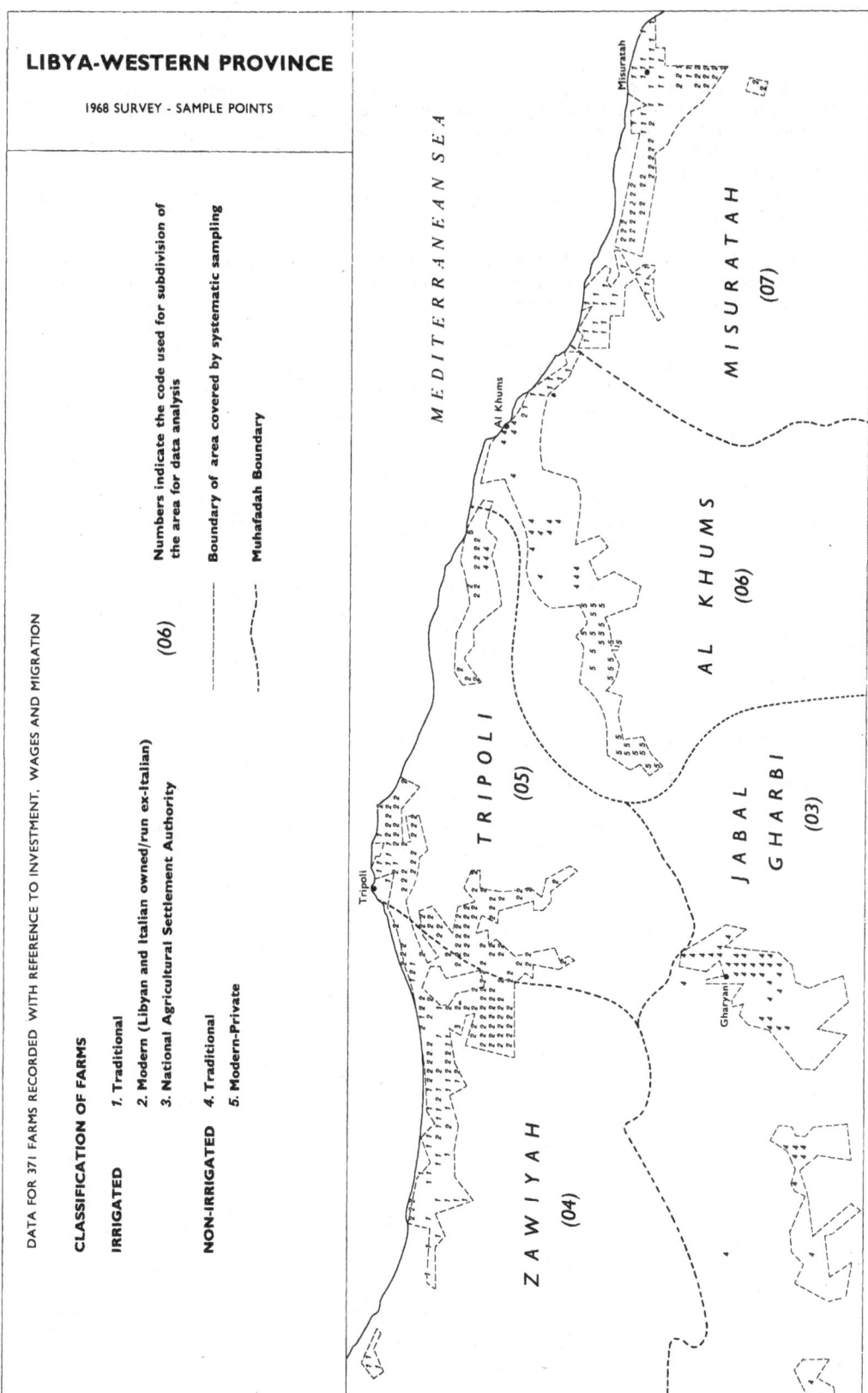

sought by ownership of large farms. In the traditional sectors, total farm size tends to be small even where land is not scarce, mainly, it would seem, because farmers consider that the greater the area farmed, the greater the risks of ruin in the event of serious failure of the rains. Modern farms are larger on average than the traditional units, though polarised around the 25-50 ha. range in the ex-demographic estates and above 100 ha. in the private concession areas.

Patterns of farm size for Western Libya in 1968 are illustrated in Symap 1.1 (see Appendix 9) showing clearly the smaller farms of the traditional oases and jabal gardens which contrast with the larger modern units in the ex-Italian settlement zones. Air photographs taken both in the 1950s and more recently allow a very easy distinction to be drawn between the traditional farms, where field patterns are irregular and date palms are a common feature, and the farms developed since 1911, with large regular field patterns and tree crops systematically planted. (These last we have called modern farms for convenience). See photograph facing page 76.

In the al Qassabat (see Symap 1.1 Appendix 9) area and also in the area south of Ajaylat, purely indigenous developments, in the former, consolidating existing traditional olive groves, and in the latter reclaiming new lands, have resulted in a large size of farm independent of Italian influence. Of total farms included in the 1968 survey, 29.7% were 5 ha. or less in area, while almost the same proportion (29.5%) was between 6 and 25 ha. Of the remaining 60.8% of farms, 31.6% were between 26 to 125 ha., 4.9% were between 126 to 625 ha. and 4.3% were 625 ha. and larger. Only 0.54% of farms (two in number of the 370 valid observations made) were larger than 3,000 ha., representing the modern Italian developed sector.

A classification of farm size by farm type for Western Libya indicates a considerable cleavage between traditional and modern sectors. Whereas traditional irrigated and dry land farms of less than 10 ha. accounted for 84% and 72% of all farms in their respective group, only 22% of irrigated and 4% of dry land farms in the modern sector were reported within this range. Dry land holdings in both traditional and modern sectors were larger on average than irrigated farms within their respective groups. (see Table 4.4)

Table 4.4

Size of Farm by Farm type - Western Libya 1967/68

Hectares

Farm Type	No. Valid Obs'ns	Number of farms in each category and %									
		0-1 ha.		1-10 ha.		10-100 ha.		100-1000 ha.		Over 1000 ha.	
		No.	%	No.	%	No.	%	No.	%	No.	%
1. Irrig. Trad.	95	16	17	64	67	14	15	1	1	-	-
2. " Mod.	181	2	1	38	21	105	58	27	15	9	5
3. " NASA	1	-	-	-	-	1	100	-	-	-	-
4. Dry Trad.	68	5	7	44	65	12	18	7	10	-	-
5. " Mod.	26	-	-	1	4	22	85	1	4	2	8
TOTAL	371	23	6	147	40	154	42	36	10	11	3

Source: Joint Research Project 1968 Questionnaire.

AL KHUMS (SAHAL/VALDAGNO) 1953

Fairey Surveys Ltd. June 1953

Approximate scale 1:25,000

Small farms, of less than ten hectares, and sometimes less than five, are characteristic of modern farms in Suwani bin Yadim, Bin Gashir and surrounding the Tripoli Oasis. This represents a break up of the original farm units, a change dating partly from independence (1951), but mainly from the period since the commencement of oil exports (1961). These developments will be examined further when the Talbighah and Suwani bin Yadim areas are studied in detail later in this chapter.

4.3.3 Extent of Cultivation of Farms

The total area of land cultivated each year on all farms other than those which are fully irrigated, varied with rainfall. In the 1967/68 season it was reported that 43.1% of farms had between 80 to 100% of their area under cultivation (see Table 4.5).

Table 4.5

Area of Farm Cultivated 1967/68 - Western Libya (including orchards)

Per cent of farm cultivated	Per cent of all farms
0	9.4
1-20	11.3
21-40	12.5
41-60	14.8
61-80	8.9
81-100	43.1
	100.0

Source: Joint Research Project 1968 questionnaire.

Some 52.0% of farms cultivated less than 60% of their area and 9.4% of farms undertook no cultivation at all. Regional variations in area cultivated were apparent, with 54.3% of farms reporting no cultivation concentrated in the region of the 'detached Gefara' between al Khums and Misuratah, though other areas, including Sabratah, Suwani bin Yadim and the Jabal west of al Qassabat were only lightly cultivated. The major areas where cultivation occupied a high proportion of farms are illustrated in Symap 4.1 (Appendix 9), which shows a high density of such farms in the western Jabal, Tarhunah and al Qassabat. Table 4.6 summarises the area of cultivated land in Western Libya by farm type, indicating that less than 5% of traditional irrigated farms held more than 10 ha. under cultivation in the year and only 22% of traditional dryland farms. By contrast, 43% of modern irrigated and 69% of modern dryland farms had more than 10 ha. under cultivation. A high percentage of cultivated area is closely associated with traditional intensive farms where much of the farm area is irrigated, emphasising vegetables. Dry land farms are often highly mechanised, with a high proportion of trees per hectare.

Table 4.6

Area of Farm Cultivated by Farm Type
Western Libya 1967/68

Hectares

Farm Type	No.Valid Obs'ns	Number of farms in each category and %									
		0-1 ha.		1-10 ha.		10-100 ha.		100-1000 ha.		Over 1000 ha.	
		No.	%	No.	%	No.	%	No.	%	No.	%
1 Irrig. Trad.	95	41	43	49	52	4	4	1	1	-	-
2 " Mod.	181	27	15	76	42	54	30	18	10	6	3
3 " NASA	1	-	-	-	-	1	100	-	-	-	-
4 Dry Trad.	68	11	16	42	62	10	15	5	7	-	-
5 " Mod.	26	5	19	3	12	16	62	1	4	1	4
TOTAL	371	84	23	170	46	85	23	25	7	7	2

Source: Joint Research Project 1968 questionnaire.

More detailed evidence concerning the extent of cultivation is shown in the crop survey maps in Table 4 in Appendix 2.2. The maps show the cropping pattern for both winter (1967/68) and summer (1968) seasons, for the study areas, which were chosen to reflect conditions on irrigated and non-irrigated, modern and traditional, as well as on private and government run farms.

The extent of cultivation can be assessed from the crop maps and from Table 4 in Appendix 2.2, which was compiled by measuring areas on the crop maps. A summary of the results is presented in Table 4.7 in this chapter, to show the proportions of uncultivated land, fallow and grazing land, and the proportion of cultivated to cultivable land.

Table 4.7

Proportions of a) Uncultivated Land b) Total Fallow plus Grazing c) Total Cultivated Land and d) Cultivated Land as % of Cultivable. All Figures are Percentages of the Total Areas included in the Field Surveys

		Uncultivated land*		Total Fallow + Grazing		Cultivable land		Cultivated as % of Cultivable	
		Sum.	Wint.	Sum.	Wint.	Sum. / Wint.		Sum.	Wint.
		%	%	%	%	%		%	%

IRRIGATED & SEMI-IRRIGATED (CROPPING CONTINUOUS THROUGHOUT THE YEAR)

1 TRADITIONAL – INTENSIVE

		Sum	Wint	Sum	Wint	Sum/Wint		Sum	Wint
Western Prov.	13 Tajura	71	75	44	47	73		39	35
	15 Suq al Jumah	66	77	41	51	74		46	31
	21 Sahal (Al Khums)	77	60	74	57	97		24	41
	41 Zawiyah	90	85	75	70	85		11	17
	42 Al Ajaylat	84	67	82	64	98		16	34
Eastern Prov.	51 Tukrah	79	58	71	51	92		23	45
	64 Darnah	74	65	22	16	50		54	71
	63 Umm ar Rizam	–	65	–	32	67		–	53
Southern Prov.	91 Sabhah	–	63	–	54	92		–	40
	92 Awbari	–	57	–	53	96		–	45
	93 Bin Haret	–	57	–	51	93		–	46
	96 Umm al Aranib	–	57	–	55	98		–	43
	97 Murzuq	–	63	–	61	98		–	38
	98 Waddan	–	79	–	62	83		–	25
	99 Sawknah	–	72	–	60	88		–	32

2 MODERN PRIVATE – INTENSIVE & EXTENSIVE

Western Prov.	11 Suwani bin Yadim	60	65	53	60	93		43	27
	14 Talbighah/Jadidah	53	47	52	46	99		47	54
	22 Taminah	74	39	72	37	98		27	62
	24 Valdagno	79	58	78	57	99		21	42
Eastern Prov.	53 Baninah	77	90	77	90	99		24	9

3	MODERN NASA (GOVERNMENT) - INTENSIVE						
	Western Prov.	12 Sa'a'idiyah	39	52	38	51	99	61	49
		22 Wadi Ki'am	50	37	42	28	92	54	69
	Eastern Prov.	52 Bu Turabah	48	70	48	70	100	52	30
NON-IRRIGATED (ONE CROP PER YEAR)								
4	TRADITIONAL - INTENSIVE							
	Western Prov.	31 Gharyan	85	59	54	29	70	22	59
5	MODERN PRIVATE - EXTENSIVE							
	Western Prov.	33 Tighrinnah	55	47	59	45	98	43	54
		35 Jandubah	–	52	–	39	87	–	55
	Eastern Prov.	72 Al Marj etc.	–	11	–	8	97	–	92
		73 Bu Zayd	–	43	–	43	100	–	57
		62 Fatiyah	–	17	–	12	95	–	88
6	MODERN NASA (GOVERNMENT) - EXTENSIVE							
	Eastern Prov.	71 Farzugah	–	72	–	69	98	–	29
		72 Al Marj etc.	–	16	–	15	99	–	85
		61 Al Qubbah	–	51	–	42	91	–	54
		65 Suluntah	–	84	–	83	99	–	16

– indicates no data

* uncultivated land includes fallow, abandoned land, other non-agricultural land, houses and graves.

Irrigated v. Non-irrigated farms

In Western Libya when comparing irrigated and semi-irrigated farms with non-irrigated farms, one is comparing coastal and Gefara farms with those of the Jabal Nafusah. The studies confirmed that farming is more continuous throughout the year on the Gefara and at that coast than on the jabal. However two jabal areas, Gharyan and Tighrinnah, where tobacco is important, show relatively high levels of cropping throughout the year, levels comparable with irrigated areas near the coast. In winter the non-irrigated farms have a higher proportion of their area under crops than do the irrigated farms. Between 50% and 60% of the jabal farms were under crops compared with only 17% to 41% for coastal traditional farms, and 27% to 69% for modern farms on the Gefara or at the coast. The high figure of 69% is for Wadi Ki'am, a government sponsored estate, and reflects the higher level of activity on such enterprises than on other farms in Western Libya.

Traditional v. Modern Farms

The extent of cultivation helps also to distinguish farms of the traditional type from those using modern methods. Both in winter and summer, but especially in the latter, more land is under crops on modern farms than on traditional. In summer traditional farms are cropped on between 11% and 46% of the cultivable area, contrasting with between 21% and 47% on modern farms. Winter figures for traditional farms ranged from 17% to 35%, while those for modern farms were between 27% and 62%, with two out of the four modern areas over 50%.

Private v. Government Run Farms

The distinction between privately and government run farms has already been noted. Unfortunately no government dry land farms were covered in Western Libya, but for irrigated farms the position is clear. Government schemes show much more continuous cropping and are especially productive in the summer. Some privately run farms have a similar level of utilisation, for example those at Talbighah/Jadidah and at Taminah, but other modern farms and all traditional farm areas examined had much lower proportions under crops than the government run farms.

4.3.4 Irrigation

With the exception of a small area around Gharyan in the Jabal Nafusah, and a number of farms in the al Qusay'ah, al Qassabat and Ghanimah region, the majority of irrigated farms are located on the Gefara plain. The greatest density of farms with a high proportion of irrigated land is mainly in the Tripoli, Misuratah and Suwani bin Yadim/Bin Gashir areas, while the sedentary farmed area of the Gefara proper stands out clearly as the major zone of irrigated agriculture (see Symap 5.1). Some 40% of farms in Western Libya did not report any irrigation in the 1967/68 season, and apart from the dry land farms of the Jabal Nafusah and the rainfed ginan in the wadi basins south of Zliten, a significant number of farms in Zliten oasis itself, and also near Misuratah and Zuwarah were reported without irrigation (see Table 4.8).

Table 4.8

Irrigated Area of Farms by Region -

Western Libya 1967/68.

Hectares

Number & % of Farms in each category

Muhafadah	None		1-3 ha.		4-11 ha.		12-40 ha.		41-130 ha.		131-450 ha.		451-1500 ha.	
	No.	%	No.	%	No.	%	No.	%	No.	%	No.	%	No.	%
Jabal Gharbi	47	96	0	0	2	4	0	0	0	0	0	0	0	0
Zawiyah	14	13	33	31	31	29	22	20	5	5	2	2	0	0
Tripoli	6	8	21	27	21	27	17	22	8	10	3	5	1	1
Al Khums	48	76	8	12	4	6	1	2	1	2	1	2	0	0
Misuratah	33	44	19	26	13	17	8	11	0	0	1	1	1	1
TOTAL	148	40	81	22	71	19	48	13	14	4	7	2	2	0

Source: Joint Research Project 1968 questionnaire.

Dependence of Libyan farms on dryland cereals, orchards and livestock herding is indicated by the fact that 52.0% of farms maintain 40% or less of their holding in irrigated and semi-irrigated culture. Only 18.4% of farms were intensively irrigated in 1967/68 with between 81-100% of their land under irrigation (see Table 4.9).

Table 4.9

Irrigation of Farms - Western Libya 1967/68

Per cent of farm irrigated	Per cent of all farms
0	39.8
0.1-20	13.2
21.0-40	11.1
41.0-60	11.3
61.0-80	6.2
81.0-100	18.4
	100.0

Source: Joint Research Project 1968 questionnaire.

Variations in the total area irrigated per farm by farm type are shown in Table 4.10. Four farms in the dryland sector reported some of their acreage under irrigated culture, though only one had more than 25 ha. In the traditional irrigated sector, 93% of farms reported less than 5 ha. under irrigation in the season 1967/68, while 52% of modern irrigated farms recorded more than 5 ha. of irrigated land (see Table 4.10).

The one NASA farm included in the survey had less than 5 ha. under irrigation, some 25% of its total area. Using data for all farms within the 1967/68 survey of Western Libya, there is a high degree of correlation between the irrigated area and the total cultivated area of farms in the traditional sector, though with strong regional bias as noted above.

Table 4.10

Irrigated Area of Farm by Farm Type -

Western Libya 1967/68

Hectares

Farm Type	No.Valid Obs'ns	Number of farms in each category and %										
		0-1		1-5		5-25		25-125		125-625		Over 625	
		No.	%	No.	%	No.	%	No.	%	No.	%	No.	%
1. Irrig. Trad.	95	54	57	34	36	6	6	1	1	-	-	-	-
2 " Mod.	181	48	27	41	23	63	35	21	12	7	4	1	1
3 " NASA	1	-	-	1	100	-	-	-	-	-	-	-	-
4 Dry Trad.	68	65	96	2	3	-	-	1	1	-	-	-	-
5 " Mod.	26	25	96	1	4	-	-	-	-	-	-	-	-
TOTAL	371	192	52	79	21	69	19	23	6	7	2	1	-

Source: Joint Research Project 1968 questionnaire.

Recent changes in irrigated farming are shown on air photos, indicating a considerable intensification of summer irrigation on farms which were growing very few summer crops in 1953. For example, fields close to Sabratah which had no summer field crops in 1953 were supporting irrigated plots in 1966. Similar evidence is available for farms of the modern type in Suwani bin Yadim, Bin Gashir, and for farms surrounding the Tripoli oasis.

It is more difficult to establish whether intensification of irrigation on the ex-Italian farms represents a return to a state existing before 1940, from which there has been a decline, because there are no air photos in existence to allow an extension of the comparison before 1953 in the Western Provinces. The 1937 Census of Agriculture, carried out with great thoroughness in the same areas of Italian farming, shows that in 1937, by the definition of that time, just under 10% of the area farmed by Italians was irrigated or semi-irrigated in this part of coastal Libya.[2] This proportion indicates that irrigated and semi-irrigated farming covered only a small part of the farmed area in the year of the census.

It also indicates that agriculture was making only limited demands upon the underground water resources. Although Italian plans included an intensification of agriculture, dry farming was always to be the main method for most of even the relatively favoured areas of coastal Libya.

In addition to the redevelopment of Italian farms there is limited but important evidence that areas not regularly used previously are being brought into production. Extensions of irrigated agriculture can be observed on air photos south of the coastal oases to the east and west of Sabratah. On 1966 air photos the newly irrigated areas show clearly. In other places, even within fifteen kilometres of Tripoli, unplanted and previously unused sandy areas have been irrigated only since 1960. It has not been possible to quantify these extensions, but they cannot be less than 500 ha., and they may be more than 2000 ha. (see illustrations overleaf). It must be noted, however, that in all cases these developments have taken place in areas where groundwater resources are suspect, and long-term prospects are poor for intensive irrigated farming.

4.3.5 Orchards

Orcharding has continued to be a major activity on all farms in Western Libya. Only 1.7% of farms were without any trees in 1967/68. No less than 58.9% of farms were planted at a density of greater than 21 trees per hectare, with 20.3% recording densities of over 60 trees per hectare (see Table 4.11).

Table 4.11

Trees in Areas of Settled Agriculture -

Western Libya 1967/68

Trees per hectare	Per cent of all farms
0	1.7
1-10	19.5
11-20	19.9
21-30	18.1
31-60	20.5
over 60	20.3
	100.0

Source: Joint Research Project 1968 questionnaire.

Since the Italian developments were based on dry farming methods, the major crops were tree crops, and over 22,000 ha. were planted on demographic farms alone. The areas thus planted are quite clear on both old and more recent photographs   (see illustrations facing page 99).

The extent of areas under tree crops changed little between 1953 and 1968 in the modern sector. Extensions of citrus planting are significant, but in total these plantings would not exceed 500 ha. in Western Libya. Most of these trees have yet to reach maturity.

Other tree crops, for example olives and almonds, were as numerous in 1968 as in 1953. Obviously yields cannot be deduced from air photographs, and it is

SOUTH OF SABRATAH 1953

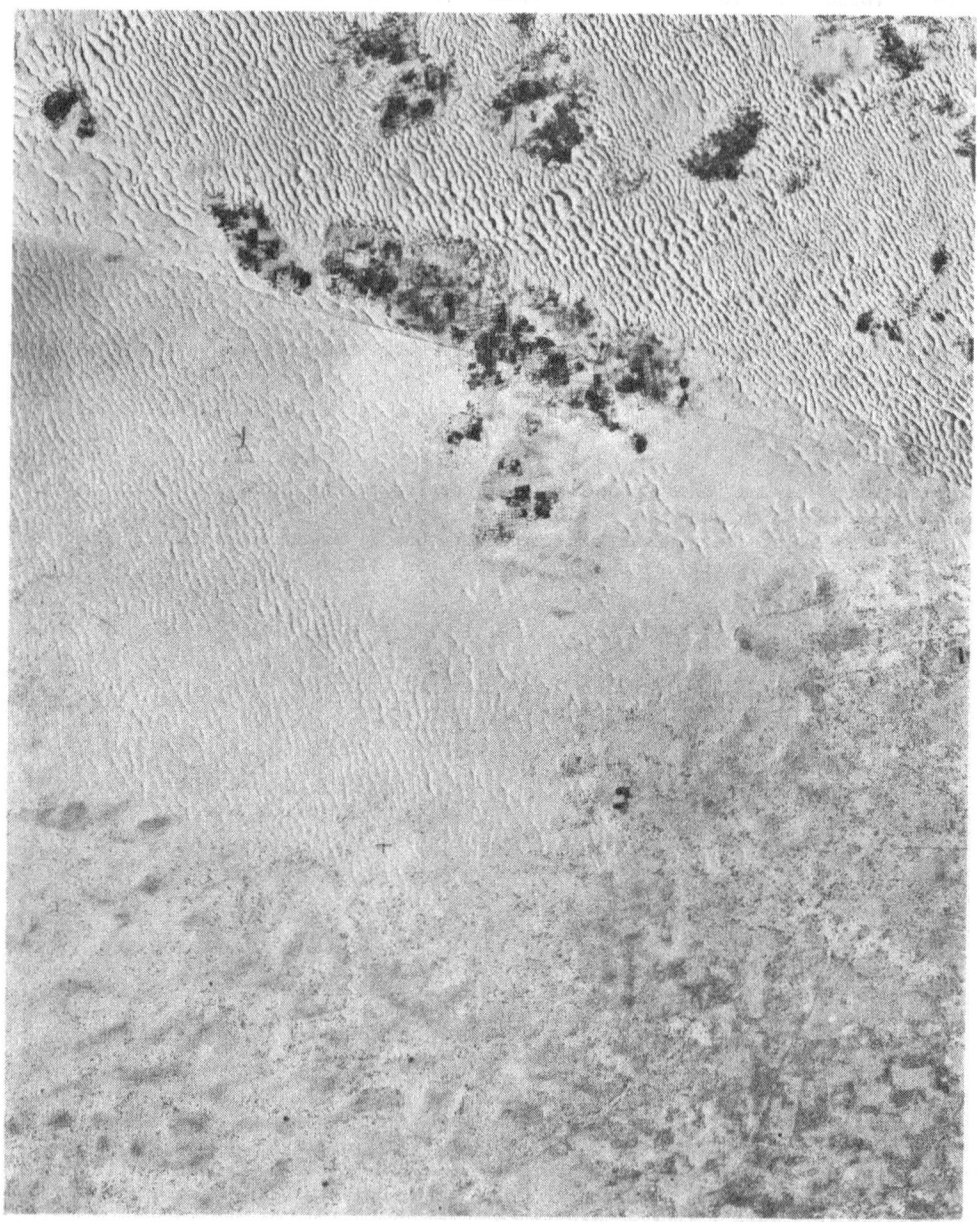

Fairey Surveys Ltd. May-July 1953

Approximate scale 1:25,000

SOUTH OF SABRATAH 1966

Aero Exploration
May 1966

Approximate scale 1:25,000

therefore data from field visits which led to the conclusion that output from tree crops was lower in 1968 than in 1953.

The same pattern is repeated for the vine. There has been little extension, and the 15,600 ha. planted by the Italians up to 1940, with an estimated yield at full production of 180,000 to 200,000 q'litres has not been reached.[3] Actual production of wine in the Western Provinces was 130,000 q'litres in 1940,[3] which compares with 37,306 tons of grapes for wine yielding less than 40,000 q'litres of wine in 1960.[4]

According to data collected in the 1967/68 survey of Western Libya, the areas with the highest densities of trees were located in the littoral steppe of the Gefara, though similar densities were found in some parts of the Jabal Nafusah, particularly between Yafran and Jadu and at al Khadra (see Symap 7.1 Appendix 9). In the Jabal Nafusah two-thirds of all farms had 33-100 trees and almost 40% had 33-185 trees per farm. In the plain areas, the Tripoli region stood out as an area with a high number of trees per farm, while Misuratah recorded a lower average (see Table 4.12).

Table 4.12

Number of Trees by Region - Western Libya 1967/68

Muhafadah	Number of Farms in each category and %													
	None		1-5		6-32		33-185		186-1000		1001-6000		6001+	
	No.	%	No.	%	No.	%	No.	%	No.	%	No.	%	No.	%
Jabal Gharbi	4	8	2	4	9	18	20	41	13	27	1	2	0	0
Zawiyah	0	0	1	1	3	3	26	24	56	52	14	13	7	7
Tripoli	1	1	0	0	5	6	14	18	22	29	19	25	16	21
Al Khums	0	0	0	0	5	8	13	21	16	25	22	35	7	11
Misuratah	1	1	1	1	11	15	29	39	24	32	6	8	3	4
TOTAL	6	2	4	1	33	9	102	27	131	36	62	17	33	9

Source: Joint Research Project 1968 questionnaire.

Although traditional irrigated farms carry a relatively high density of trees, their absolute importance is less than that for other sectors, with 54% of farms having 10-100 trees per unit and only two per cent recording more than 1,000 trees. In the modern irrigated sector, 42% of farms possessed more than 1,000 trees per unit. Traditional dryland tree holdings, though larger on average than traditional irrigated orchards, returned only 10% of farms with more than 1,000 trees per unit against 8% in the modern sector (see Table 4.13).

Table 4.13

Number of Trees on the Farm by Farm Type –
Western Libya 1967/68

Farm Type	No.Valid Obs'ns	Number of farms in each category and %												
		0-1		1-10		10-100		100-1000		1000-10000		10000-100000		Over 100000	
		No.	%	No.	%	No.	%	No.	%	No.	%	No.	%	No.	%
1 Irrig.Trad.	95	1	1	3	3	51	54	38	40	2	2	-	-	-	-
2 " Mod.	181	1	1	1	1	15	8	88	49	54	30	20	11	2	1
3 " NASA	1	-	-	-	-	-	-	1	100	-	-	-	-	-	-
4 Dry Trad.	68	5	7	1	1	24	35	31	46	7	10	-	-	-	-
5 " Mod.	26	-	-	-	-	-	-	5	19	18	69	3	12	-	-
TOTAL	371	7	2	5	1	90	24	163	44	81	22	23	6	2	1

Source: Joint Research Project 1968 questionnaire.

Areas near Jandubah (south-west of Gharyan) and Bir Mijji (south-west of Tarhunah) have been allocated for development by NASA. Some planting and replanting of olives has taken place at Jandubah, and some experimentation has been carried out at Bir Mijji. The limited nature of these activities is confirmed by air photos, which cover the Jandubah area properly, and the Bir Mijji area incompletely.

A high density of trees per hectare is associated closely with modern, mainly dryland farms, where a high degree of mechanised cultivation is carried on. (see Symap 7.1 and 7.2, Appendix 9). At the other pole, a high density of trees per hectare is correlated with well-established traditional irrigated farm units with mechanised means of water lifting and a large work force.

4.3.6 Cereals and Vegetables

Although cereal farming is important in both modern and traditional sectors in Western Libya and 1967/68 was a fair rainfall year, 41.7% of farms reported that cereals had not been cultivated in that season. Of those which did undertake cereal cultivation, however, 47.2% had more than one third of their land under grain crops, representing 27.5% of total farms (see Table 4.14).

Table 4.14

Per cent of Farm Under Cereals on Settled
Farms - Western Libya 1967/68

Percentage of farm under cereals	Percentage of all farms
0	41.7
0.1-10	9.2
10.1-20	11.1
20.1-30	10.5
30.1-40	5.4
40+	22.1
	100.0

Source: Joint Research Project 1968 questionnaire.

Excluding the area of shifting cultivation, the main areas with a high percentage of farms under cereals were concentrated in the Yafran, Gharyan and al Qassabat districts of the Jabal Nafusah, though smaller areas of the same kind in the eastern Sahal al Ahmad, western and southern Zliten and at Misuratah were also discernable (see Symap 4.2, Appendix 9). On the Jabal Nafusah the high proportion of farms given over to cereals was partly a function of the small size of farms. Most farms in Western Libya retain only a small absolute area under cereals, and with the exception of the Jabal Nafusah, where 59% of farms were recorded with a cereal acreage of between one and seven hectares, and Misuratah (43%), an almost consistently high proportion of farms fell in the 1-7 ha. range - 38% at Zawiyah, 36% in Tripoli and 36% at al Khums. Farms reporting large absolute cereal acreages were confined to al Khums and Tripoli where 11% and 9% respectively of total farms had more than 65 ha. under grain crops (see Table 4.15).

Table 4.15

Area Under Cereals by Region - Western Libya 1967/68

Muhafadah	Number of farms in each category and %													
	None		1-2 ha.		3-7 ha.		8-21 ha.		22-65 ha.		66-175 ha.		176-500 ha.	
	No.	%	No.	%	No.	%	No.	%	No.	%	No.	%	No.	%
Jabal Gharbi	13	27	16	32	13	27	3	6	4	8	0	0	0	0
Zawiyah	57	53	18	17	23	21	5	5	4	4	0	0	0	0
Tripoli	37	48	15	20	13	17	5	6	2	2	2	2	3	5
Al Khums	21	33	7	11	16	25	17	19	5	8	1	2	1	2
Misuratah	27	36	13	17	19	26	15	20	1	1	0	0	0	0
TOTAL	155	42	69	19	84	22	45	11	16	4	3	1	4	1

Source: Joint Research Project 1968 questionnaire.

Analysis of the cereal acreage by farm type indicates the same conclusions (Table 4.16), with only 3% of farms in the traditional irrigated category reporting more than five hectares under cereals.

Table 4.16

Area Under Cereals by Farm Type - Western Libya 1967/68

Farm Type		No. Valid Obs'ns	Number of farms in each category & %									
			0-1 Ha.		1-5 ha.		5-25 ha.		25-125 ha.		Over 125 ha.	
			No.	%	No.	%	No.	%	No.	%	No.	%
1 Irrig.	Trad.	95	68	72	24	25	3	3	-	-	-	-
2 "	Mod.	181	85	47	49	27	36	20	8	4	3	2
3 "	NASA	0	-	-	-	-	-	-	-	-	-	-
4 Dry	Trad.	68	27	40	25	37	10	15	6	9	-	-
5 "	Mod.	26	11	42	5	19	10	38	-	-	-	-
TOTAL		370	191	52	103	28	59	16	14	4	3	1

Source: Joint Research Project 1968 questionnaire.

There is a generally held notion that the traditional Libyan farms were worked less intensively in 1968 than in the 1950s. This is confirmed in many irrigated areas where recent air photos show that field crops do not cover as great a proportion of these farms as they did in 1953. Examples can be seen in areas west of Sabratah, as well as in the gardens of Surman and Zawiyah. The evidence is especially strong near Zawiyah. South and east of Tripoli in the Tripoli oasis, and on the Sahal between al Khums and Zliten, there is further evidence that the area under field crops fell between 1953 and 1966/68. Air photos do show that there has been an increase in the area under citrus on the traditional irrigated farms, but this is not a major change, nor can the economic implications of the change be easily assessed, as only a small proportion of the production reaches an already overcrowded seasonal market. In the non-irrigated traditional farms it appears that winter grain, mainly barley, was grown over much the same area in 1968 as in 1953. This is not an easy matter of interpretation, but the evidence from air photos, as well as field visits in 1968, confirm the impression.

Vegetable growing is of greatest importance in the Tripoli area, especially in Tajura and Suq al Jumah oases and the Jadidah region. Whereas 43.9 per cent of farms had not undertaken vegetable growing in 1967/68 in Western Libya as a whole, only 23.4% of farms in the Tripoli area reported no vegetable crops. Other areas of intensive vegetable growing included Surman, Zawiyah and Sahal al Ahmad/Zliten oases (see Symap 5.2, Appendix 9). A large group of farms accounting for 30.7% of the total devoted small parts (less than 20%) of their acreage to vegetables, while 25.4% devoted more than 20% of the total farm to this purpose (see Table 4.17). Absolute acreages are not large and only 13.5% of farms reported more than five hectares under vegetables (Table 4.18) against 77.3% with between one and two hectares.

Table 4.17

Vegetable Cultivation on Settled Farms – Western Libya 1967/68

Percentage of farm under vegetables	Percentage of all farms
0	43.9
0.1-10	20.8
11.1-20	9.9
21.1-30	7.3
31.1-40	5.7
40+	12.4
	100.0

Source: Joint Research Project 1968 questionnaire.

Table 4.18

Area Under Vegetables by Region – Western Libya 1967/68

Hectares

Muhafadah	Number of farms in each category and %														
	None		1-2 Ha.		3-5 ha.		6-13 ha.		14-33 ha.		34-80 ha.		81-200 ha.	
	No.	%	No.	%	No.	%	No.	%	No.	%	No.	%	No.	%
Jabal Gharbi	39	80	9	18	1	2	0	0	0	0	0	0	0	0
Zawiyah	25	23	50	47	22	20	8	8	1	1	0	0	1	1
Tripoli	18	23	28	37	23	30	6	8	1	1	1	1	0	0
Al Khums	43	68	13	21	5	8	2	3	0	0	0	0	0	0
Misuratah	38	51	26	34	9	12	2	3	0	0	0	0	0	0
TOTAL	163	44	126	34	60	16	18	5	2	1	1	0	1	0

Source: Joint Research Project 1968 questionnaire.

The dryland sector makes little contribution to the vegetable acreage and only 8% of modern dryland farms reported more than one hectare under such crops, while less than two per cent of traditional dryland farms had significant amounts of land given over to vegetables (Table 4.19). Traditional irrigated farms possessed relatively small areas in vegetables and 6% of farms in the group reported more than 8 ha. against 17% of modern irrigated farm units. Farms with a large proportion of land devoted to vegetable growing tend to be those where irrigation is practised over much of the area of the farm and where a high proportion of land is under general cultivation in the traditional sector.

Table 4.19

Area Under Vegetables by Farm type - Western Libya 1967/68

Hectares

Farm Type		No. Valid Obs'ns	Number of farms in each category and %										
			0-1 ha.		1-2 ha.		2-4 ha.		4-8 ha.		8-16 ha.		Over 16 ha.	
			No.	%	No.	%	No.	%	No.	%	No.	%	No.	%
1 Irrig.	Trad.	95	71	75	10	11	8	8	4	4	1	1	1	1
2 "	Mod.	181	94	52	23	13	34	19	23	13	5	3	2	1
3 "	NASA	1	-	-	-	-	1	100	-	-	-	-	-	-
4 Dry	Trad.	68	66	97	1	1	1	1	-	-	-	-	-	-
5 "	Mod.	26	24	92	-	-	-	-	-	-	-	-	-	-
TOTAL		371	255	69	34	9	44	12	27	7	6	2	3	1

Source: Joint Research Project 1968 questionnaire.

Modern irrigated farms, on the other hand, were recorded with 26% of the total owning more than 5 ha. of cereals. Whereas some 40% of dryland farms in both traditional and modern sectors reported no or negligible cereal acreages, traditional farms encompassed a wider range of areas under cereals than modern farms, 9% of farms having more than 25 ha. of grain crops, while no modern units were larger than 25 ha. Farms administered by NASA in Western Libya have a high crop area/farm area ratio, and a high population density. This results from the generous government investment on these farms.

Table 4.20 Analysis of Farming Types and the Extent of Cultivation 1949/1953/1957 to 1966/68 Showing the Proportions of Various Farming Types & Land Use. All Figures are Percentages

		IRRIGATED(& SEMI-IRRIGATED)		UNIRRIGATED		GRAZING	WOODS/ PLANTA- TIONS/ TREE CROPS	CITRUS	DUNES & DESERT	SEA, FLOWING WADI & SABKHAH	AREA NOT PHOTO- GRAPHED OR STUDIED	BUILT UP AREA	MILIT -ARY AREAS
		CROPLAND											
		Trad.	Modern	Trad.	Modern								
WESTERN LIBYA													
1 Talbighah	1953	12	11	–	47	15	2	2	9	–	–	1	1
	1968	12	37(-2*)	–	20(-2*)+	14(-7*)	5	5	2(-2*)	–	13	1	1
2 West of al Ajayalat	1953	5	–	–	–	95	–	–	–	–	–	–	–
	1966	5	27	–	–	68	–	–	–	–	–	–	–
3 Suwani bin Yadim	1953	–	45	–	34	13	6	1	–	–	–	1	–
	1968	–	44	–	37	8	9	1	–	–	–	1	–
4 Gefara (Foot of Jabal)	1953	–	–	25	–	75	–	–	–	–	–	–	–
	1968	–	–	9	–	91	–	–	–	–	–	–	–
5 Jabal Nafusah	1953	–	–	15	11	71	1	–	–	–	–	2	–
	1968	–	–	10	14	72	1	–	–	–	–	2	–
6 Wadi Ki'am	1953	38	0	–	–	40	–	–	7	14	–	1	–
	1965	38	9	–	8	23(-3*)	–	–	7(-1*)	14(-2*)	6	1	–
EASTERN LIBYA													
7 Al Marj	1957	–	–	–	72	25	–	–	–	–	–	3	–
	1967	–	–	–	93	6	–	–	–	–	–	3	–
8 Farzugah	1957	–	–	–	23	76	–	–	–	–	–	1	–
	1967	–	–	–	21	59(-19*)	–	–	–	–	19	1	–
9 Al Qubbah (5.5 km² only)	1949	–	–	–	77	19	–	–	–	–	–	4	–
	1967	–	–	–	78	15	3	–	–	–	–	4	–

Table 4.20 - continued

SOUTHERN LIBYA											
10 Sabhah	1958	16	-	2	-	-	-	-	81	-	-	-	2	1
(20 km² only)	1966	17							77(7)		7	3	1

Source: air photos.

* *Figures in brackets indicate estimated %
not photographed*

\+ *Includes 5% new scattered cultivation.*

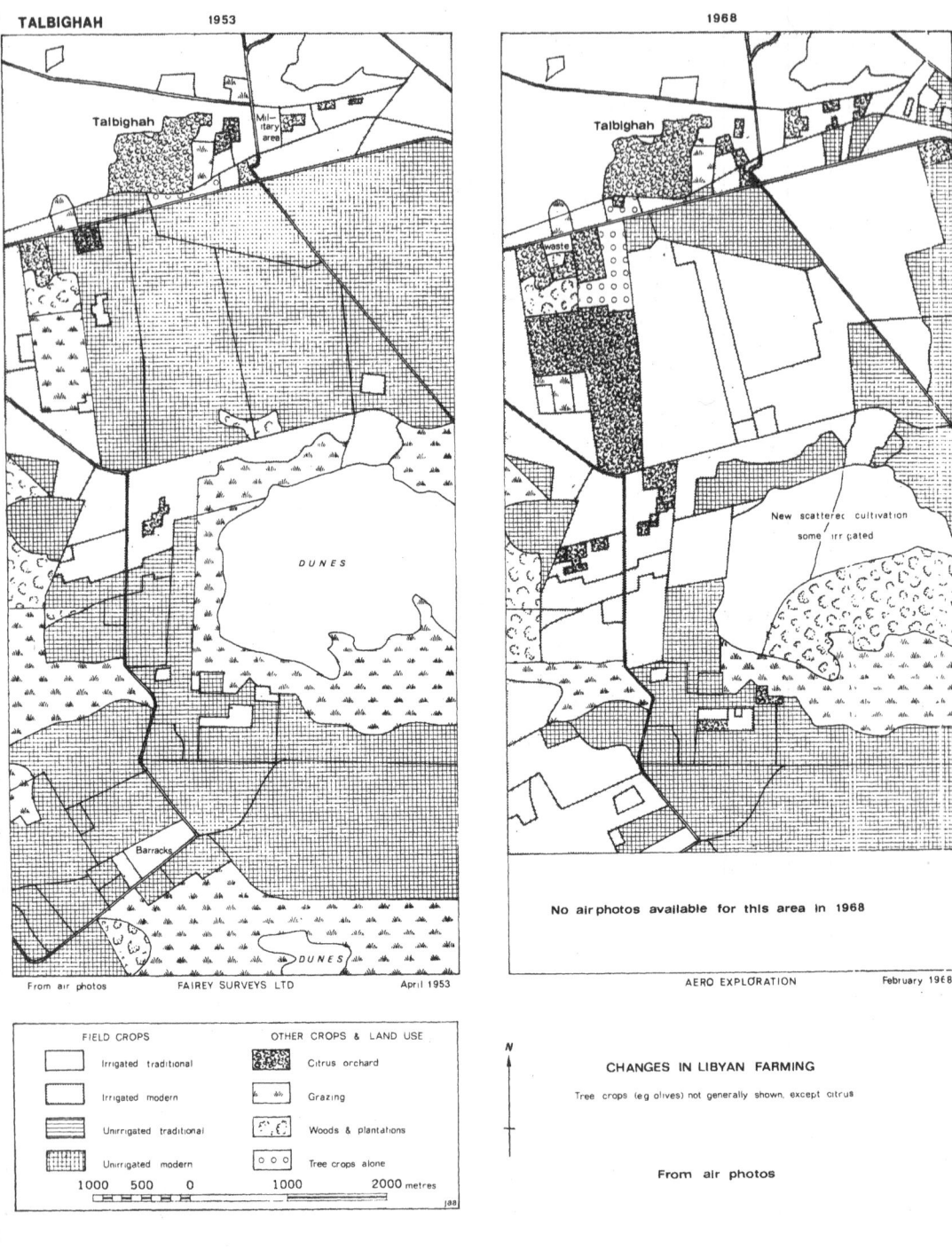

4.3.7 Detailed Analysis of Six Selected Areas

The land-use and farming types of six areas in Western Libya have been analysed and the results of these analyses are summarised in Table 4.20. Each area will be described briefly, and the evidence provided by air photo analysis will be related to other information about the areas, deduced from field visits and other sources.

1. Talbighah (Map facing page 97; photos facing page 99 ; also Crop Maps 3 & 4, (Appendix 9).

Talbighah lies 10 kilometres east of Tripoli, and the 40 square kilometres studied extend south from Mellahah to include areas of traditional irrigated farming and ex-Italian farms. The latter are situated further inland, to the south, where deeper wells were, and are required. Still further south, areas previously unutilised have been examined. Twelve per cent of the total area was under traditional irrigated gardens in 1953, and this proportion was unchanged in 1968. The intensity of farming was different, however, with a 40% reduction in the area of field crops by 1968, partly compensated by an extension of citrus planting, which reflects the high level of total investment confirmed by the 1968 questionnaire survey for small farms near Tripoli (see Appendix 7, Symaps 9.1 & 9.2 - Investment per Hectare). The same questionnaire showed, however, that most investment on these traditional farms was going into housing (see also section - 'Housing development in rural areas', which concludes the section on Talbighah). One, and sometimes two, houses have replaced older dwellings, and since the farms are situated close to Tripoli they are considered pleasant places in which to live, and from which to commute if necessary. Indeed, in some, their use as a residence has completely superseded their use as farms. Agricultural production from the Talbighah traditional gardens must have gone down between 1953 and 1968, except possibly for citrus fruit. Whether this fruit could be successfully marketed in an already crowded seasonal market is not clear, and the importance of the extensions of citrus planting should not be overestimated.

Remarkable changes which can be seen in the map facing page 97 and on photos facing page 99 have taken place further to the south on the ex-Italian farms. 47% of these areas do not seem to have been irrigated in 1953 and much of this land was unused or under-utilised; only 11% was irrigated or semi-irrigated. By 1968 these proportions had almost been reversed, with approximately 35% irrigated or semi-irrigated, and the non-irrigated area down to 18%. Also areas which were used only for rough pasture in 1953 had shrunk from 15% to 5% in 1968. This resulted from the extension of woodland (plantations) from 2% to 5%, and the development of irrigated and dry farming on land classified in 1953 as rough pasture or dune.

The most significant developments have taken place in the central part of the area where the ex-Italian farms have been sold in large and small lots. The most important commercial development is the 180 ha. citrus farm, with a turnover of approximately £L 600 per hectare in 1968. This farm had only just been purchased in 1953, and the citrus trees were being planted at the time of the photography.

Nearby to the east, the ex-Italian farm has been sold as much smaller farms of two to ten hectares, with a turnover about £L 100 or less per hectare on average. This low figure is still much higher than in 1953, when very little agricultural activity of any kind could be identified there.

TALBIGHAH 1953

Fairey Surveys Ltd. April 1953

1968

Aero Exploration   Approximate scale   February 1968

Two other changes should be emphasised. Afforestation is going ahead throughout Western Libya, and one such area has been picked up by this 'case study'. Almost two square kilometres of previously unutilised dune is now planted with eucalyptus. Secondly much of the rest of the dune area, unused before 1953, has been used agriculturally at some time during the past fifteen years. By 1968 at least four permanent dwellings had been built in the former dune area, and over fifty shanty dwellings could be identified, mainly associated with the agricultural development described. Only between ten and twenty hectares were irrigated, the rest being dry farmed in the winter only, and not in every year.

Talbighah is, therefore, an area where farming activity has increased since the revenues from oil have trickled down to the farmer, either as wages from other employment, agricultural bank loans, or from engagement in business enterprises. Development has mainly taken the form of extensions of irrigated farming on farms originally set up between 1911 and 1939 and which were severely run down in 1953.

Mention should be made of the underground water resources upon which these developments have been based. It has been shown that the most important extensions have been in irrigated farming. Detailed measurements of underground water levels were taken in this area during the field work of the joint project, and these showed the fluctuations during a hydrological year. These measurements have been compared with figures recorded ten years before, and in one case thirty years before.

The overall level of underground water is declining from year to year. Even at points within two kilometres of the sea levels have declined 0.2 metres in ten years.[5] Further inland, at a well 6.6 kilometres from the coast, the distance from the ground to the surface of well water in the summer fell from 16.4 metres in 1939 to 26.3 metres in 1968[6], and most significantly, the rate of decline between 1960 and 1968 was almost twice as great as during the preceding twenty years. Similar rates of decline have been identified two kilometres further to the south.[6]

Housing Developments in Talbighah

New and replacement housing is evident throughout rural Libya. The photos facing page 99 show such development for an area of modern farming where a large farm sold as small lots of between four and ten hectares (between 1960 and 1965) each lot now having a new dwelling. It has also been shown in chapter 5 that in 1967-68 most farm investment was going into housing, especially in Western Libya.

In areas of traditional farming, both irrigated and dry, many new houses are being built. In the irrigated coastal gardens rehousing was observed in the field in Eastern, Western and Southern Libya. To illustrate this development, an area near the coast in the Tripoli oasis, some ten kilometres east of the city has been analysed from air photographs available for 1953, 1965 and 1968 (map facing page 101). The area examined covers approximately half a square kilometre. The following table summarises the changes which have taken place:-

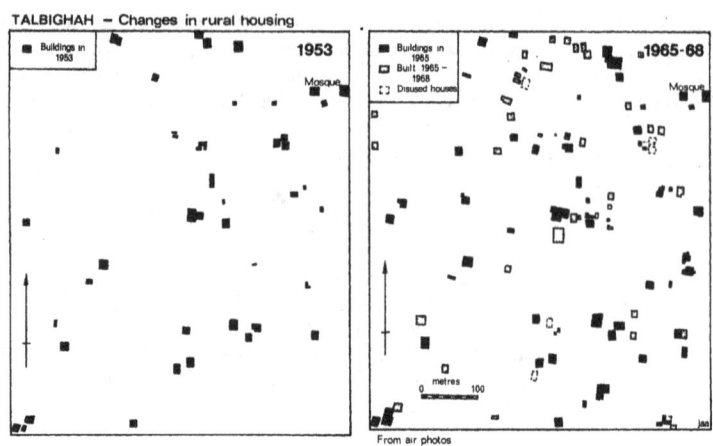

Table 4.21

Changes in the Numbers and Size of Buildings in an Area ($\frac{1}{2}$ km^2)
Ten Kilometres to the East of Tripoli 1953 - 1968

	1953	1965	1968
Number of buildings	41	63	99
Average size of buildings (including courtyards) square metres	222	168	246
Estimated area covered by buildings (including courtyards) square metres	9100	10575	15500
Per cent of total area built over	2.3%	2.7%	3.9%

Source: air photos.

Clearly house replacement and additional housing is in progress in such areas close to the major settlements, and it has been found that many farmers and their families prefer to reside in these pleasant garden areas than to move into the city. Commuting to work in the city is relatively easy and living conditions are good, so that these small farms are often valued more for their living amenities than as a source of agricultural income.

One other point of interest which is indicated in the above table concerns the size of the houses being built. It would appear that in the early part of the building boom up to 1965 houses being constructed were smaller than those built in 1968.

2. **West of Ajaylat** (Map and photos following)

As the general comparison of air photos revealed that new areas were coming into cultivation south and west of Sabratah, a forty square kilometre area was selected west of Ajaylat for an examination of these changes in more detail. Photos only are shown for an area south of Sabratah following page 85.

Only 5% of the area was under traditional irrigated gardens in both 1953 and 1966 and little change could be detected between the earlier and later periods for this type of farming.

The rest (95.1%) of the area has been classified as grazing land, which was of poor quality, being partly dunes. By 1966 27% of the total area was raising irrigated crops, and has been classified as modern semi-irrigated and irrigated farming, in that the development has taken place in the recent past, although the layout of the farms more resembles the traditional Libyan garden. The method of water distribution differs from the traditional method, in that spray pipes are being used to advantage on these irregular areas. The productivity of these new farms cannot be estimated, but it would appear likely that generally poor yields would be the rule in 1966. However, the existence of such enterprise confirms again the wish of some elements at least of the Libyan farming community, (and in some cases amongst families recently returned from Tunisia), to maintain and extend Libyan agriculture.

WEST OF AL AJAYLAT 1953

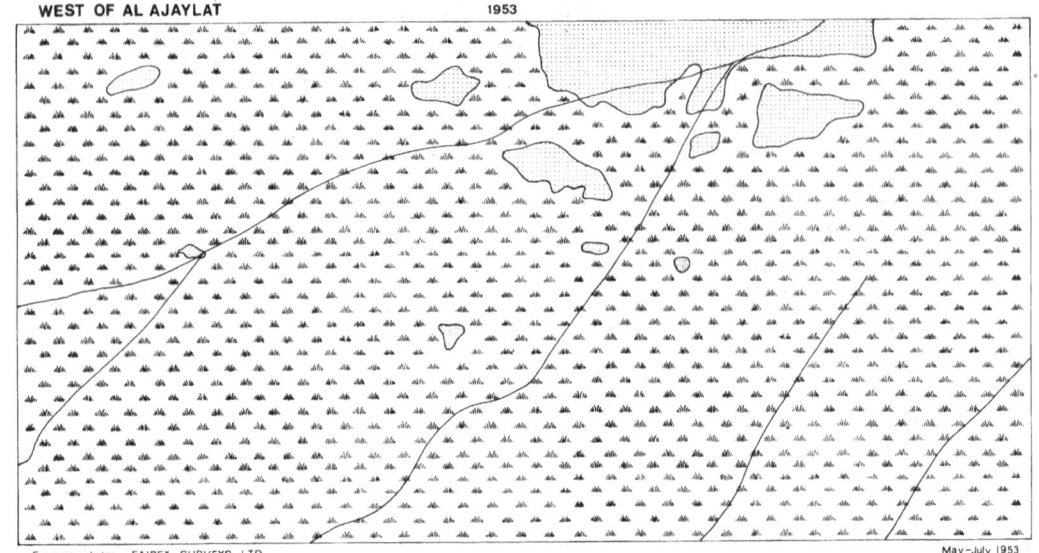

1966

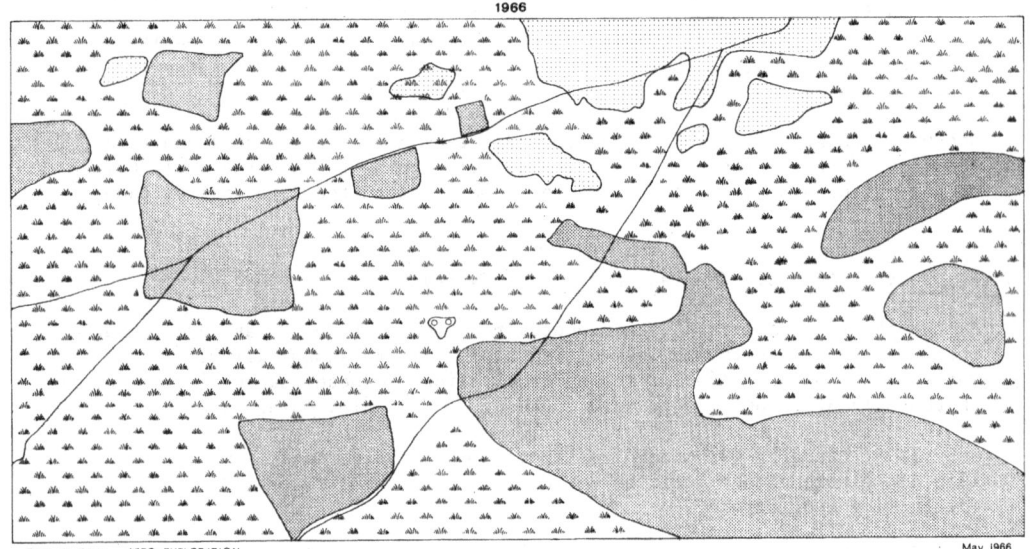

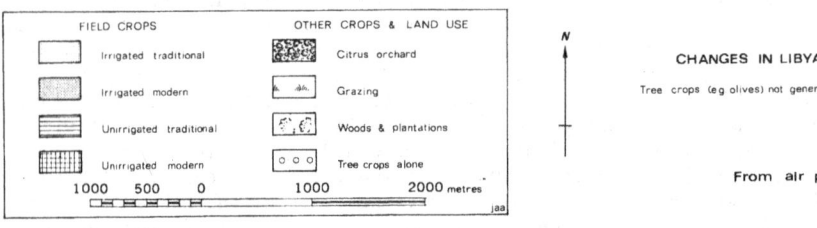

CHANGES IN LIBYAN FARMING

Tree crops (e.g. olives) not generally shown except citrus

From air photos

WEST OF AJAYLAT

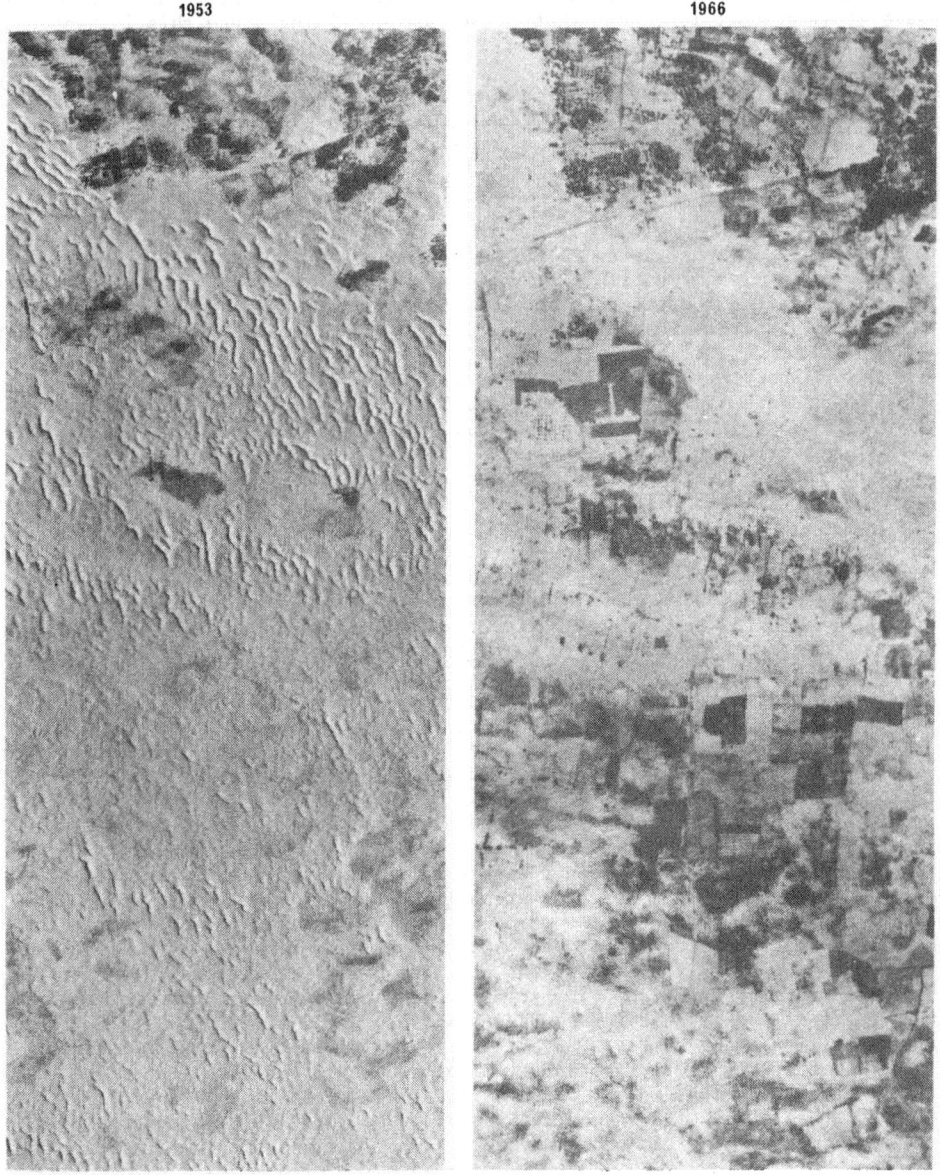

1953   1966

Fairey Surveys Ltd.   May–July 1953   Aero Exploration   May 1966

Approximate scale 1:25,000

It must be mentioned in this second case study that the resources upon which this new irrigation has been based cannot be relied upon in the long term. Salt water has already been pumped in wells on coastal farms to the west of Sabratah, and although there are no data which indicate declining water levels west of Ajaylat it is likely that levels are declining since this is happening throughout coastal Libya.

Additional illustrations of the changes outlined above can be seen for an area south of Sabratah shown on photographs following page 85.

3. <u>Suwani bin Yadim</u>   (Map and photographs overleaf)

Suwani bin Yadim is situated 21 kilometres south of Tripoli. It did not exist as a settlement until 1911, when railway and other buildings were erected Farms were laid out after this date, mainly as dry farms based on olives and winter grain, with some vines.

Air photos show that in 1953 the farms were under-utilised as at Talbighah. Photographs were taken in June 1953 and 1968, and estimates have been made of the areas of irrigation (Table 4.20). These indicate that there has been little change in the proportions, with a 2% total increase in cultivated area and a 1% fall in the irrigated and semi-irrigated area, the latter including much of the olive groves.

These figures conceal a considerable intensification of full irrigation on most of the farms which have been bought by Libyan farmers in the past fifteen years. The 1968 photos (overleaf) show this clearly, especially just to the south of Suwani bin Yadim itself. As at Talbighah, the production of irrigated summer crops must have been higher in 1968 than in 1953, and field work in 1967 indicated a similar summer intensity. The main summer crops at Suwani bin Yadim are tomatoes and ground-nuts both of which require a great deal of water. No attempt has been made to measure the likely usage of water for summer agriculture, as the effect of this increased irrigation upon underground water levels can be demonstrated without exact figures of withdrawal.

Underground water resources are being depleted at Suwani bin Yadim extremely rapidly. (See diagram facing page 40.) By 1968 the rate of decline had reached one metre per year, and reliable measurements over ten years,[7] show that the rate of decline has been steadily increasing since 1959. Geological evidence[8] shows that the depth of mainly saturated strata can only extend at most to 50 metres below the present water level. Since rates of decline seem likely to move quickly to two metres and more per year, increasingly expensive irrigated farming at Suwani bin Yadim can only continue for between 20 and 30 more years unless new water resources are discovered. Other changes in the area result from the utilisation of former grazing land for arable farming. The area of grazing fell from 13% to 8% between 1953 and 1968. Woodland in turn increased from 6% to 9%, and numerous small plots on the edge of poor grazing areas were being farmed on a dry land basis in 1968, amounting in all to approximately 2% of the total area.

4. <u>Gefara (Foot of Jabal)</u> (Map facing page 106).

The forty square kilometres selected to demonstrate some of the changes in agriculture in regions of dry (including wadi) farming areas on the Gefara plain, lie close to the foot of the Jabal Nafusah to the north west of Gharyan. It includes an area through which drain a number of small wadis, which flow when winter rains are sufficient on the Jabal Nafusah.

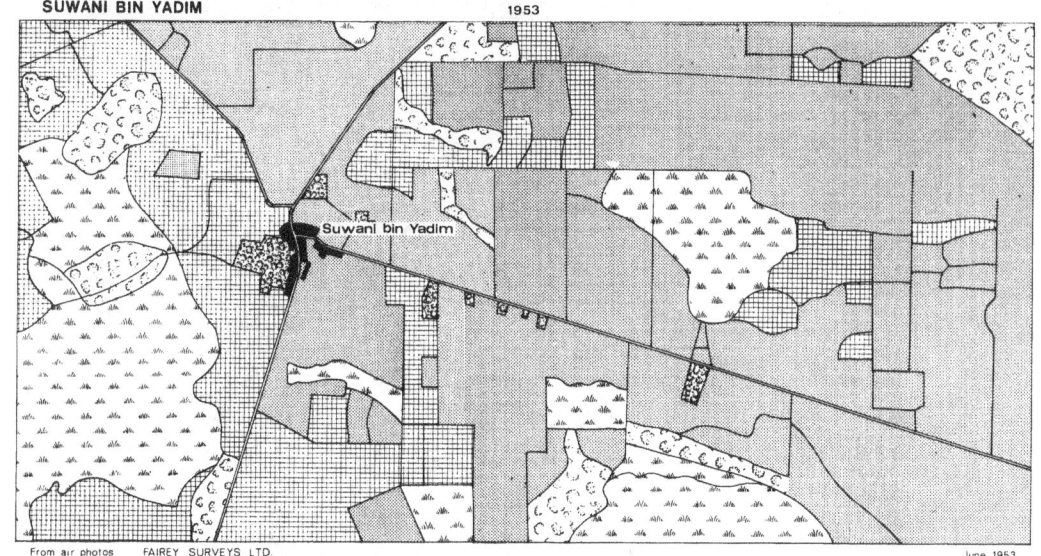

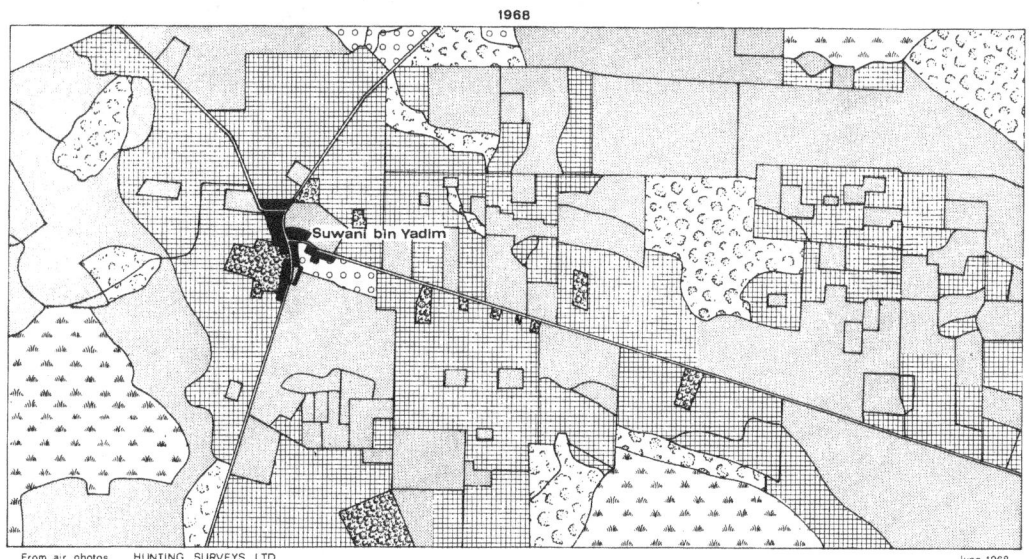

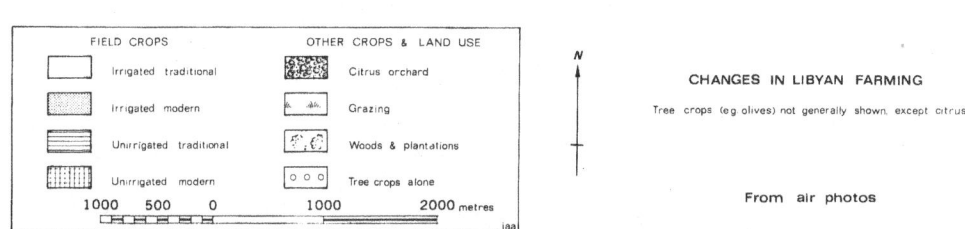

CHANGES IN LIBYAN FARMING

Tree crops (e.g. olives) not generally shown, except citrus.

From air photos

SUWANI BIN YADIM 1953

Fairey Surveys Ltd. June 1953

1968

Hunting Surveys Ltd   Approximate scale 1:25,000   June 1968

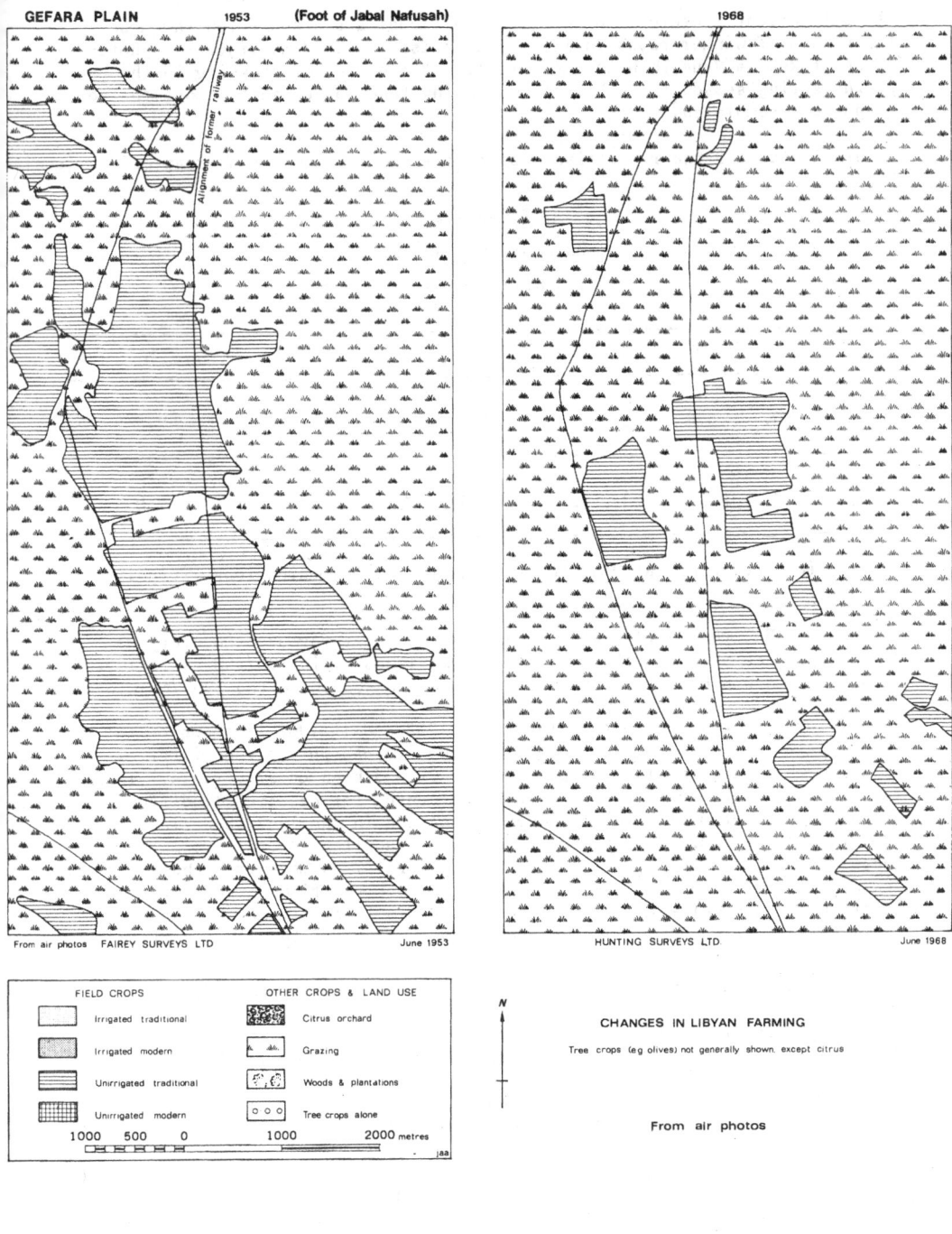

It is important therefore to consider the amount and disposition throughout the season of winter rains in 1952/53 and also in 1967/68, since the photographs taken in June in both cases reflect the extent of cropping in the preceding spring season, with harvesting having taken place just before the photography was completed.

Rainfall data for the respective seasons are shown below for Gharyan on the jabal.

Table 4.22
Rainfall at Gharyan
millimetres

	S.	O.	N.	D.	J.	F.	M.	A.	M.
1952/1953	6.7	5.8	33.2	4.0	54.0	38.0	4.0	3.5	2.2
1967/1968	47.0	88.5	13.2	22.5	54.5	75.0	0	5.5	7.0

Source in Meteorological Department, Ministry of Communications, Tripoli.

These show that the 1967/68 winter season was better favoured in every way. More than twice as much rain fell in the jabal nearby in 1967/68 as in 1952/53. Also the rain was better distributed through the season in the 1967/68 winter.

The difference between the area farmed in 1953 and in 1968 is shown on the maps facing page 106. 25% of the total had been cropped during the winter of 1952/53, while for the 1967/68 period only 9% had been under cereals. This fall in hectarage under crops cannot be accounted for by rainfall differences, or by disposition of the rain through the season in the 1967/68 period. There is evidence therefore that there has been some decline in dry farming at the jabal foot. The jabal farmers, and it is generally farmers from the top of the scarp who farm these areas, either no longer have the time, or do not feel it profitable, to utilise these lands as much as in 1953. It may be that their permanent off-farm jobs prevent journeys to the foot of the jabal to farm there.

5. Jabal Nafusah-Tighrinnah (Map facing page 108, photographs facing page 110)

An area of hill land of Western Libya has been selected to show changes in traditional farming, as well as developments in modern farms. In this case the modern farms were laid out before 1939 for tobacco growing. The forty square kilometres studied lie to the south and west of Tighrinnah, and are not irrigated, with the most important field crops being raised after the commencement of the winter rains.

The average size of the traditional jabal gardens is normally small. Data collected in 1968 showed the average size for this farm type to be 31.5 hectares, but this average includes areas to the west and east where such farms are larger. Also it is possible for the farmer on the jabal to have additional parcels of land some distance from his dwelling either on the Gefara or on the jabal further to the south. These farms were also the most fragmented according

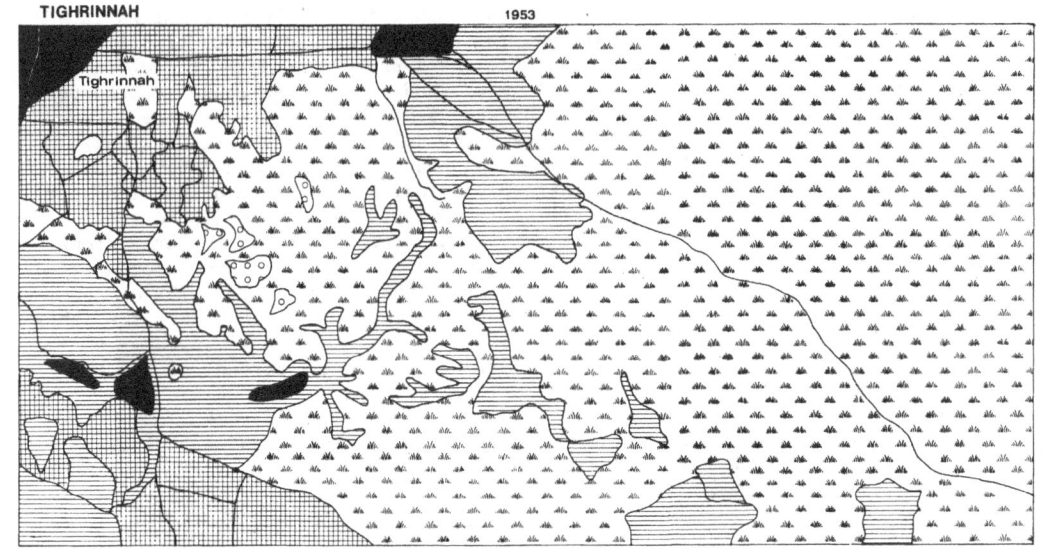

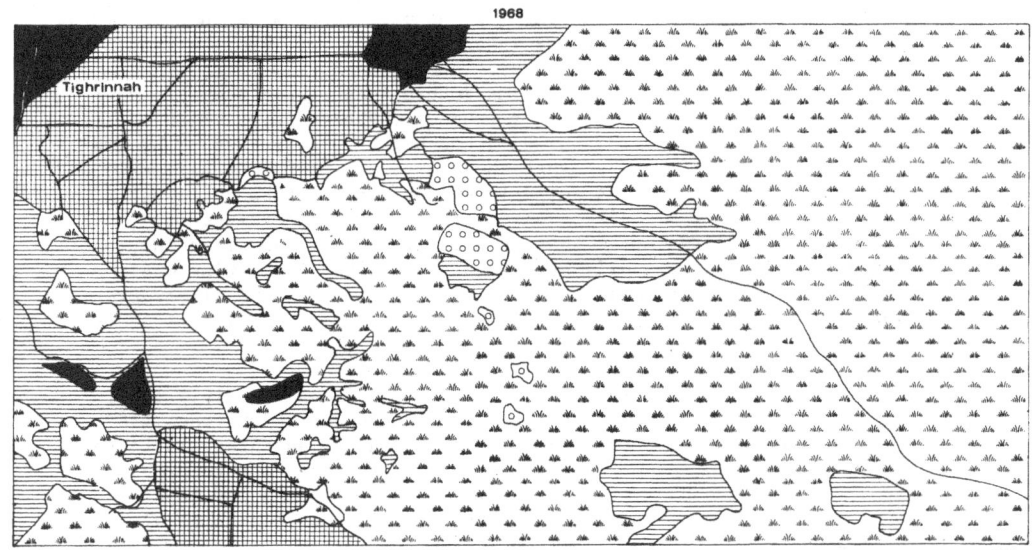

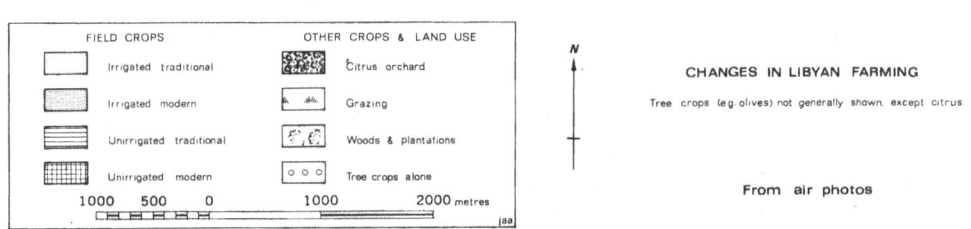

to the 1968 survey. Thus the areas of traditional farming being examined in these air photos may represent part only of the land farmed by the traditional jabal farmer. Between 1953 and 1968 there was a decline from 15% to 10% in the total area identified as traditional farming, and the land no longer cultivated has reverted to grazing. It has already been noted when discussing the Gefara (jabal foot) area that rainfall was more favourable in 1967/68 than in 1952/53, and so any apparent reduction in cultivation cannot be accounted for by poor rainfall in 1967/68. Field visits before and during the period of the 1968 air photos showed that despite an overall decrease in the area farmed, the area being utilised was being used intensively; a high proportion of the traditional gardens had been, or were under winter grain, mainly barley. This was confirmed by the 1968 questionnaire survey which recorded that approximately 70% of these farms were cultivated mostly with cereals. The traditional gardens of the jabal are much less neglected than those of the coast, and the incentives to grow grain locally rather than use imported varieties are still strong, as there is a strong consumer preference for the local barley flour.

Investment was shown to be relatively high in the jabal gardens, especially near Gharyan, where over £L 150 per hectare was recorded by the 1968 questionnaire survey (see Symaps 9.1 & 9.2 - Investment per hectare). Old houses and underground dwellings are being replaced very quickly, and it is this type of investment which was most common in 1968. The main source of investment is the off-farm employment of one or more of the extended family in the administrative or educational establishements in the main centres, such as Gharyan. This is confirmed by a fall-off in the investment rate away from Gharyan.

In the areas which have been classified as modern farms there seems to have been an increase in activity. Three per cent of the total area which could only be described as grazing land in 1953, had begun to be re-farmed by 1968. This is described as re-farming in that these are areas laid out before 1939 as tobacco farms. The government actively encourages the tobacco industry, and approximately half of Libya's requirements are grown in the country. The photographs taken in 1968 confirm that an extension has taken place in tobacco hectarage, and output has steadily grown since 1959 when production was estimated at 855,000 kilogrammes. By 1963 output was 1,068,000 kilogrammes, and by 1966 it had risen another 30%, as a result of the licensing of additional areas.

Meanwhile the consumption of cigarettes in Libya is rising rapidly. Total imports of tobacco and tobacco manufactures more than doubled between 1965 and 1967,[9] while unmanufactured tobacco imports increased threefold in the same period.[10] There is scope for even further expansion of Libyan tobacco production. At present, however, the local production is heavily subsidised by the state tobacco monopoly, and the Libyan product cannot compete with imported varieties.

6. <u>Wadi Ki'am</u> (Map facing page 112)
      photograph (1953 only) facing page 114

Wadi Ki'am, one of the few perennial rivers in Libya, is fed by flood flow from the Wadi Tareglat system draining the dip slope of the eastern Jabal Nafusah and by spring water flow near its mouth. The area included within the confines of the air photo cover interpreted on the map facing page 112 takes in the lower wadi more or less from the spring to the mouth together with the easterly extension of the Sahal al Ahmad, Zliten and the western outskirts of the Zliten sub-district. Lying on the borders of the al Khums and Zliten sub-district, relatively distant from established market villages and subject to

TIGHRINNAH　　　　　1953　　　　　(JABAL NAFUSAH)

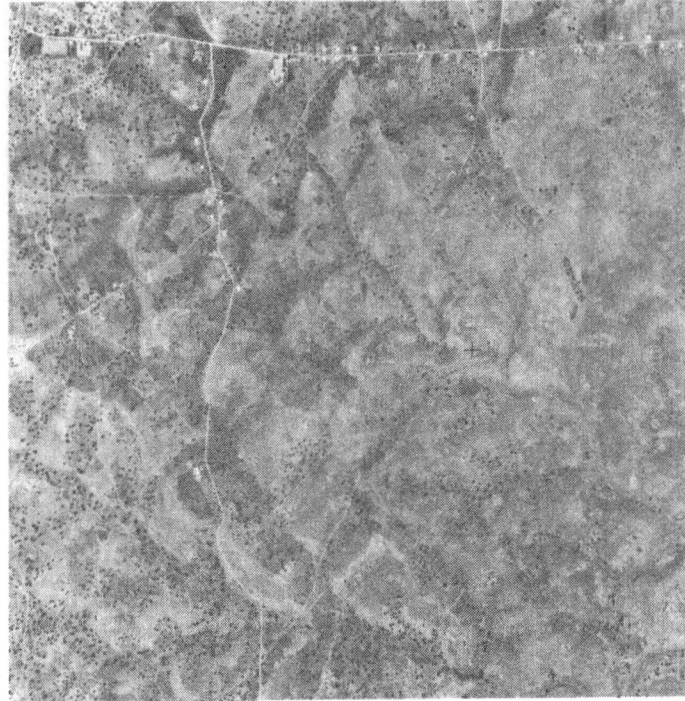

Fairey Surveys Ltd.　　　　　　　　　　　　　　　　June 1953

1969

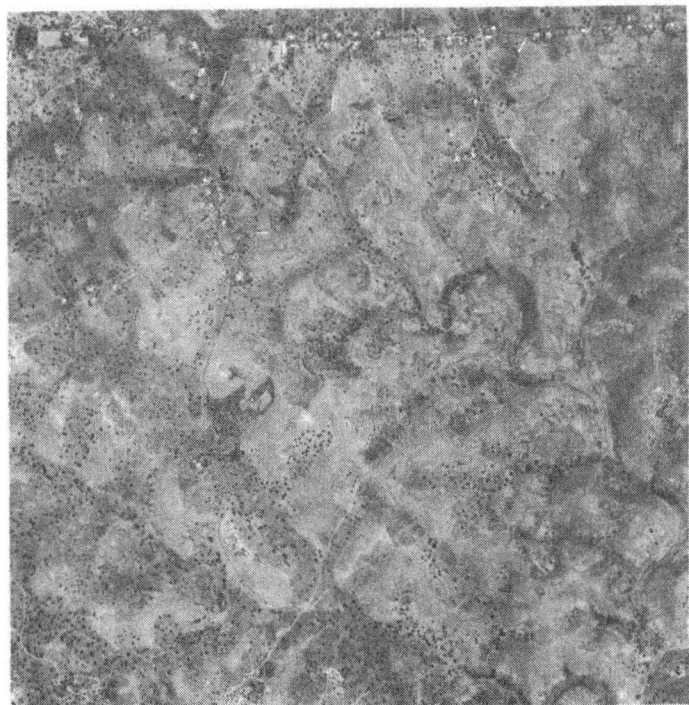

Hunting Surveys Ltd.　　　　　　　　　　　　　　　June 1968

Approximate scale 1:25,000

occasional flooding, the area has been comparatively neglected until recent years.

The marginal nature of the site is clearly indicated on the photo facing page 114, 1953, when the more fertile areas of land (38% of land) were enclosed in the form of oasis gardens irrigated from the shallow aquifer and farmed in a traditional manner. Irrigation water was drawn to the surface by the dalu system of water raising and the donkey ramps associated with the individual farm wells may be discerned from stereoscopic scrutiny. Of the grazing land in 1953, representing some 40% of total land under review, the best endowed was that lying adjacent to the wadi. There is little evidence that the grazing area was ploughed on any great scale at that time, though the year in question was rather dry with rainfall for the agricultural year totalling 182.5 mm (of which only 175.1 mm had fallen by April when the air photo was taken). Grazing of livestock in the traditional economy represented an important element in farm income. In addition to small livestock holdings by the oasis dwellers kept on farm throughout the year and pastured in the environs of the oases the grazing land would also be used seasonally by nomadic groups.[11]

Of remaining land, 7% was taken up by coastal dunes and sand spits, while sea, wadi and sabkhah accounted for a further 14% of the review area. Apart from an Italian-built road house and a number of dispersed farm settlements, accounting for less than one per cent of total land, Wadi Ki'am has few outstanding settlement characteristics. The main road, traversing the area east-west, has been paved since the 1930s, and provided access to Zliten, Suq al Khamis and al Khums, lying at 15, 11, and 23 kilometres distance, respectively. In 1953 goods would have been transported by donkey-cart to market, putting farmers at a disadvantage compared with those closer to the centres of population.

Two major and immediately obvious changes have taken place since 1953 as shown on the map facing page 112, the first encompassing the creation of an estate of small modern irrigated farms on the western bank of the wadi and the second the extension of the cultivated areas adjacent to the oases of the Sahal al Ahmad. These developments have resulted in an increase of nine per cent in the area under irrigated agriculture and eight per cent in the area under dryland agriculture, all of the reclaimed land taken in from the former grazing area. Taking into account adjustments to compensate for the slightly less comprehensive photo cover in 1965 than in 1953, all other land use types have remained unchanged (see Table 4.20).

In statistical terms, the physical area of irrigated lands in the traditional oases has remained static, though even from air photo interpretation it is possible to discern that the ramps formerly used by dalu system water raising have almost entirely fallen into disuse, and since irrigated cultivation is still carried on in these areas it is fair to deduce that diesel pumping of water for irrigation has replaced the dalu. Intensiveness of use of the oasis gardens has tended to become more patchy and in aggregate less in 1965 than in the earlier year, though this change is less marked here than in other oasis areas of the littoral of Western Libya such as Zliten and Zawiyah.

An insignificant amount of reclamation of land on the periphery of the oasis has taken place since 1953, mainly confined to one area in the north-west of the survey area. Much of this land is utilised in a way almost identical to that in the traditional areas. The major land reclamation project in the area (though dwarfed by the existing ex-Italian estates of the east of the survey area including al Dafiniyah, Taminah and al Kararim) is the 240 hectare Wadi

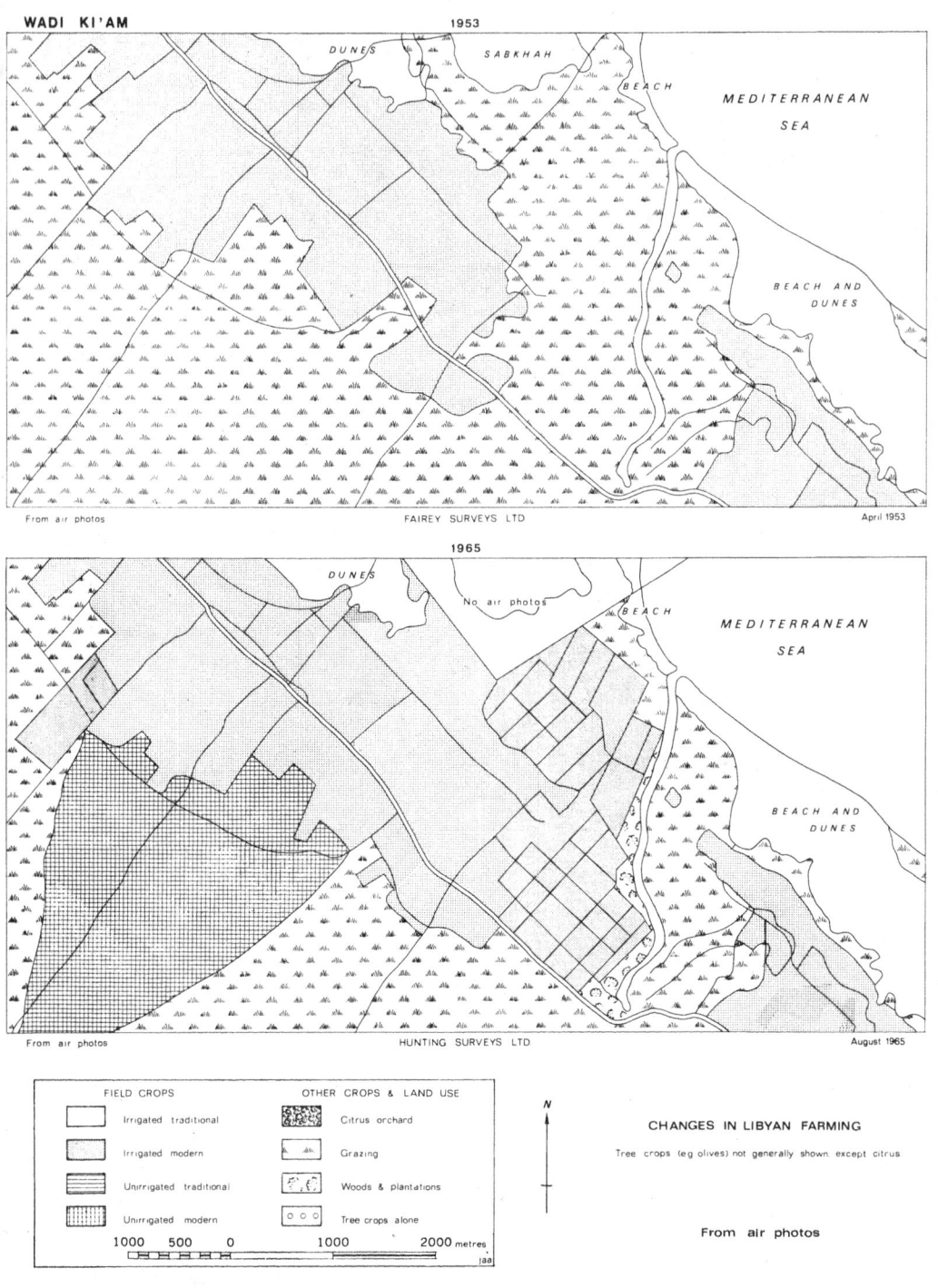

Ki'am settlement developed under the terms of a United States aid programme. It draws its water supply for irrigation from wells adjacent to the natural reservoir impounded between the spring (occurring close to the point where the main highway crosses the wadi) and a sand bar across the wadi mouth. Farm management is based on individual rotations for each, separately owned, two hectare plot, which is fully irrigated. It is significant that the estate was created in the period preceding the oil boom when a two hectare plot was assumed to be large enough to support a farm family at then acceptable standards, though initial optimism was not matched by performance even in the early period before 1961. In recent years the estate has become a responsibility of NASA, which provides financial aid, some administrative support and extensive service facilities. In many ways the estate reflects land use characteristics encountered on other NASA-controlled settlements, with a much more intensive use of land and water resources than in the surrounding oases. Summer cropping is practised on a high proportion of the farm units though the relatively rich variety of high value cash crops cannot be appreciated from the black and white air photos. Detailed analysis of the cropping situation on the estate for 1968 may be found on Table 4.7, page 81, while the estate is also covered by Maps 3 and 4 in Appendix 7. The pattern of land use on the estate is anomalous in the setting of the Sahal al Ahmad and is sustained only by the financial support of NASA.

Comparison between the survey area in 1953 and 1965 in the non-irrigated sector indicates a substantial change towards reclamation, though in fact the position is less clear. The tractor-farmed areas indicated in the south-west quadrant of the map facing page 112 and utilised for winter cereals may reflect merely the response of local farmers to an average rainfall year (see table following) with a good distribution of the fall in the winter and early spring months:

Table 4.23

Rainfall - Sahal al Ahmad in Agricultural Years 1952/53 and 1964/65

Millimetres

	S	O	N	D	J	F	M	A	M	J	J	A	Total
1952/53	2.6	0.0	19.3	28.7	85.9	20.6	14.6	6.3	23.2	1.3	0.0	0.0	182.5
1964/65	0.0	12.8	79.4	31.4	15.4	27.9	26.1	11.1	0.5	0.0	0.0	4.0	208.6

Source: Ministry of Communications - Meteorological Service. Tripoli.

However with an increased supply of tractors available to farmers in the area, it is not unlikely that larger areas are more frequently being sown in the steppe lands immediately surrounding the oases than formerly.

Grazing lands are still used and scavenging by oasis kept animals remains as much a feature of the farming scene in 1965 as in the earlier year. Seasonal in-movement of semi-nomadic pastoralists has become less important and the grazing lands are now slightly less intensively utilised than in the preceding decade. A project for developing centrally managed grazing lands to the south of the estate, launched in the late 1950s, has been discontinued and no evidence of pasture land improvement is apparent from the air photo cover.

WADI KI'AM 1953

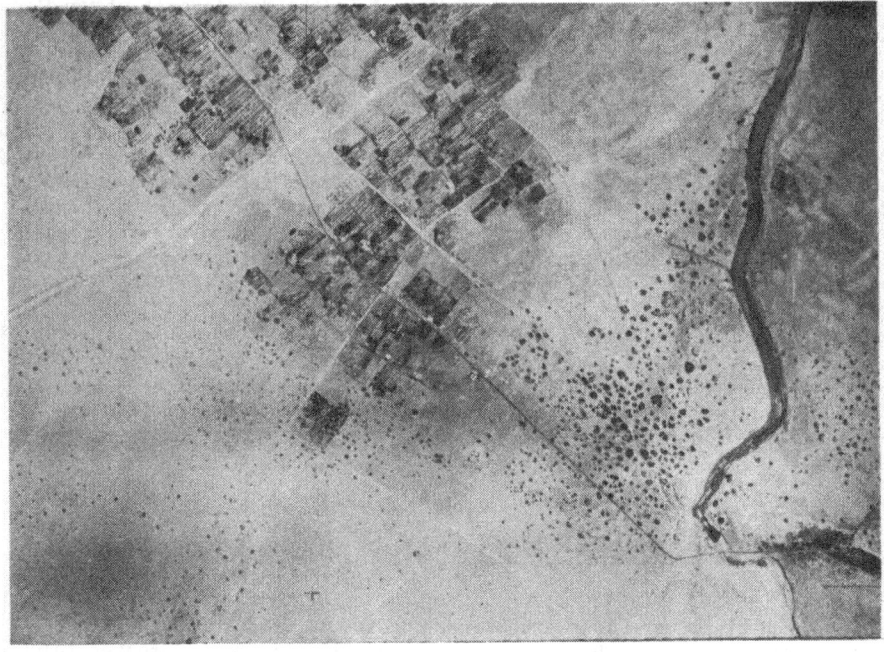

Fairey Surveys Ltd June 1953

Approximate Scale 1:25,000

Small changes have been brought about in the non-agricultural lands of the area under review, of which the most important is the development of woodland shelter belts mainly of tamarisk/acacia associations along the west bank of the wadi, the estate perimeter and tracks traversing the farmland. The surface area under trees is insufficient to register in the Table 4.20. Growth of the estate has prompted the construction of administrative and service buildings in the area, while an appreciable amount of new building within the traditional oases has taken place over the twelve year period between the taking of the air photos. Close study of the housing on the Wadi Ki'am estate shows considerable extension of the original house units reflecting both the general trend in Libya as a whole for new wealth to be dispersed on house improvements, and local dissatisfaction with the house style chosen by the foreign consultants who planned them.

The particular interest of the Wadi Ki'am estate lies in the demonstration of the official attitude to land utilisation in the 1950s, though despite this, the estate in particular exhibits characteristics in common with those noted on NASA farms elsewhere in Western Libya, with intensive use of land at all seasons supported by full irrigation.

4.4 Eastern Libya

4.4.1 General Distribution of Land Use

The changes in the agricultural scene brought about in Eastern Libya by the Italian occupation, were less extensive than in the West.[3] The development of the al Marj and Farzugah areas for dryland agriculture was pressed through for reasons of expediency during the drive for demographic settlement in the late 1930s despite the poor rainfall endowment of the region. By 1940 2206 families had been settled on 145,000 hectares (compare 3,960 families on 231,090 hectares in Western Libya.)[3] Finally the conflicts of the 1940-42 period brought about the evacuation of all the Italian farming community from the east.

Apart from very limited areas of irrigated agriculture of the traditional pattern at the coast, settled agriculture did not exist significantly in the province before the Italian invasion. The neglect of the traditional irrigated farms is evident in Eastern Libya, as in Western, a position confirmed by an examination of farms near the settlements along the coast between Benghazi and Tukrah, especially near the latter settlement, but also at Daryanah. A similar pattern was evident in photographs taken of Darnah and Umm ar Rizam in 1966. The other most obvious change was in housing. New houses have increased at the same rate as in Western Libya.

Only around Benghazi are there significant areas of modern irrigated farming. Those on the Jabal Akhdar, for example on the al Marj Plain are never more than two or three hectares. So far searches for underground water resources for agriculture have not been successful, and to this the air photographs bear witness, in that no significant extension of irrigated agriculture can be detected between 1954 and 1966.

Non-irrigated traditional farms are limited to some small areas of the central Jabal Akhdar. The definition is not very useful, however, in Eastern Libya as traditional irrigated agriculture was and is frequently of a 'shifting' character. The rainfall cereal areas of Western and Eastern Libya worked under shifting cultivation have little in common, for all such land in Eastern Libya is located in regions receiving more than 200 mm. rainfall each year, including the discontinuous mountain areas of the Jabal al Akhdar and the plains south of Benghazi.

As already indicated, 145,000 hectares could be described as modern unirrigated farmland in 1940. These differed from similar areas in Western Libya, in that the emphasis was on grain production. Fewer trees were planted, 6,272 ha. (compare 75,250 ha. in Western Libya), and vines covered only 1,782 ha. (compare 15,600 ha. in Western Libya).[3] The extent of development up to 1938 as well as a comparison with that in Western Libya can be seen on the maps facing pages 120 and 122. Considering the dry basis of agriculture on the Jabal Akhdar and the correspondingly lower returns per hectare, as well as a landscape that lends itself to mechanisation, the farms laid out by the Italian colonists of 50 ha. and sometimes of 25 ha. seem uneconomically small.

Regional variations in farm size in Eastern Libya, including cultivated gardens but excluding shifting cultivation areas, were reported in 1967 to range from 2.71 ha. in the Benghazi region to 3.28 ha. in al Marj and 7.36 ha. in the Darnah-al Qubbah area (1967 questionnaire).

In recent years there has been an increase in mechanisation but up to 1968 little progress has been made with reclamation, and in few areas was activity at the pre-1940 level. Air photos guide us to this conclusion; certainly between 1954 and 1966 little change can be detected. By 1968, however, house reconstruction had been commenced both at Farzugah and at Girnadah, this being a preliminary to the further reclamation of the old Italian farms.

4.4.2 Extent of Cultivation of the Farms

The crop surveys of the summer of 1967 (July/August) and the winter of 1968 (February), indicate the proportion of farm areas under crops for these seasons. The maps were measured and the percentage for each crop is tabulated in Table 4 in Appendix 2.2. Important totals have been deduced from this table and set out in Table 4.7 in this chapter.

Table 4.7 allows a comparison of the Eastern and Western parts of the country. Two things should first be noted, first the absence of a modern irrigated/semi-irrigated case study in Eastern Libya reflecting the slight importance of this type of agriculture in these Muhafadat, and second the very high proportion of the farm which is cultivated in the dry farming areas of the Jabal Akhdar, namely al Marj, Farzugah, Bu Zayd, al Qubbah, Fatiyah and Suluntah. Suluntah seems exceptional, but its low percentage of cultivated area is mainly accounted for by its low and unreliable rainfall.

In Eastern Libya there is no equivalent of the large irrigated and semi-irrigated farms of the Gefara Plain, and conversely there is no counterpart in Western Libya for the non-irrigated al Marj Plain, which extends to the north-east of the town, with another similar flat area to the south-west at the foot of the second scarp.

The 1967/68 case studies were less comprehensive for the Eastern than for the Western part of Libya, and although this renders the scheme which we followed when discussing the West less complete, it is still felt to be viable. The scheme was to compare the proportions of the farm cultivated for irrigated v.

dry farms, for traditional v. modern farms, and for the private v. the government sponsored farms.

Irrigated v. Non-irrigated Farms

Irrigated farming is of minor importance in Eastern Libya, but those areas where it is carried out have the same proportions cultivated as in Western Libya. But whereas in the West dry farms show only a slightly higher area utilised than for irrigated farms, in Eastern Libya the dry farms studied recorded very high farm utilisation especially for grain crops. At al Marj the percentage utilised is 95% or 85% depending on whether the farms are privately or government run; elsewhere lower proportions are recorded, but always over 50%, except at Farzugah where redevelopment was not fully under way by 1968. There is very little continuous cropping as was evident earlier when considering the Jabal Nafusah in Western Libya where grain crops and tobacco may be raised at different seasons.

Traditional v. Modern Farming

As already indicated it is not possible to distinguish between traditional and modern farming in Eastern Libya as no case studies were completed for irrigated modern nor for non-irrigated traditional farms. It is possible, however, to compare the types which are represented with their equivalents in Western Libya.

Traditional, intensively worked, coastal farms show the same high proportion of fallow land in both parts of the country, especially in summer. The case of Darnah is special in that the gardens studied are very close to the town and building is rapidly superseding farming. At Darnah of the land available, high proportions are used for crops in both summer and winter, with 54% and 71%, respectively. Here as in other places in Eastern Libya the emphasis on winter crops is more marked than in similar irrigated areas of the Western part of the country.

Turning to the modern dry land farms which can be compared in both Eastern and Western Libya, Table 4.7 indicates that such farms in Eastern Libya support a greater area under crops than those in Western Libya. This is certainly the case in respect of privately run farms. On these farms the cropped area is between 57% and 92% for the case studies completed, and in Western Libya only 54% to 55%. It should, however, be noted that the figure for Tighrinnah should be modified to take into account the continuous cropping which is practised there; tobacco being grown after the winter grain crop. The total cropped area for the year would amount to about 80% if this were taken into account.

There is some other evidence which should be remarked, which concerns the high level of utilisation of dry land farms known to be traditional in Western Libya. These are located near Gharyan and al Qassabat, and are shown clearly on Symaps 4.1 and 4.2 in Appendix 9. Levels of utilisation of over 80% are indicated, a similar proportion to that recorded for the case studies for modern farms on and near the al Marj Plain of Eastern Libya. The same symaps show that the modern dry land farms in Western Libya have a generally lower proportion of the farm under crops, both at Jandubah and at Tarhunah.

The explanation of the lower level of utilisation on the modern dry land farms of Western Libya than on those of the East lies in the circumstances of their early development. Such farms on the Jabal Nafusah of Western Libya were

AL MARJ   **1957**

Hunting Surveys Ltd.   July 1957

FARZUGAH   **1957**

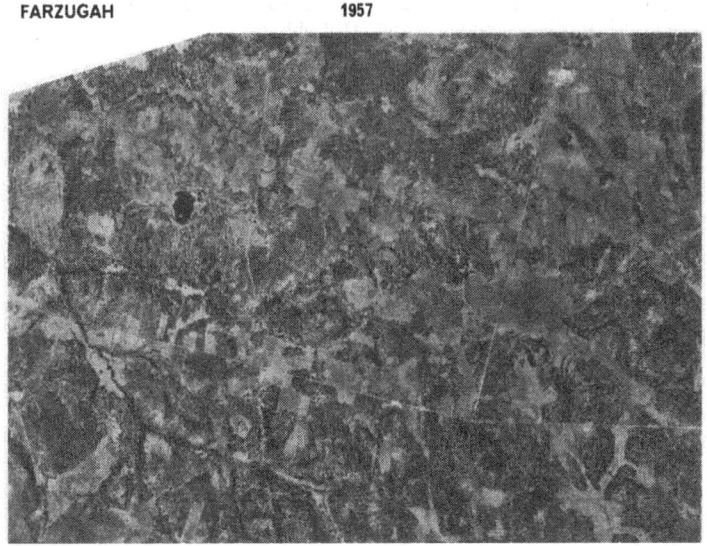

Hunting Surveys   July 1957

Approximate scale 1:50,000

developed in places less favoured in respect of rainfall and soils than the older traditional farms. On the Jabal Akhdar of Eastern Libya, however, which had not been an area of settled agriculture before the arrival of the colonists, relatively well favoured areas were taken over for permanent farming for the first time.

Private v. Government Run Farms

In Eastern Libya government run farms were less highly utilised than privately owned farms at the time of the 1968 survey. The National Agricultural Settlement Authority have taken over a number of marginal areas, for example Farzugah, al Qubbah and Suluntah, and these are not yet fully developed, but in any event being in areas of lower rainfall, and where terrain is more difficult for farming, it is unlikely that they will compare favourably with the private farms located on better land.

So far in discussing the private and government farms of Eastern Libya we have referred to the dominant dry land sector. Only one minor scheme of government irrigated farming was covered in 1968, that at Bu Turabah, to the east of Tukrah. The figures given in Table 4.7 do not reflect the very scattered nature of farming on this poor site, which is in no way comparable with government developments at Wadi Ki'am and Sa'a'idiyah in Western Libya, nor is farming activity as vigorous as on the traditional privately owned irrigated farms at nearby Tukrah for example.

4.4.3 Detailed Analysis of Three Selected Areas

Reference should be made to Table 4.20 on page 94 where are listed the percentage changes in activity and farming methods (1957-1967) for the three selected area, al Marj, Farzugah and al Qubbah.

7. <u>Al Marj</u> (Map opposite)
   and photograph facing page 118

For the al Marj area of 40 square kilometres air photographs taken in July 1967 have been used as well as field work completed in the same month of 1967. The area selected is part of the al Marj Plain, where extensive dry land farming is carried out. The south-west corner of the area included the relatively low lying 'al Gharig', which frequently floods in winter, to allow the cultivation of crops, normally associated with the irrigated coastlands, such as melon.

The Italian development of the area left a rectangular road and track pattern, with one dwelling per 50 ha., this being the size of farm selected for the Italian demographic settlement. Most of the houses are empty, partly as a result of the destruction caused by the 1963 earthquake, but also because the large expanse of the Marj Plain can as easily be farmed by farmers living some distance away, since cultivation and harvesting are mechanised.

The areas set out before 1939 have been taken over by the National Agricultural Settlement Authority, and these comprise 60% of the area studied. The balance falls mainly in the 'al Gharig' area which is farmed privately by people from the town of al Marj.

Since this is a region of predominantly dry farming, it is helpful to have data on the rainfall during the months before the photography and the field work.

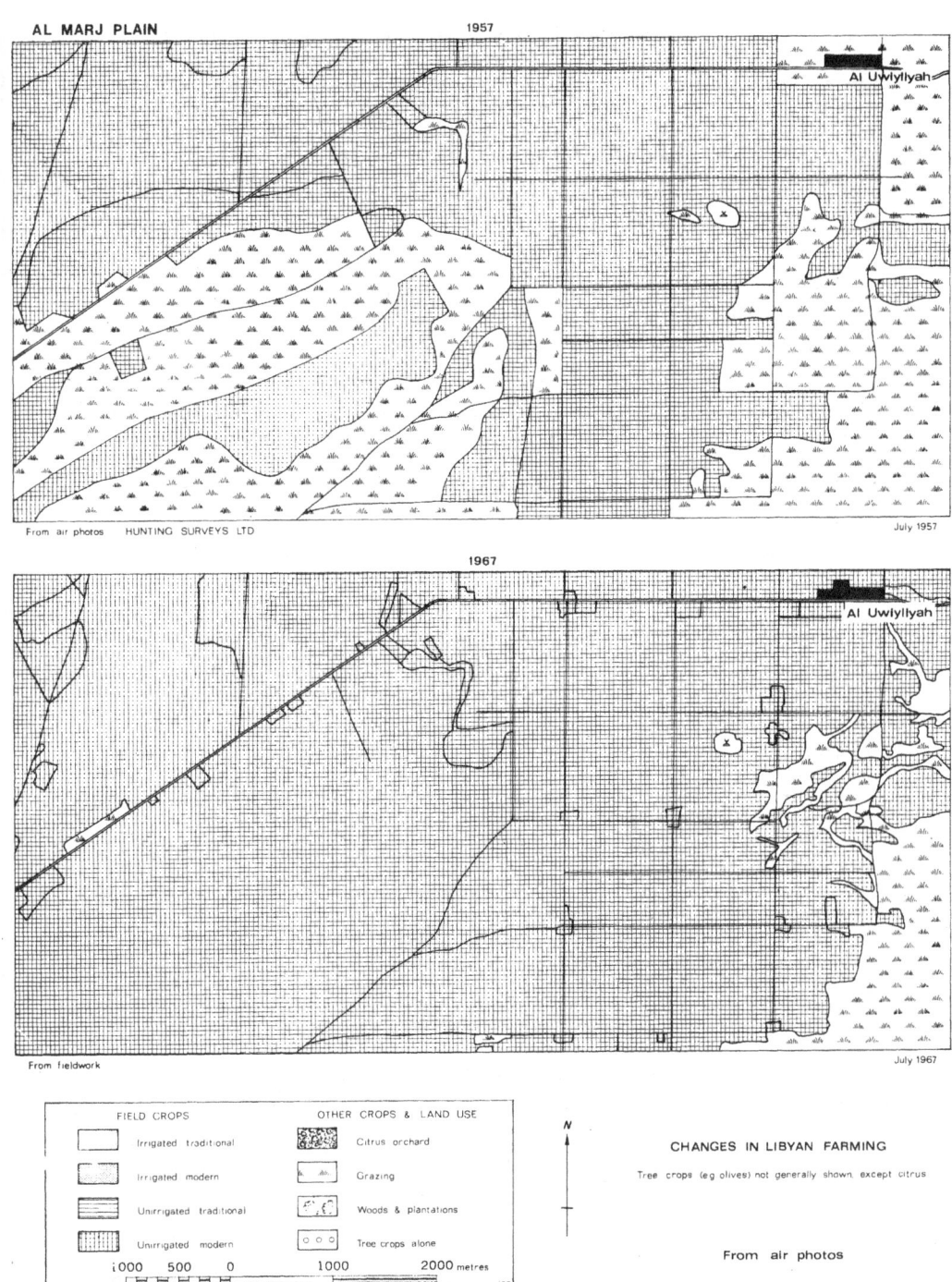

The average rainfall for al Marj is 448.1 mm. year. Unfortunately precise data for 1957 are not available, but an examination of the figures for the station at Shahhat, further to the east on the Jabal Akhdar, indicate the rains were slightly above average during the 1956/57 season (634 mm. against 588 mm. mean annual). An examination of data for both Shahhat and al Marj for the 1930s, shows that 70% of the time above average rainfall at Shahlat was reflected in above average figures at al Marj.[12] For the period September 1966 to June 1967 rainfall was 397.0 mm. in other words close to the mean. The seasons 1956/57 and 1966/67 are therefore comparable, and deficient rainfall can be discounted as an inhibiting factor for either season.

Land use in the al Marj area has been divided into two types, non-irrigated modern cropland and grazing land. The field work of July 1967 showed that a very high proportion (93%) of the study area was under cereals, reflecting the good and well-distributed rains of the preceding winter and spring seasons.

Photographs for 1957 indicate that a smaller area, amounting to 72% of the total, was or has been under crops at that time. It would appear that the al Marj area, like many areas in Western Libya, was being under-utilised in the 1950s. In recent years there has been an increase in the hectarage of dry farming, which is in line with the claims and intentions of the National Agricultural Settlement Authority, which is charged with the responsibility of redeveloping former Italian farms, and increasing the arable area further where possible.

8. <u>Farzugah</u> (Map facing page 122)
     and photograph facing page 118

Farzugah lies some twenty kilometres to the west of al Marj, and an area of forty square kilometres has been selected mainly to the south of the main road. The area has been studied for 1957, the year for which photography is available, and for 1967 when field work was completed by the joint research project. In 1967 the area covered in field work was 19% less than in 1957. In both years the month of July was considered.

Rainfall at Farzugah is on average slightly lower than at al Marj, and certainly in 1967, at 291 mm[12] it was approximately 30% lower. Figures for 1957 are not available, but as for al Marj, rainfall for this earlier period was probably about 10% lower than average.

Farzugah was an area laid out in the late 1930s by the Italian authorities and the air photos show the rectangular pattern of roads and farm boundaries. This area of former Italian activity comprises some 80% of the area outlined on the map facing page 122, the rest being rough pasture. Settled farming had only been in progress for a few years at most when the colonists left in 1942, and their impact cannot have been great. By 1957 23% of the total area studied was under cereals, which was approximately 30% of the area laid out as farms by the Italian colonists.

Field work in 1967 indicated that there had been no significant change in the area farmed. Despite rather better rains on the Jabal Akhdar the total area under crops had fallen slightly to 21% of the total. Such a change cannot be considered significant, and it is reasonable to conclude that up to 1967 there had been no increase in the area farmed at Farzugah. It is another dry land area where changes are taking place more slowly than in areas where irrigation is possible. It has already been shown that dry farming in Western Libya is

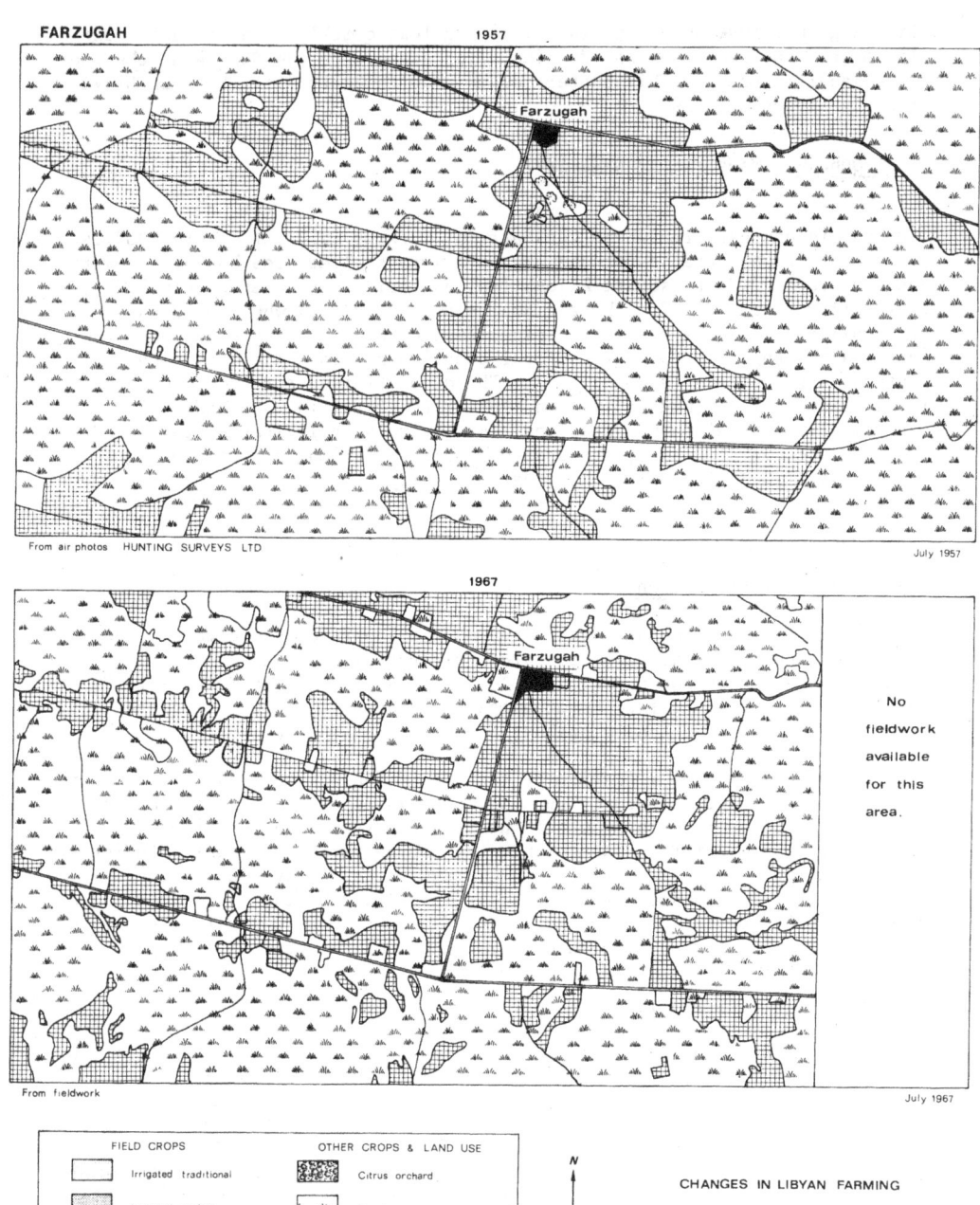

attracting less investment and is developing less quickly than irrigated agriculture, and in some cases has declined (for example on the Gefara at the foot of the Jabal Nafusah). This pattern seems also to be true for Eastern Libya, certainly for NASA farms.

9. Al Qubbah (Maps facing page 124)

Al Qubbah is another area where the pattern of farms laid out before 1939 is visible on air photographs for the area. A much smaller area has been covered than the standard forty square kilometres, as field work covered only 5.5 square kilometres in 1967. The air photos and field work when compared on the compilations on the map facing page 124 indicate that there have been no significant changes in the agricultural practice nor in the area farmed in the eighteen years between 1949 and 1967. The area utilised for crops, mainly grain, was relatively high at 77% and 78% of the total in 1949 and 1967, respectively. The al Qubbah area confirms the relatively static state of dry farming on the Jabal Akhdar, at least on farms for which the National Agricultural Settlement Authority have responsibility.

4.5 Southern Libya

4.5.1 General Introduction

Air photographs indicate that, as in the northern part of the country, there has been a general extension of the area cultivated. This also is true at Sabhah, Awbari and in the oases of al Jufrah (Waddan, Hun and Sawknah). Field visits showed that mechanical water pumps were replacing dalu wells permitting the extension of irrigation throughout Southern Libya.

This extension and intensification of the traditional as opposed to the modern type of irrigated agriculture is unusual in Libya as a whole. In total the extensions would be less than 10% of the area cultivated in the mid-1950s, but they serve to confirm a move within the Libyan farming community to invest in the farm and to extend cultivation. In the south of the country the opportunities for expansion are especially restricted by the environment, and as the south Libyan farmers have not been exposed to modern farming techniques the methods used to extend irrigated farming are of the traditional type.

4.5.2 Extent of Cultivation of Farms

As field work was completed in only one season in Southern Libya, that of the winter of 1967/68 (February), it is only possible to assess the extent of cultivation partially.

All farms are of one type and therefore it is not appropriate to adopt the treatment which was used in discussing this topic in relation to farms in Eastern and Western Libya, when farm types were contrasted, that is irrigated with non-irrigated, or traditional with modern. The farms for which crop surveys were completed were all of the traditional irrigated type.

The results of measuring the areas of particular crops are summarised in Table 4 in Appendix 2.2 and also in Table 4.7 in this chapter. In respect of the proportion cultivated the figures show a remarkable consistency, especially as the areas examined are widely dispersed (see map facing page 124). Five out of the seven areas shown on Map 8, Appendix 7, had between 38% and 46%

AI QUBBAH 1949

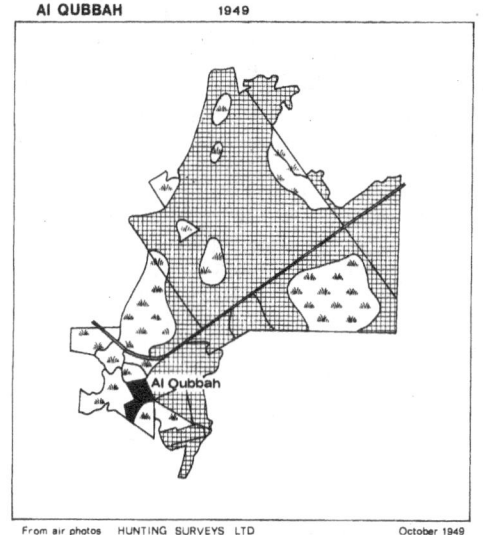

From air photos   HUNTING SURVEYS LTD   October 1949

1968

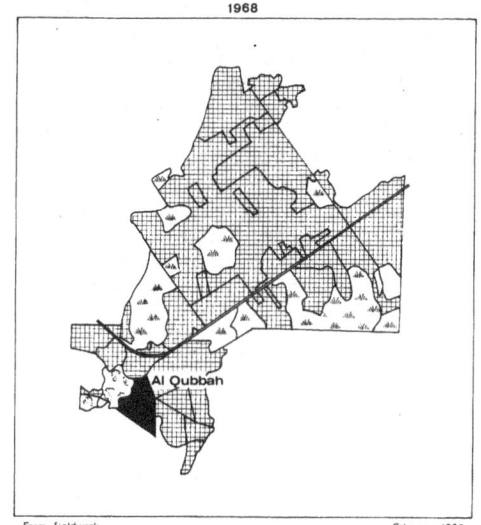

From fieldwork   February 1968

SABHAH 1958

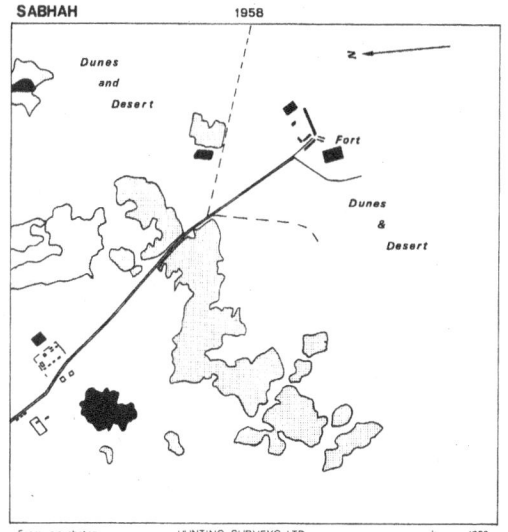

From air photos   HUNTING SURVEYS LTD   January 1958

1966

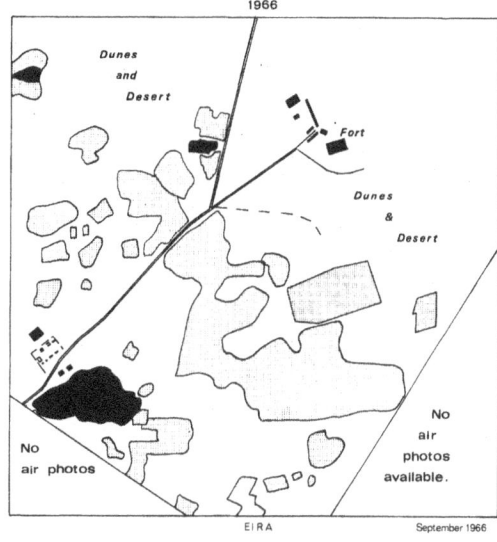

EIRA   September 1966

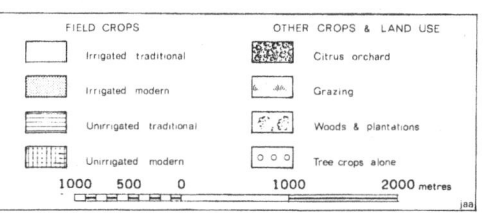

FIELD CROPS
- Irrigated traditional
- Irrigated modern
- Unirrigated traditional
- Unirrigated modern

OTHER CROPS & LAND USE
- Citrus orchard
- Grazing
- Woods & plantations
- Tree crops alone

1000 500 0 1000 2000 metres

CHANGES IN LIBYAN FARMING

Tree crops (e.g. olives) not generally shown, except citrus

From air photos

under crops in the winter of 1967/68. The other two areas, both in al Jufrah (Waddan and Sawknah) show lower utilisation figures, and a very significant absence of cereals. They had only 25% and 32% respectively under crops, and these lower proportions may reflect their closer proximity to alternative sources of food and agricultural products. Misuratah is 450 kilometres away, while it is a further 300 kilometres to Sabhah, and further again along unmetalled roads to the other places studied.

This level of winter cropping (30 to 45% in general) is similar to that in Eastern and Western Libya, but shows a much smaller range. No equivalent traditional coastal areas show a higher level of cropping, except the oasis of Darnah, and generally there is more evidence of the neglect of traditional farms at the coast, especially near the towns, for example at Zawiyah and al Ajaylat. There is therefore evidence that farms in Southern Libya are being run with greater enthusiasm than similar farms in better favoured areas near the coast. More will be said of this in the analysis of the Sabhah area which follows.

4.5.3 Detailed Analysis of the Selected Area

Reference should be made to Table 4.20 where are listed the percentage changes in activity and farming methods between 1958 and 1966 for the area selected for detailed study, Sabhah.

10. Sabhah (Map facing page 124)

Agriculture in the southern part of Libya is very dispersed, and any area of forty square kilometres would include a large proportion of desert. The area selected for study at Sabhah is less than half this size, and still includes more than 75% of desert and dunes, usable only as very poor pasture.

Photography for 1958 and 1966 is available, and the comparison of these years shows that changes in agriculture in Southern Libya are different from those in the north. Crops can only be raised where water for irrigation is available, and the farms are essentially traditional in character, and very similar to those near the coast in Western Libya. Any investment in agriculture cannot be directed towards the redevelopment of modern farms, as is the case in Western Libya, and so former traditional farms, and sometimes previously unfarmed land, have been brought back into use. These changes are illustrated in the map facing page 124, which shows that between 1958 and 1966 the area being farmed has been extended from 16% to 19% of the area studied. In absolute terms these changes are very small; in the Sabhah region the total extensions cannot amount to more than 30 ha. The contribution of these farms is also therefore small, and in relation to the total Libyan agricultural production, insignificant. The evidence of enterprise and the will to develop the poor agricultural resources are of importance, and have been remarked on here and in other parts of this section, as it is felt that attention should be drawn to the varied reactions of the Libyan farmer to the availability of additional resources. In Southern Libya the reaction has been to extend the areas farmed, even of traditional irrigated farming, which in almost all other areas of Libya is a farming type in which activity is declining.

4.6 Notes on the air photos and on the diagrams derived from them

Selection of the map and photo scales

It should be noted that the air photographs used to illustrate Chapter 4 include in general only part of the area covered by the comparative maps, which show forty square kilometres at 1:50,000. Photographs at 1:25,000, though ideal for illustrating the character of most Libyan agriculture, would have been too large for inclusion in the text in a normal way, if the whole forty square kilometres of each area had been shown. For each area studied approximately half of the mapped area has been selected for photographic presentation, at the 1:25,000 scale.

Exceptions are the extensive farming areas of al Marj and Farzugah, which have been shown on photographs adjusted to a scale of 1:50.000, which is also the scale of the comparative maps.

It should also be noted that the air photos have only been adjusted approximately to a consistent scale of 1:25,000 and there has been no attempt to accurate rectification.

1:50,000 maps from the A.M.S. Series P 761 were used as base maps for all areas, except Sabhah, for which an uncontrolled photo mosaic has been used.

Comparison of changes in Libyan agriculture using air photos has been carried out at two levels. First there has been an examination of air photographs of most agricultural (60% approximately) areas of Libya, in order to obtain a general impression of changes at the national level. Secondly, photographs covering a number of selected areas, generally forty square kilometres each, were examined stereoscopically in great detail. These areas have been carefully selected to demonstrate particular features of change in Libyan agriculture.

Complete details of sources and dates of air-photos are shown on each map or illustration. Much of the earlier material has been drawn from the useful 1:24,000 cover, flown by Fairey Surveys Limited in 1953 in north-west Libya. However, in Eastern Libya, the general comparison for the earlier period was on the basis of photographs flown as a preliminary to the compilation of the 1:50,000 United States Army Map Service P 761 series of maps. The detailed work was based on material flown by Hunting Surveys Limited in 1957, with some photos for 1949. The same company provided photographs for Southern Libya for 1957/58.

More recently most of agricultural Libya has been covered by aerial photography, between 1965 and 1968; Eastern Libya by Aero Exploration on behalf of the National Agricultural Settlement Authority in 1965, and the same company covered much of Western Libya in 1966 (western part) for the Ministry of Planning/Ministry of Municipalities, and also a number of marginal agricultural areas on behalf of the National Agricultural Settlement Authority (NASA). In some cases special photography was flown for the Project, notably covering the Jabal Nafusah area of Western Libya. These special photographs were completed by Hunting Surveys Limited and Aero Exploration.

Photo quality

The air survey companies which so generously gave permission for the reproduction of their prints have asked that attention should be drawn to the following points:-

128

Aero Exploration took the photographs dated 1966, and our illustrations have been enlarged from the 1:65,000 original prints. Inevitably these compare unfavourably with prints produced at a scale of 1:24,000 shown on the same page (facing pages 86 and 102).

AL QUBBAH
1949

Approximate scale 1:25,000

SABHAH   **1958**   Hunting Surveys Ltd   October 1949

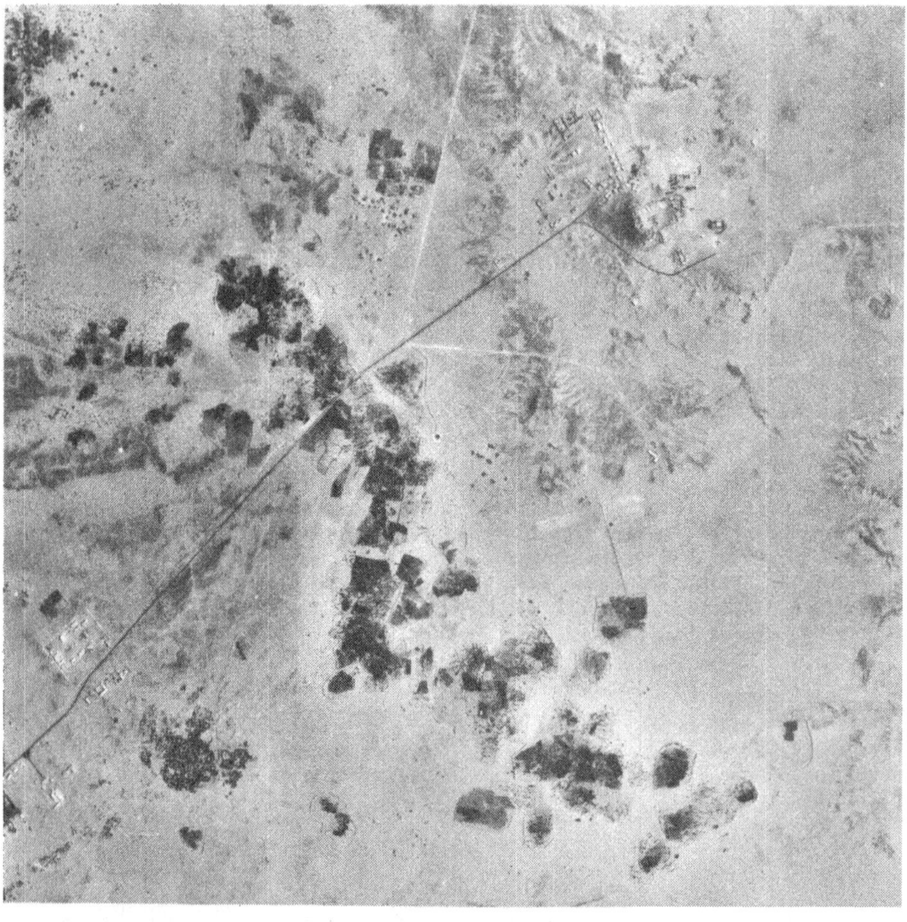

Chapter 4

References

1. British Military Administration <u>Handbook on Tripolitania</u> Appx. T. p.93, Tripoli 1947.

2. <u>Primo censimento generale delle aziende agrarie metropolitane della Libia</u> pp.34-35, Tripoli 21 April 1937.

3. Instituto Agricola Coloniale, <u>Some data on the Italian activity in the colonies</u> Plate XVI, Firenze 1945.

4. Ministry of Agriculture, <u>Census of Agriculture</u>, p.247, Tripoli 1960.

5. Ministry of Agriculture - Soil and water conservation department. <u>Figures for observation well at Mellahah (1374-352. M-4)</u>, Tripoli 1960-1968.

6. Cederstrom and Bertaiola, <u>Groundwater in the Tripoli area</u>, Records for well no.420, Tripoli 1960. Also field work completed by J. A. Allan (SOAS) University of London, 1967/1968.

7. Ministry of Agriculture - Soil and water conservation department. <u>Figures for observation well at Suwani bin Yadim (3242-1302-1)</u> Tripoli 1960-1968.

8. Cederstrom and Bertaiola, <u>Groundwater in the Tripoli area</u>, Well logs for well 815, three kilometres north-west of Suwani bin Yadim. Tripoli 1960.

9. Figures provided by the Tobacco Monopoly. Tripoli.

10. Ministry of Planning. <u>Trade statistics</u> (Department of Statistics) 1965, 1966, 1967 Tripoli.

11. McLachlan, K. S. The Wadi Caam Project in 'Field Studies in Libya' edited by Willimott, S.E. and Clarke, J.I., Durham 1960.

12. Fantoli, A., <u>Le pioggie della Libia</u>, Roma 1952.

Chapter Five

INVESTMENT IN LIBYAN AGRICULTURE

5.1 Introduction - some comments on the survey

The growth of the oil industry in recent years has created opportunities for the modernisation of Libyan agriculture on a scale which was unthinkable only a few years ago. The climatic conditions in Libya and its water resources are such that a great deal of investment is required for the expansion of agricultural output, as shown by the Italian experience up to 1939. Revenues from oil have removed a great deal of the financial restraint in a number of ways. First, part of the enlarged government budget has been earmarked for agricultural projects and for financing and subsidising the purchase of agricultural equipment, fertilisers, and irrigation pumps. (See Table 1.5 in Chapter 1.) Secondly, the expansion of trade, commerce, construction, and civil services, as a consequence of the rapid rise in oil income, have attracted a large number of migrants from the villages to the towns, and have increased the average earnings of the workers. (See Chapter 6.) A part of the incremental income of the town dwellers, many of whom have retained their links with villages from which they come, has been remitted back to the family farms. Thirdly, increased earnings of the town dwellers have also been translated into increased demand for agricultural products, which have boosted earnings of farmers, and a part of these earnings are being ploughed back to finance investments in machinery and tools. The development of institutions such as the Agricultural Bank and rural co-operatives have aided the mobilisation of savings, and have influenced the direction of investment in agriculture.

In our 1968 survey of Western Libya we attempted to measure the relative importance of various sources of agricultural finance with little success. Slightly more than one-tenth of the respondents stated that they had had loans during the previous year, almost all through the National Agricultural Bank, but the statements by the farmers of the amounts received were not always reliable. Moreover, it was not possible to measure adequately the money received as remittances from family members living in towns, or the amount of profit reinvested in agriculture.

It is clear, however, that the level of mechanisation, as measured by the number of tractors, irrigation pumps, and other tools, per head of agricultural population or per unit of cultivable land, is high when compared with that of earlier years in Libya and also with that in most other developing countries of the world. Government trade statistics for the years of the present decade show a continuous stream of imports of agricultural machinery, fertilisers, and other equipment and materials required for the modernisation of agriculture.

In this chapter we shall analyse the results of our 1968 survey of Western Libya with respect of the pattern of current investment. For analytical purposes, the 370 farms that constitute our sample, have been grouped according to region, type of farming, and size of cultivated area. Data for 371 farms were collected, but as only one government farm was visited, it has been decided to analyse only the material from the 370 private farms enumerated.

The five regions are Jabal Gharbi, Zawiyah, Tripoli, al Khums, and Misuratah. Farms have been divided into four size groups according to cultivated areas - "very large" (350 ha. or more), "large" (between 80 ha. and 349 ha.), "medium" (between 20 ha. and 79 ha.), and "small" (less than 20 ha.). Farms have also been classified into "irrigated" and "non-irrigated", and "modern" and "traditional". (See Table 5.1)

The questionnaire from which the data on investment are derived relates to the period August 1967 to July 1968. An inventory was made of farm buildings, equipment etc., which reflect previous investment, but no attempt was made to relate this to specific periods.

Investment expenditures have been grouped under the following heads:
(1) Real Property and Construction, (2) Irrigation, (3) Machines and Tools, (4) Transport, and (5) Land Reclamation. Expenditures on weddings, travel, and furniture have been grouped in a separate item as "Other Expenditures". "Real Property and Construction" include investment of a durable nature which is tied to land. It includes expenditures on land, houses, rooms, yards, sheds, workshops and storage bins, as well as on other buildings and construction works. Of these, the expenditure on "homes and rooms" is partly for "consumption" purposes and partly for "investment", and hence, we have shown this item of expenditure separately, and in parenthesis. "Irrigation" includes expenditure on durable machines, like irrigation pumps (electric or diesel) and/or electric generators, as well as on cisterns, wells, pipes, and expenses incurred for deepening wells. "Machinery" includes tractors, combine harvesters, ploughs, harrows, mats for olive picking, insecticide sprays, and other equipment. "Transport" includes items such as cars, carts, and pick-up vans. Costs for "Land Reclamation" are mainly wage expenditures.

It is important to note at this stage that there are some important omissions from our list of investment expenditures by Libyan farmers. Wage cost as part of the total cost of investment was not separately examined, although it is certainly a very important item of expenditure. In our survey, the respondents were asked to provide data on the volume of employment, on the nature of employment, as also on average wage rates. But in view of seasonal fluctuations in the level of employment and wage rates, and of the differences between family labour and hired labour, the wage rates reported could not be used to calculate the total annual wage bill of the farmer. However, some of the items mentioned above, such as "Land Reclamation", or "Costs of Deepening Wells", contain a large wage component.

Another omission is that of investment in livestock and poultry. We found that the farms constituting our sample did not purchase more than two sheep-equivalents per farm in a year, and that the expenditure on livestock purchase (net of sales) was a very small proportion of total investment. Even where the total stock of sheep, goats, cattle, camels, donkeys, and horses was high, the actual net addition to the stock through purchase was negligible, and as far as the sample of farms from Western Libya is concerned, the omission of livestock purchases has virtually no bearing on our conclusion. This is not as significant as it might seem in view of the fact that the joint project has been examining settled farms, on which livestock rearing is not an important activity. We also excluded expenditure on fertiliser, although its importance as an input in Libyan agriculture is growing over time.

5.2 Investment and the Size of Farm

Table 5.1 gives for each area the size distribution of farms according to the four out of six categories, used elsewhere in the report. (For the definition of the six categories refer to Chaper 4, page 67). It is clear from these figures that the larger farms tend to be modern, and the smaller the farm the larger is the probability of it being traditional. On the other hand, there is no such clear relationship between irrigation and farm size. Among various regions, Tripoli and al Khums contain a greater proportion of larger farms than Zawiyah, Misuratah, and Jabal Gharbi, in that order.

Table 5.4 gives the average amount of investment per farm for each size category for each type of farming, as also for the whole of Libya. Ignoring the very large farms, it is seen that the large farms invest more than the smaller farms. The very large farms generally spend more than the medium and small farms, but less than the large farms. The only important exception to this is the one very large farm in the traditional unirrigated category, which has a very high investment figure compared to that obtained for the large farms of that category, and also considerably influences the total figure for farms in the very large traditional and non-irrigated categories. The positive relationship between size and investment per farm is also more or less confirmed when various regions are separately considered, (Table 5.16), and when size categories with small proportion of farms are ignored. The only important exception to this generalization is Jabal Gharbi, where 90% of the farms are small and which shows relatively high investment figures.

If, on the other hand, instead of investment per farm, we take investment per unit of cultivated land into account, a diametrically opposite conclusion emerges. As seen from Table 5.5, the very large farms invest very little per unit of land, and the amount of investment per hectare increases substantially as the size of farm declines. For the whole of Libya, the smallest farms invest, on average, at least thirty times more than the very large farms, at least three times more than the large farms, and about twice as much as the medium farms. This conclusion applies to modern, traditional, irrigated, and non-irrigated farms separately as well as to composite types. There are two exceptions, first the very large traditional non-irrigated farm, and the large modern semi-irrigated farm. (Table 5.5/Table 5.1) This conclusion is confirmed when various regions are examined, although there is little difference between the medium and small farms in Zawiyah and Misuratah in this respect. (Table 5.16)

It can be concluded that although owners of large farms invest more per farm, investment per hectare is much higher on small farms. In this connection it should be noted (Table 5.17) that 71% of cultivated land is owned by 4% of farmers, while only 9% is owned by 77% of farmers.

The distribution of investment in various categories also varies according to the size of farm. The percentage of investment in real property increases as one moves from the largest to the smallest of farms. (Table 5.3) Whereas the very large farms spend as little as one-tenth of their investment on this item, it absorbs more than half of the expenditure of the small farms. This negative association between the size of the farm's cultivated area and the percentage of investment in real property is also observed when various types of farming are taken into consideration, with the two exceptions noted previously - the one large traditional irrigated farm and the very large traditional non-irrigated farm. (Tables 5.6 - 5.9) The same phenomenon is observed again, when the regions are examined, with the exception of Jabal Gharbi. (Tables 5.11 - 5.15) In general, slightly more than half of the investment in real property goes into the building of new homes and rooms. The medium farms generally spend less than half, and the small farms far more than half of their investment in real property, on homes and rooms. It is certainly not surprising that the small farms spend more of their investment on better living conditions than the larger farms, in view of the poor housing which was general on small farms. Their need for more land, sheds, and storage bins is also likely to be higher than that for the larger farms, as the latter tend already to possess many of these facilities.

A second feature of the distribution of investment among various heads is the overall association of larger farms with a higher percentage invested on machinery and tools. The very large farms put about half of their investment on this item, the large farms more than one-fifth, but the medium and small farms do not spend more than one-eighth of their funds on this. (Table 5.3) In absolute terms, a very large farm spends on average twenty times more than a small farm, nine times more than a medium farm, and more than double the amount spent by the large farms on machinery tools, and other investment going for machinery also holds for various regions and types of farming with few exceptions. (Table 5.6 - 5.9 and 5.11 - 5.15) Not only does the amount or percentage of total investment spent on this item vary consistently according to size, but there are also remarkable differences between farms of various size categories in the quality of their tools. The small farms use ploughs and harrows and sometimes small tractors, the larger farms use heavier equipment, such as tractors or combine harvesters.

If one ignores the very large farms, which spend a low percentage of their investment on irrigation, the share of investment in irrigation is on average, positively associated with size. (Table 5.3) In absolute terms also the large farms are seen to spend three times as much as the very large or medium farms, and about fourteen times as much as the small farms, on average, on irrigation equipment. (Table 5.2) However, when the data are analyzed by regions and types of farming, no clear pattern emerges, except in Zawiyah and for modern irrigated farms. (Tables 5.6 - 5.9 and 5.11 - 5.15) As in the case of machinery, the larger farms use better quality equipment - such as electric or diesel pumps - and the smaller more on wells, cisterns, and sometimes, on pumps of small capacity.

No clear picture emerges from our data about the relationship between size and the share of transport in total investment, except that the very large farms devote a higher percentage to this item than the other three categories. (Table 5.3) However, an examination of the regional data and the figures for various types of farming show that even this conclusion holds only for Tripoli and for the modern irrigated farms. (Tables 5.6 - 5.9 and 5.11 - 5.15)

Because of the disproportionate distribution of very large farms among various regions and types of farming, the higher percentage allocated to transport by the very large farms in Tripoli and by modern irrigated farms have also influenced the overall percentage accounted for by transport for the entire sample. In absolute terms, however, a very large farm spends on transport, on average, twice as much as a large farm, more than four times as much as a medium farm, and about ten times as much as a small farm. The overall figures clearly show an association between size and investment per farm on this item.

No clear trend is discernible for the percentage share accounted for by land reclamation and other expenditures in relation to size, except that the small farms spend a larger share of their total expenditure on items such as weddings, travelling, or furniture, than do farms in other size categories.

To sum up, the larger farms spend more on machines and irrigation, and less on real property and construction. Even where there is little difference in the percentage shares of various items, the larger farms tend to use tools or equipment of better quality than those used by the smaller farms. Whereas the larger farms, on average, invest more in agriculture than the smaller farms, the latter invest relatively much more intensively on their smaller plots.

5.3 Investment and the Type of Farm

As is to be expected, the modern farms invest, on average, more than the traditional farms, and to a lesser extent the irrigated farms do more investment than the non-irrigated farms. (Table 5.4) But, in terms of investment <u>per unit of land</u> the irrigated farms spend more than the non-irrigated categories and the traditional farms (which are generally smaller) tend to spend more <u>per unit of land</u> than their modern counterparts. (Table 5.5)

When the share of various items in the total investment expenditures of various types of farm is examined, the following general conclusions emerge. (Tables 5.6 - 5.9) First, the traditional farms spend proportionately more on real property than the modern, and, to a lesser extent the non-irrigated farms spend a higher percentage on this item than do the irrigated farms. But the difference between various types of farming on this account are not so pronounced as the differences according to size. Of the total expenditures on real property, a large part is spent by all types of farm on homes and rooms, but the modern irrigated farms spend a relatively smaller proportion of their budget on real property.

Second, as one would expect, the irrigated farms spend a larger proportion on irrigation equipment than the non-irrigated farms. Moreover, the non-irrigated farms devote a larger part of their investment to machinery than do the irrigated farms. The irrigated farms naturally give relatively more attention to irrigation equipment, and the non-irrigated farms to machinery. As between the modern and the traditional farms, the former spend a larger proportion on machinery than the latter. Ignoring the modern non-irrigated farms, which spend a negligible amount on irrigation, the modern farms, on average, also spend more on irrigation than the traditional farms - both in absolute terms, and as a percentage of total investment.

Third, there is virtually no difference between the traditional and the modern farms, on the one hand, and the irrigated and the non-irrigated farms, on the other, in the percentage spent on transport. There is no obvious explanation for the larger allocations to transport made by the two extremes of farming type, namely traditional irrigated and modern non-irrigated farming.

There is no clear difference between the types of farm with respect to the percentage spent on land reclamation; the non-irrigated farms generally spend a relatively larger proportion on other items such as weddings, travel, and furniture.

For the entire sample, the modern irrigated farm exerts the largest influence on the percentage of investment going into various items. Although about half of the farms belong to this category, it accounts for three-fourths of the total investment by all farms together. (Table 5.18) In absolute terms, the modern irrigated farms spend, on average, two-and-half times as much as the modern non-irrigated farms, and about four times as much as both types of traditional farms. (Table 5.4) On every item the average expenditure of the modern irrigated farms is considerably higher than that of the other types. (Table 5.6 - 5.9) Between irrigated traditional and non-irrigated traditional

farms, there is little difference in total investment per farm, but the
average expenditure on irrigation and transport in the former is higher than
that in the latter. Again, the non-irrigated traditional farms spend much
more on machinery than the irrigated traditional farms. Expenditure per farm
on real property is very similar for both types. The modern non-irrigated
farms, on the other hand, spend far less than the traditional farms on irrigation, far more on machines and transport, and slightly more on real
property.

Broadly speaking, differences in the investment pattern between various
types of farms are not so clear-cut as the differences according to size.

5.4 Regional Pattern of Investment

The pattern of agricultural investment as covered by this survey differs
considerably between regions. In terms of size, the farms of Tripoli and
al Khums are, on average, much larger than those of other regions. These
two regions also contain all but three of the very large farms, and two-
thirds of the large farms. But whereas Tripoli is wholly irrigated, or
semi-irrigated, more than two-thirds of the farms of al Khums are non-irrigated, and all the modern non-irrigated farms are in this region. (Table 5.1)
The farms of Zawiyah and Misuratah are, on average, one-third the size of
the farms in Tripoli and al Khums, and, except for one farm in Zawiyah, all
the farms of these two regions are irrigated. But whereas the farms of
Zawiyah are mostly modern, those of Misuratah are traditional. Moreover,
there are only two farms in Misuratah in the two largest size categories,
while there are seven such farms in Zawiyah. Jabal Gharbi is the least
developed of all the regions, most of the farms being very small, and none
irrigated or modern.

To compare Zawiyah with Misuratah first, the farms of these two regions
differ mainly in the degree of modernisation; in both they are irrigated
and differ only slightly in size distribution. But a farmer in Zawiyah
invests, on average, more than twice as much as a farmer from Misuratah.
A closer inspection shows that the difference in investment between the two
regions, when only traditional farms are taken into account, is negligible,
while among modern farms, those from Zawiyah invest three times as much as
those from Misuratah. (Tables 5.10, 5.12, and 5.15)

The percentage distribution of investment among various items is not radically
different from these two regions, except for the fact that Zawiyah invests
a larger proportion on machinery and a smaller proportion on transport, than
Misuratah. The percentage figures for Zawiyah are close to those for the
entire sample, while in the case of Misuratah the figure for machinery is
less, and that for transport is a good deal more than the average for the
whole sample.

The scale of investment per farm or per unit of cultivated land in Tripoli
is twice as much as in al Khums. (Table 5.16) This is largely because about
two-thirds of the farms of al Khums are non-irrigated, while all the farms
of Tripoli are irrigated. When only the irrigated farms are considered, there
is only a slight difference between the two regions in the amount of investment per farm, although the farms in Tripoli invest three times as much
per unit of land as those in al Khums.

It is interesting to note that the farms in Tripoli invest a relatively larger
percentage on irrigation, and the farms in al Khums invest a relatively

larger percentage on machinery, and this conclusion also applies when only the modern irrigated farms of these two regions are considered. Moreover, there exists a striking difference in the percentage of investment in real property for these two regions, as well as in investment per farm or per unit of land on this item. A major explanation for both of these two features is perhaps the fact that the very large farms contribute more than half of the total investment for al Khums, whereas these account for less than 5% of the total investment for Tripoli. (Table 5.19) The dominance of very large farms in al Khums, perhaps, accounts for the relatively larger share of machinery and the smaller shares for irrigation and real property in total investment. The very large farms of al Khums are also seen to invest more - per farm as well as per unit of land - than the corresponding farms of Tripoli.

Jabal Gharbi shows the lowest figures for investment - per farm or per unit of land - and almost its entire investment is on real property. Perhaps the fact that its farms are neither modern nor irrigated explains the very low figures for machinery and irrigation equipment. Moreover, the small average size of farm in that region largely accounts for the proportionately large expenditures on real property.

5.5 Summary and conclusions

One of the most striking results of this survey is the extremely high degree of inverse relationship between the size of a farm and level of investment per unit of cultivated area. This is also the most consistent result when various regions and types of farming are separately examined. In consequence, the small farms which account for less than one-tenth of the total cultivated area, contribute almost half of the total investment, and the very large farms, which account for about three-fourths of the cultivated area, contribute only one-eighth of the total investment. It is not clear which factors in the agricultural life of Libya lead to this kind of relationship in such extreme form. One possible explanation is the grossly skewed distribution of cultivated land among various farms. The larger farms are too large in land area in relation to their resources to invest on a scale comparable to those existing for the smaller categories. It is also possible that the larger farms are the ones which introduced mechanisation of agriculture at earlier dates, and hence have to invest a smaller amount from year-to-year today than do the smaller farms which have begun using machinery only recently. In so far as many of the larger farms are owned and operated by persons of Italian origin this is possibly true. On the other hand, a close examination of the existing capital stock on the larger farms* shows that this is not large enough to explain away the disparities among farms of varying size in investment per unit of cultivated land. Clearly large farms have the advantage of the economies of scale with reference to the utilisation of equipment. A smaller farm may suffer the effects of the "indivisibility" of major items of equipment, such as tractors. It is also not known to what extent investment is financed by loans, and whether the larger farms can more easily obtain loans.

---

* *An inventory of buildings, machinery, etc. was made of all farms. These data are available in the School of Oriental and African Studies, University of London.*

It is also important to note that the pattern of investment, as well as its scale, is influenced more by "size" than either by type of farming or regional location. The traditional farms (which are usually small) tend to invest more <u>per unit of land</u> than their modern counterparts, although on a per farm basis, the opposite conclusion emerges. At the same time the irrigated farms invest more than the non-irrigated, both on the <u>per farm basis</u> and on the <u>per unit of land</u> basis. Among the regions, Jabal Gharbi, Tripoli, and Misuratah invest about as much per unit of cultivated land as the sample average, while the farms of Zawiyah invest more, and those of al Khums less than the sample average. But when size is taken into account, and per farm estimates are compared, differences between the regions and various types of farming become more pronounced. The regions with a high proportion of larger farms, (for instance al Khums) show higher per farm investment figures than regions (such as Jabal Gharbi) with low average size farms. Among various types of farming, the modern farms, because of their much larger average size, have three times as much investment per farm as the traditional farms.

The irrigated farms allocate a larger proportion of their investment to irrigation equipment, and the modern farms allocate a larger proportion to machinery. The percentage going into real property and construction has a clear negative link with size, irrigated farms and modern farms. The larger farms are also found to favour investment on machinery but generally also tend to be modern. The very large farms spend a large percentage on transport, while the small farms devote a relatively larger share of their expenditure to weddings, travel, or furniture. The percentage distribution of investment for differing regions is largely influenced by the size distribution of the farms in them and also by the distribution of various types of farm.

Table 5.1 Frequency Distribution of Farms According to Size, Type of Farming and Region – Western Libya 1968
(Cultivated Area in Hectares Given in Parenthesis)

		Jabal Gharbi	Zawiyah	Tripoli	al Khums	Misuratah	Total
Traditional Irrigated	Small	0	34 (449)	9 (13)	9 (32)	40 (109)	92 (603)
	Medium	0	2 (45)	0	0	0	2 (45)
	Large	0	1 (150)	0	0	0	1 (150)
	V.Large	0	0	0	0	0	0 (0)
	Total	0	37 (644)	9 (13)	9 (32)	40 (109)	95 (798)
Modern Irrigated and Semi-Irrigated	Small	0	51 (914)	44 (75)	3 (58)	29 (237)	127 (1284)
	Medium	0	10 (363)	12 (417)	3 (62)	4 (88)	29 (930)
	Large	0	5 (722)	6 (985)	1 (120)	1 (250)	13 (2077)
	V.Large	0	2 (1300)	6 (8362)	3 (3110)	1 (2000)	12 (14722)
	Total	0	68 (3299)	68 (9839)	10 (3350)	35 (2575)	181 (19063)
Traditional Non-irrigated	Small	44 (207)	1 (0)	0	12 (71)	0	57 (278)
	Medium	4 (160)	0	0	2 (64)	0	6 (224)
	Large	1 (240)	0	0	3 (420)	0	4 (660)
	V.Large	0	0	0	1 (400)	0	1 (400)
	Total	49 (607)	1 (0)	0	18 (955)	0	68 (1562)
Modern Non-irrigated	Small	0	0	0	10 (71)	0	10 (71)
	Medium	0	0	0	13 (475)	0	13 (475)
	Large	0	0	0	1 (99)	0	1 (99)
	V.Large	0	0	0	2 (2400)	0	2 (2400)
	Total	0	0	0	26 (3045)	0	26 (3045)
Total	Small	44 (207)	86 (1363)	53 (88)	34 (232)	69 (346)	286 (2236)
	Medium	4 (160)	12 (408)	12 (417)	18 (601)	4 (88)	50 (1674)
	Large	1 (240)	6 (872)	6 (985)	5 (639)	1 (250)	19 (2986)
	V.Large	0	2 (1300)	6 (8362)	6 (5910)	1 (2000)	15 (17572)
	Total	49 (607)	106 (3943)	77 (9852)	63 (7382)	75 (2684)	370 (24468)

Source: 1968 Questionnaire Survey

Table 5.2 Expenditure per Farm According to Size and Items of Expenditure for the Entire Sample - Western Libya 1967/68

£ Libyan

	Small(286)*	Medium(50)*	Large(19)*	V.Large(15)*	Total(370)*
% of total farms	77%	14%	5%	4%	100%
% of total cult'd area	9%	7%	12%	72%	100%
HECTARES	0 - 20 ha.	21 - 80 ha.	81-350 ha.	> 350 ha.	-
Real property & construction	557	1146	1471	600	685
(Homes & rooms)	(424)	(200)	(832)	(407)	(407)
Irrigation Equipment	193	966	2776	863	457
Machinery	129	310	1356	2802	325
Transport	93	200	485	951	162
Land Reclamation	25	83	190	94	44
Total Investment	996	2704	6278	5310	1673
Other Expenditure	103	57	132	179	101
Total Expenditure	1099	2761	6410	5489	1774

B.K.D.

Note: 'Real property and construction' includes 'homes and rooms', and this last item should not be counted twice in checking total investment.

Source: 1968 Questionnaire Survey.

* *Number of cases shown in brackets.*

Table 5.3 Expenditure per Hectare of Cultivated Land According to Size and Items of Expenditure for the Entire Sample - Western Libya 1967/68

£ Libyan

(Percentage Distribution of Investment Given in Parenthesis)

	Small (286)*	Medium (50)*	Large (19)*	V.Large (15)*	Total (370)*
% of total farms	77%	14%	5%	4%	100%
% of total cult'd area	9%	7%	12%	72%	100%
Hectares	0 - 20 ha.	21-80 ha.	81- 350 ha.	> 350 ha.	—
Real property & construction	71 (56%)	34 (42%)	9 (23%)	0.5 (11%)	10 (41%)
(Homes & rooms)	(54) (43%)	(6) (7%)	(5) (13%)	(0.3) (8%)	(6) (24%)
Irrigation Equipment	25 (19%)	29 (36%)	18 (44%)	.7 (16%)	7 (27%)
Machinery	16 (13%)	9 (11%)	9 (22%)	2.4 (53%)	5 (19%)
Transport	12 (9%)	6 (7%)	3 (8%)	.8 (18%)	2 (10%)
Land Reclamation	3 (3%)	2 (3%)	1 (3%)	.1 (2%)	1 (3%)
Total Investment	127 (100%)	81 (100%)	40 (100%)	4.5 (100%)	25 (100%)
Other Expenditure	13 (9%)	2 (2%)	1 (2%)	.2 (3%)	2 (6%)
Total Expenditure	140	83	41	5	27

Notes 1. 'Real property and construction' includes 'homes and rooms', and this last item should not be counted twice in checking total investment.
2. 'Other Expenditures' are expressed as % of 'Total Expenditure'.
3. Percentages contain rounding errors.

* Number of cases shown in brackets.

Source: 1968 Questionnaire Survey.

B.K.D.

Table 5.4 Investment per Farm According to Size and Type of Farming for the Entire Sample
Western Libya 1967/68

£ Libyan

	Small	Medium	Large	Very Large	Total
Irrigated Traditional	714	1137	2560	0	743
Modern	1498	3893	8226	5229	2620
Non-irrigated Traditional	318	804	1322	16399	656
Modern	931	1172	4506	250	1137
Total Traditional	563	887	1570	16399	707
Total Modern	1457	3050	7960	4518	2434
Total Irrigated	1175	3715	7821	5229	1974
Total Non-irrigated	409	1056	1949	5633	789
Total	996	2704	6278	5310	1693

Source: 1968 Questionnaire Survey.

B.K.D.

Table 5.5 Investment per Hectare of Cultivated Land According to Size and Type of Farming for the Entire Sample - Western Libya 1967/68

£ Libyan

	Small(286)*	Medium (50)*	Large (19)*	Very Large (15)*	Total (370)*
Irrigated Traditional	109	51	17	0	88
Modern	149	121	51	4	25
Non-irrigated Traditional	65	22	8	41	29
Modern	131	32	46	1	10
Total Traditional	95	27	10	41	49
Total Modern	148	92	51	4	23
Total Irrigated	136	118	49	4	27
Total Non-irrigated	79	29	13	6	16
Total	127	81	40	5	25

Source: 1968 Questionnaire Survey

* *Number of farms shown in brackets.*

B.K.D.

Table 5.6 Expenditures per Farm According to Size and Items of Expenditure for TRADITIONAL IRRIGATED FARMS Western Libya 1967/68

£ Libyan

(Percentage Distribution of Investment for Each Size Category is Given in Parenthesis)

	Small (92)*		Medium (2)*		Large (1)*		V.Large (0)*		Total (95)*	
% of total farms	96%		2%		1%		1%		100%	
% of total cult'd area	22%		2%		5%		71%		100%	
Hectares	0 – 20 ha.		21 – 50 ha.		81 – 350 ha.		> 350 ha.			
Real property & construction	421	(59%)	100	(9%)	2500	(98%)	0	(0%)	436	(57%)
(Homes & rooms)	(383)	(58%)	(100)	(9%)	(2500)	(98%)	(0)	(0%)	(371)	(49%)
Irrigation Equipment	124	(17%)	5	(1%)	60	(2%)	0	(0%)	121	(16%)
Machinery	44	(6%)	850	(75%)	0	(0%)	0	(0%)	60	(8%)
Transport	116	(16%)	155	(14%)	0	(0%)	0	(0%)	116	(17%)
Land Reclamation	9	(1%)	27	(2%)	0	(0%)	0	(0%)	9	(1%)
Total Investment	714	(100%)	1137	(100%)	2560	(100%)	0	(0%)	742	(100%)
Other Expenditure	75	9%	0	0%	0	0%	0	0%	72	9%
Total Expenditure	£L 789		£L 1137		£L 2560		£L 0		£L 814	

B.K.D.

Notes 1. 'Real property and construction' includes 'homes and rooms', and this last item should not be counted twice in making up total investment.
2. 'Other Expenditures' expressed as percentages of Total Expenditure.
3. Percentages may have rounding errors.

Source: 1968 Questionnaire Survey.

*Number of farms shown in brackets.

Table 5.7 Expenditures per Farm According to Size and Items of Expenditure for MODERN IRRIGATED & SEMI-IRRIGATED FARMS Western Libya 1967/68

£ Libyan shown for Total Expenditure

Percentage Distribution of Investment by Item

	Small (127)*	Medium (29)*	Large (13)*	V.Large (12)*	Total (181)*
% of total farms	71%	16%	7%	6%	100%
Hectares	0 – 20 ha.	21 – 80 ha.	81 – 350 ha.	> 350 ha.	–
Real property & construction	52%	43%	22%	4%	37%
(Homes & rooms)	(36)	(2)	(12)	(3)	(18)
Irrigation Equipment	22	42	49	19	32
Machinery	15	7	20	54	20
Transport	8	5	6	21	8
Land Reclamation	3	3	3	1	3
Total Investment	100	100	100	100	100
Other Expenditure	10%	2%	1%	2%	5%
Total Expenditure	£L 1665	£L 3959	£L 8337	£L 5324	£L 2763 B.K.D.

Notes
1. 'Real property and construction' includes 'homes and rooms', and this last item should not be counted twice in making up total investment.
2. 'Other Expenditures' are expressed as percentages of 'Total Expenditure'.
3. Percentages may have rounding errors.

Source: 1968 Questionnaire Survey.

* *Number of farms shown in brackets.*

Table 5.8 Expenditures per Farm According to Size and Items of Expenditure for TRADITIONAL NON-IRRIGATED FARMS Western Libya 1967/68

£ Libyan Shown for Total Expenditure

Percentage Distribution of Investment by Item

	Small (57)*	Medium (6)*	Large (4)*	V.Large (1)*	Total (68)*
% of total farms	84%	9%	6%	1%	100%
% of total Cult'd area	18%	14%	42%	26%	100%
Hectares	0 -20 ha.	21-80 ha.	81 - 350 ha.	> 350 ha.	—
Real property & construction	86%	48%	20%	38%	56%
(Homes & rooms)	(79)	(27)	(0)	(24)	(44)
Irrigation Equipment	10	4	11	6	8
Machinery	1	26	38	49	26
Transport	0	22	25	6	8
Land Reclamation	2	1	6	1	2
Total Investment	100	100	100	100	100
Other Expenditure	1%	16%	16%	9%	8%
Total Expenditure	£L 321	£L 954	£L 1572	£L17949	£L 710

B.K.D.

Notes
1. 'Real property and construction' includes 'homes and rooms', and this last item should not be counted twice in making up 'total investment.'
2. 'Other Expenditures' are expressed as percentages of 'total expenditure'.
3. Percentages may have rounding errors.

Source: 1968 Questionnaire Survey.

*Number of farms shown in brackets.

Table 5.9 Expenditures per Farm According to Size and Items of Expenditure for MODERN NON-IRRIGATED FARMS Western Libya 1967/68
£ Libyan Shown for Total Expenditure
Percentage Distribution of Investment by Item

	Small (2)*	Medium (1)*	Large (13)*	V.Large (10)*	Total (26)*
% of total farms	8%	4%	50%	38%	100%
% of total Cult'd area	2%	16%	3%	79%	100%
Hectares	0 - 20 ha.	21 - 80 ha.	81 - 350 ha.	> 350 ha.	—
Real property & construction	51%	45%	16%	0%	42%
(Homes & rooms)	(39)	(38)	(0)	(0)	(32)
Irrigation Equipment	0	3	1	0	2
Machinery	31	29	50	0	32
Transport	15	20	35	0	20
Land Reclamation	3	3	1	100	4
Total Investment	100	100	100	100	100
Other Expenditure	10%	0%	1%	0%	3%
Total Expenditure	£L 1031	£L 1172	£L 4556	£L 250	£L 1177 B.K.D.

Notes
1. 'Real property and construction' includes 'homes and rooms', and this last item should not be counted twice in making up total investment.
2. 'Other Expenditures' are expressed as percentages of 'Total expenditure'.
3. Percentages may have rounding errors.

Source : 1968 Questionnaire Survey.

* Number of farms shown in brackets.

Table 5.10 Expenditure per Farm According to Type of Farming
FOR THE ENTIRE SAMPLE Western Libya 1967/68
£ Libyan Shown for Total Expenditure
Percentage Distribution of Investment by Item

	Traditional (163)*	Modern (207)*	Irrigated and Semi-irrigated (276)*	Non-irrigated (94)*
% of total farms	44%	56%	75%	25%
% of total cult'd area	18%	82%	81%	19%
Real property and construction	58%	37%	40%	51%
(Homes & rooms)	(48)	(19)	(22)	(39)
Irrigation Equipment	13	31	30	6
Machinery	15	20	18	28
Transport	12	9	9	13
Land Reclamation	2	3	3	3
Total Investment	100	100	100	100
Other Expenditure	8	5	6	6
Total Expenditure	£L 771	£L 2561	£L 2093	£L 839

B.K.D.

Notes 1. 'Real Property and construction' includes 'homes and rooms', and this last item should not be counted twice in making up total investment.
2. 'Other Expenditures' are expressed as percentages of 'Total expenditure'.
3. Percentages may have rounding errors.

Source: 1968 Questionnaire Survey.

*Number of farms shown in brackets.

Table 5.11 Expenditures per Farm According to Size and Items of Expenditure for
JABAL GHARBI Western Libya 1967/68
£ Libyan Shown for Total Expenditure
Percentage Distribution of Investment by Item

	Small (44)*	Medium (4)*	Large (1)*	V.Large (0)*	Total (49)*
% of total farms	90%	8%	2%	0%	100%
% of total cult'd area	34%	26%	40%	0%	100%
Hectares	0 – 20 ha.	21 – 80 ha.	81 – 350 ha.	> 350 ha.	
Real property & construction	91%	100%	0%	0%	92%
(Homes & rooms)	(87)	(0)	(0)	(0)	(81)
Irrigation Equipment	5	0	0	0	5
Machinery	1	0	0	0	1
Transport	0	0	0	0	0
Land Reclamation	3	0	100	0	3
Total Investment	100	100	100	0	100
Other Expenditure	1	17	0	0	1
Total Expenditure	£L 346	£L 300	£L 20	£L 0	£L 332

Notes 1. 'Real property and construction' includes 'homes and rooms', and this last item should not be counted twice in making up total investment.
2. 'Other Expenditures' are expressed as percentages of 'Total Expenditure'.
3. Percentages may have rounding errors.

Source: 1968 Questionnaire Survey.

*Number of farms shown in brackets.

B.K.D.

Table 5.12 Expenditure per Farm According to Size and Items of Expenditure for
ZAWIYAH Western Libya 1967/68
£ Libyan Shown for Total Expenditure
Percentage Distribution of Investment by Item

	Small (86)*	Medium (12)*	Large (6)*	V.Large (2)*	Total (106)*
% of total farms	81%	11%	6%	2%	100%
% of total cult'd area	35%	10%	22%	33%	100%
Hectares	0 – 20 ha.	21 – 80 ha.	81 – 350 ha.	> 350 ha.	–
Real property & construction	59%	43%	6%	0%	42%
(Homes & rooms)	(48)	(4)	(6)	(0)	(29)
Irrigation Equipment	11	26	65	3	25
Machinery	16	21	25	85	22
Transport	12	9	4	9	9
Land Reclamation	2	2	1	3	1
Total Investment	100	100	100	100	100
Other Expenditure	13	3	0	5	8
Total Expenditure	£L 1394	£L 2715	£L 7012	£L 4747	£L 1924

Notes 1. 'Real property and construction' includes 'homes and rooms', and this last item should not be counted twice in making up total investment.
2. 'Other Expenditures' are expressed as percentages of 'Total Expenditure'.
3. Percentages may have rounding errors.

* *Number of farms in brackets.*

Source: 1968 Questionnaire Survey.

B.K.D.

Table 5.13 Expenditure per Farm According to Size and Items of Expenditure for
TRIPOLI Western Libya 1967/68
£ Libyan Shown for Total Expenditure
Percentage Distribution of Investment by Item

	Small (54)*	Medium (12)*	Large (6)*	V.Large (6)*	Total (77)*
% of total farms	69%	15%	8%	8%	100%
% of total cult'd area	1%	4%	10%	55%	100%
Hectares	0 – 20 ha.	21 – 80 ha.	81 – 350 ha.	> 350 ha.	–
Real property & construction	51%	50%	35%	3%	44%
(Homes & rooms)	(27)	(0)	(19)	(0)	(16)
Irrigation Equipment	30	41	37	50	36
Machinery	10	3	16	15	10
Transport	6	1	7	31	6
Land Reclamation	4	5	5	2	4
Total Investment	100	100	100	100	100
Other Expenditure	10	1	1	1	5
Total Expenditure	£L 2077	£L 5536	£L11270	£L 1991	£L 3336

B.K.D.

Notes 1. 'Real property and construction' includes 'homes and rooms', and this last item should not be counted twice in making up total investment.
2. 'Other Expenditures' are expressed as percentages of 'Total Expenditure'.
3. Percentages may contain rounding errors.

Source: 1968 Questionnaire Survey.

* *Number of farms in brackets.*

Table 5.14 Expenditure per Farm According to Size and Items of Expenditure for
al KHUMS Western Libya 1967/68
£ Libyan Shown for Total Expenditure
Percentage Distribution of Investment by Item

	Small (34)*	Medium (18)*	Large (5)*	V.Large (6)*	Total (63)*
% of total farms	54%	29%	8%	10%	100%
% of total cult'd area	3%	8%	9%	80%	100%
Hectares	0 - 20 ha.	21 - 80 ha.	81 - 350 ha.	> 350 ha.	
Real property & construction	57%	42%	20%	15%	27%
(Homes & rooms)	(40)	(37)	(3)	(11)	(20)
Irrigation Equipment	9	14	6	12	11
Machinery	23	25	41	56	43
Transport	9	17	29	15	16
Land Reclamation	2	2	3	2	2
Total Investment	100	100	100	100	100
Other Expenditure	7	4	9	2	4
Total Expenditure	£L 493	£L 1350	£L 2225	£L 9716	£L 1753

Notes 1. 'Real property and construction' includes 'homes and rooms', and this last item should not be counted twice in making up total investment.
2. 'Other Expenditures' are expressed as percentages of 'Total Expenditure'.
3. Percentages may contain rounding errors.

* Number of farms in brackets.

Source: 1968 Questionnaire Survey

B.K.D.

Table 5.15 Expenditure per Farm According to Size and Items of Expenditure for
MISURATAH Western Libya 1967/68

Percentage Distribution of Investment by Item

£ Libyan Shown for Total Expenditure

	Small (68)*	Medium (4)*	Large (1)*	V.Large (1)*	Total (75)*
% of total farms	92%	5%	1%	1%	100%
% of total cult'd area	13%	3%	9%	74%	100%
Hectares	0 - 20 ha.	21 - 80 ha.	81 - 350 ha.	> 350 ha.	-
Real property & construction	49%	0%	0%	0%	37%
(Homes & rooms)	(43)	(0)	(0)	(0)	33
Irrigation Equipment	22	73	0	0	32
Machinery	13	9	0	13	12
Transport	14	18	0	87	17
Land Reclamation	2	1	0	0	1
Total Investment	100	100	0	100	100
Other Expenditure	4%	0%	0%	0%	3%
Total Expenditure	£L 758	£L 3241	£L 0	£L 1600	£L 892 B.K.D.

Notes 1. 'Real property and construction' include 'homes and rooms', and this last item should not be counted twice in making up total investment.
2. 'Other Expenditures' are expressed as percentages of 'Total Expenditure'.
3. Percentages may have rounding errors.

Source: 1968 Questionnaire Survey.   * *Number of farms in brackets.*

Table 5.16 Investment per Farm and per Hectare
by Muhafadah and by Farm Size
Western Libya 1967/68
£ Libyan

		Small	Medium	Large	V.Large	Total
JABAL GHARBI	Per Farm	342	250	20	0	328
	Per Hectare	73	6	0.1	0	26
ZAWIYAH	Per Farm	1212	2636	7013	4497	1764
	Per Hectare	76	78	48	7	47
TRIPOLI	Per Farm	1876	5519	11187	1981	3718
	Per Hectare	1130	159	68	1	25
AL KHUMS	Per Farm	461	1300	2015	9528	1687
	Per Hectare	68	39	16	10	14
MISURATAH	Per Farm	731	3241	0	1600	867
	Per Hectare	146	147	0	1	24
TOTAL	Per Farm	996	2704	6278	5310	1693
	Per Hectare	127	81	40	5	25

Source: 1968 Questionnaire Survey.

B.K.D.

Table 5.17 Percentage Share of Various Size
Categories in Cultivated Land & Investment
Western Libya 1967/68
Per Cent & £ Libyan

SIZE	No. of Farms	% of Farms	Size of cultivated area (hectares)	% of total cultivated area	Investment £ Libyan	% of total Investment
Small	286	78%	2236	9%	284,837	46%
Medium	50	13	1674	7	135,219	22
Large	19	5	2986	12	119,289	19
V. Large	15	4	17572	72	79,647	13
Total	370	100	24468	100	618,992	100

Source: 1968 Questionnaire Survey.

B.K.D.

Table 5.18 Percentage Share of Various Farm Type in Cultivated Area & Investment
Western Libya 1967/68
Per cent and £ Libyan

FARM TYPE		No. of Farms	% of Farms	Size of cultivated area (hectares)	% of Cultivated Area	Investment £ Libyan	% of Total investment
Irrigated	Traditional	95	26%	798	3%	70549	11
	Modern	181	49	19063	78	474257	77
Non-irrigated	Traditional	68	18	1562	6	44632	7
	Modern	26	7	3045	13	29554	5
Total	Traditional	163	44	2360	10	115181	19
"	Modern	207	56	22108	90	503811	81
"	Irrigated	276	75	19861	81	544806	88
"	Non-irrigated	94	25	4607	19	74186	12
TOTAL		370	100	24468	100	618992	100

Source: 1968 Questionnaire Survey.

B.K.D.

Table 5.19 Percentage Share of Various Muhafadahs in Cultivated Land and Investment Western Libya 1967/68
Per cent.

Regions	Farm size	% of Farms By Muhafadah	% of Farms By Size	% of Cult'd Area By Size	% of Cult'd Area By Muh'dah	Investment-£ Libyan By Size	Investment-£ Libyan By Muh'dah	% of Total Investment By Size	% of Total Investment By Muh'dah
Jabal Gharbi	Small		90	34		15035		94	
	Medium		8	26		1000		6	
	Large		2	40		20		0.1	
	V.Large		0	0		0		0	
	Total	13.2	100	100	2.5		16055	100	2.6
Zawiyah	Small		81	35		104255			
	Medium		11	10		31630			
	Large		6	22		42075			
	V.Large		2	33		8993			
	Total	28.7	100	100	16.1		186953	100	30.2
Tripoli	Small		69	1		99438			
	Medium		15	4		66232			
	Large		8	10		67119			
	V.Large		8	85		11887			
	Total	21.1	100	100	40.3		244676	100	39.5
al Khums	Small		54	3		12712			
	Medium		29	8		23392			
	Large		8	9		10075			
	V.Large		10	80		57167			
	Total	17.0	100	100	30.2		106303	100	17.2
Misuratah	Small		92	13		50440			
	Medium		5	3		12965			
	Large		1	9		0			
	V.Large		1	75		1600			
	Total	20.0	100	100	11.0		65005	100	10.5
Total		100			100				100

Percentages may have rounding errors.   Source: 1968 Questionnaire Survey.   B.K.D.

Chapter Six

EMPLOYMENT AND WAGE RATES

6.1 Introduction

This chapter is concerned with employment, wage-determination and migration, especially with regard to rural Libya. In Libya, capital is relatively abundant in the form of financial revenues that accrue to the Government. But capital alone cannot induce economic progress. Complementary resources are required, the most important, no doubt, being labour.

The role of labour in relation to economic growth and development has been consistently emphasised in the economic literature, with respect both to the amount and quality of the labour force. The emergence of a modern industrial sector in developing countries can be seriously hampered by workers' attitudes. Rural migrants attracted to the factories are often not "committed" to the new environment, and may retain strong links with the countryside. As a result, the rates of labour turnover may be high, the workers lacking industrial discipline and employers incurring excessive costs. The development of the modern sector may thus be retarded. Here labour is identified as a bottleneck to growth. Emphasis is also placed on the qualitative aspects of the labour force, on the formation of "human capital". Education, skills and manpower planning are deemed necessary for economic growth. Inadequate supplies of skilled and educated personnel in the present and inadequate provisions for the future may act as a brake on the development effort.

A number of questions thus arise. Is labour a bottleneck in the economic development of Libya and, if so, which particular type of labour? Is it true to say that all sectors of the Libyan economy are affected by shortages of both skilled and unskilled workers? The question is particularly interesting in relation to agriculture. It has been widely held that in many developing countries agriculture is a reservoir of redundant workers. More recently, some economists have argued that labour surpluses are to be found in the Government sector and in urban services rather than in the rural areas of overpopulated countries. But Libya is sparsely populated, and one may be tempted to contend that neither of these propositions is relevant. Our findings indicate, however, that contrary to certain appearances, a hidden surplus of labour does exist in Libya. Its reallocation to sectors where workers are in demand may contribute to economic growth. Evidence collected by the Joint Project indicates that the shortage of <u>unskilled</u> labour within and outside agriculture - about which many employers have complained in interviews - is not a consequence of the low population density but of certain employment policies.

In this connection we would like to emphasize an important analytical point concerning the concept of labour shortages. It is wrong to assume that a drift of rural workers to the towns, even if it depletes the agricultural reserve of labour, is necessarily a bad thing. The problem must not be looked at through the farmers' eyes (they may regret the days when labour was abundant and cheap) but in the broader context of allocation and growth in the whole economy. If the labour market is competitive and if obstacles to mobility are not too obstructive, workers will tend to move from the relatively inefficient to the relatively more efficient sector of the economy.

The latter is likely to offer higher wages. Re-allocation favours the efficient activities and thus benefits both the individual worker and the economy, and there is no necessary reason why a drift to the towns should have adverse effects on the economic performance of the country. The actual problem, however, is more complex as we shall see in the course of this chapter. The difficulties arise because (a) an element of expectation enters the migrant's decision to leave the rural areas, and in a booming economy expectations tend to be over-optimistic, and (b) the Government intervenes in the labour market through wage legislation and employment policies. Because of these psychological factors and of the policies pursued, the market may fail to allocate workers efficiently. A situation in which labour shortages and labour surpluses would obtain simultaneously in various sectors of the economy may well result.

The essence of the argument is that the real problem - as far as unskilled labour is concerned - is not so much an issue of quantitative supplies but one of allocation and policies. But even if we accept this view, the question of qualitative performance would still arise. The expansion of a modern sector in Libya - oil, manufacturing industry, transport and trade - as well as the development of a progressive agriculture, depends on the existence of a pool of professional and skilled workers and on the presence of a stable and disciplined group of unskilled workers. It is well-known that in Libya today the former type of worker is extremely rare.

6.2 Quantitative Supplies of Labour

6.2.1 Total Population

That Libya is a sparsely populated country needs hardly to be emphasized. The total population may have reached the level of 1.7 or 1.8 million inhabitants but the area covered by the Republic is immense (1760 thousand sq. kms). Whether Libya is underpopulated from an economic point of view is a more difficult question. It is generally held that labour is short in Libya and shortages are sometimes attributed to the small size of the population and to the low geographical density. This is not necessarily so. Inadequate supplies of labour may be related to more immediate causes: the under-utilisation of existing manpower and its inefficient distribution among the various regions of the country or the different sectors of the economy. We shall examine the available evidence to see whether this is the case.

6.2.2 Participation in Labour Force

The 1964 Population Census - the only comprehensive source on employment in Libya - suggests that manpower resources are under-utilised. The broad picture is as follows: The recorded labour force includes some 400,000 workers. Slightly less than 26% of the population participates in the labour force. This is rather low. The participation of children is smaller than in most developing countries and than in other Middle-Eastern countries; that of women, according to the census, is almost negligible. The low participation rates for children are due to the expansion of schooling, which is generally construed as a sign of progress.

The problem is more complex in the case of women. Tradition may play an important role, but traditions are affected also by economic conditions. However, the almost negligible rate of female participation disclosed by

the 1964 Population Census is misleading. A census usually includes only
full-time workers in the category "economically active persons". In rural
areas, women and children may work for short periods only during the
seasonal peak of agricultural demand, and this work, though limited in
time, is usually very significant in terms of its contribution to output.
But it will escape the attention of the census-taker. Moreover, many agricultural operations, such as tending animals or processing farm products
are part of the normal duties of the housewife, and are not considered as
"employment" by the Census - nor even for that matter, by the farmer or
the housewife herself. From an economic point of view, however, these
duties represent a genuine contribution to the productive effort of the
community. The 1967 Questionnaire Survey of the Project reveals a much
larger participation of females in agricultural work than is shown by the
Population Census.

Although women work fewer hours than men per week their participation
cannot be deemed negligible. This qualification is important and the
questionnaire survey is valuable in correcting the false impression that
may be derived from the Census. There is nothing to suggest, however, that
labour reserves are fully utilised in Libya. We know that very few females are engaged in the urban labour force, and in agriculture participation is either seasonal or occasional.

6.2.3 Utilisation of the Labour Force (Employment/Unemployment)

A more immediate problem is that of the utilisation of the labour force
itself - the problem of unemployment and underemployment. For not only is
a relatively small fraction of the population now engaged in the labour
force, but the labour force itself is not fully employed. In the 1964
Population Census 8.6% of the labour force was recorded as unemployed, and
analysis of these figures suggests that many of them were new workers.[1]
But we cannot assume that young men just reaching working age, school
leavers, self-employed workers closing down their business, or rural
migrants seeking first employment account for the bulk of the unemployed.
The age distribution of unemployed workers shows that 18.5% only are under
20 years of age. It is highly unlikely that a significant proportion of
the remaining 81.5% - by far the largest group - are students. A regional
distribution by muqata'ah suggests that some 25% of unemployed workers live
in urban areas, the rest - and thus a large majority - in the villages, and
are thus rural adults.

The fact that these adults are seeking jobs for the first time indicates
that they are not part of the wage-labour force but members of peasant
families. Two possibilities come to the mind (a) these workers were idle
at the time of the Census, because of the seasonality of agriculture, and
registered as unemployed, or (b) they chose to be recorded as unemployed
in order to enhance their chances of getting a subsidy or some form of
employment in the Government sector.

Our analysis leads us therefore to place greater reliance on the rate of
urban unemployment (6%) than on the overall rate of 8.6%. It is also
possible that some portion of the urban unemployed are recent migrants who
have not had the chance to settle in the towns. Seasonal - and not "structural" - unemployment is the important phenomenon in rural areas (it is
wrong to dismiss the possibility of seasonal unemployment appearing in the
Census on the grounds that the returns were taken in July. Seasonal peaks
do not fall uniformly in the same month everywhere in Libya).

Thus, unemployment is a significant problem. A rate of 6% in the urban areas of an economy allegedly short of labour, with a booming modern sector located in the towns, is disturbing. The important point, however, is that a small surplus of labour seems to exist. If it is true that despite this fact employers meet serious difficulties in recruiting workers, we must infer that some institutional forces are interfering with the proper functioning of the market. Among these are opportunities for government employment at high wages. This encourages the drift to the towns. New migrants add to the urban pool and since the expectations of finding an attractive job with some public organisation are high, labourers tend to wait for these opportunities and fail to respond to the demand of the private sector.

As pointed out earlier, it may be misleading to attribute the shortage of labour in the private sector to the paucity of the country's endowment. The problem is not primarily due to a deficiency in numbers. It is also related to socio-economic factors and to policy.

6.3 Wage Rates

It is suggested that there is some misallocation of labour as between government employment and industry and construction, where extra workers are required for efficient expansion. An analysis of the sectorial structure of wage-rates may help us to understand the nature of this problem. We have collected a certain amount of data on wage-rates in the various sectors of the economy. It may be appropriate to stress that these data are the first of their kind. As such, they are extremely valuable despite certain limitations in coverage and quality.

As regards <u>agriculture</u>, the picture is as follows. Wage rates for temporary (male) workers range between £L 0.400 and £L 2.000 a day. The frequencies at £L 0.400 and above £L 1.500 are very low, almost negligible. The frequencies are concentrated in the range £L 0.500 - 1.500 with a very high mode (30%) at £L 1.000. The median falls also at £L 1.000 and the mean is around £L 0.950, slightly below the critical value of £L 1.000 (in other words, there is a higher density of frequencies for values below, than for values above £L 1.000). We can thus conclude, notwithstanding some variability in the spread of the distribution, that in 1968 the £L 1.000 daily wage was fairly representative for unskilled temporary labour in Libyan agriculture.

It is interesting to note that the number of questionnaire replies for the wages of permanent workers is less than the number for temporary workers (199 as against 330). Permanent workers are generally recruited from the members of the household while temporary labour is hired from outside, and since many of the former are not paid in cash, the wages questionnaire may understate their numbers. 40% of all farms in the sample seem to have recourse to temporary labour during the seasonal peaks.

The survey discloses that the wage rates for permanent workers are not significantly different from those of their temporary counterparts. Here again, both the mode and the median of the distribution fall at £L 1.000; the range is £L 0.400 - 1.500 with very low frequencies at the tails. The average wage is around £L 0.930. The frequencies are more concentrated than in the previous case: 30% falling at the mode (£L 1.000), 15% at £L 0.700 and another 15% at £L 0.800. Clearly, the representative wage rate (allowing of course for some variability) is again one Libyan pound a day.

The similarity of the two wage-distributions (permanent and temporary) is rather surprising. Normally, we would expect lower rates for permanent than for temporary workers. The reasons are well-known: (a) the uncertainty involved in temporary work may raise the supply price of labour, and (b) temporary labour is hired mainly during the seasonal peak when demand is buoyant. Can we assume that our statistical results are suspect? One thing is certain: there is no evidence of a systematic bias in farmers' replies (in other words, individual farmers did not quote systematically the same wage-rates for temporary and permanent workers). It is possible, however, that our treatment of the data has introduced some form of bias. We have aggregated the replies to two separate questions: what is the highest and what is the lowest paid to a worker? This is not a very satisfactory procedure, but the absence of data on the complete wage distribution in each individual farm does not leave much scope for more refined techniques.

We could examine, however, four separate distributions (highest/lowest for permanent and temporary workers) and interpret their characteristics. The following table summarises the main factors of the distribution.

Table 6.1

Characteristics of the Wage Distribution in Agriculture 1968

£L per day

		(1) lowest temporary	(2) lowest permanent	(3) highest temporary	(4) highest permanent
range	£L	0.400-1.500	1.400-1.500	0.500-2.000	0.600-1.800
mode	£L	1.000	1.000	1.000	1.000
median	£L	0.800	0.800	1.000	1.000
mean	£L	0.820	0.820	1.120	0.900

The main statistics of distributions (1) and (2) are identical; (3) and (4) are very similar, except for an important difference in the means. The mean of (3) (highest-temporary) is significantly larger than that of (4) (highest-permanent). In other words, the frequencies of certain high rates - namely £L 1.200, 1.250, 1.500 and 2.000 - are larger for temporary workers.

We can interpret our global results in the following manner:

(a) With caution, the wage-rate of £L 1.000 can be taken as the representative wage for both temporary and permanent workers.

(b) Although there are few instances when the wage-rates seem to fall as low as £L 0.500 - 0.600, the lowest wage paid to either temporary or permanent workers can be assumed to fall around £L 0.800 (mean) and £L 1.000 (mode). In other words, the minimum wage at which a farmer can hire labour does not vary significantly with the type of contract (permanent or temporary). We are not prepared to argue that there is a rigid floor to wage-rates or that institutional factors have a strong influence - the available evidence is too restricted to allow such an inference. There are several alternative explanations. The most plausible is that lowest wages are paid to temporary workers hired during the "slack" season. If this were the case we would not expect significant differences between temporary and permanent rates.

(c) As for maximum wages, the greater frequencies of high rates for temporary workers suggest that some farmers find it difficult to recruit labour during the seasonal peak and these difficulties tend to push the rates upwards.

Let us add two important remarks. We did not find any significant correlation between either regions or types of farms and the level of wages, except for government farms, where statutory wages of £L 1.000 and £L 1.500 are paid to permanent and temporary workers respectively. These are higher than any of the "average" rates computed above. Whether the government is the "wage-leader" in agriculture and in the rest of the economy is a question worth posing. We shall elaborate this point later. The second remark relates to the influence of foreign migrant labour (mainly Tunisian) on the wage-rates. In a number of instances we were able to identify the presence of migrants on low-wage farms. Foreign labour is generally cheaper than Libyan workers.

If we compare the agricultural wage-rate of £L 1.000 with what seem to be the most common hiring rates for unskilled labour in the other sectors of the economy, unusual results would arise. Typical rates are shown in the following table:

Table 6.2

Average Wages in the Main Sectors (1968)

	£L
Agriculture	1.000
Oil	0.750
Government	0.7000 - 0.800
Construction	1.200

Sources: Interviews and firm surveys conducted during the course of the project.

The typical wage for the oil industry has been derived from a survey of seven large firms. The figures are very reliable and the sample relatively large (both in terms of number of firms and of the proportion of workers included in the survey). The distribution has the following characteristics:-

Table 6.3

Statistics of the Wage-Distribution in the Oil Industry

range:	£L 0.55 – £L 1.150
mean:	£L 0.750
median:	£L 0.750
mode:	£L 0.650
coverage:	1028 workers

The typical wage can be taken as £L 0.750 a day.

For construction, we have to rely on the results of interviews conducted during the course of the Project in Benghazi and Tripoli. We were concerned with Libyan workers only, for the conditions of employment of foreign labour vary considerably from case to case. Sometimes earnings include some form of payments in the country of origin and many entrepreneurs provide foreign labour with free accommodation and other types of facilities.

There is, of course, some variation in the hiring rates of Libyan unskilled labour in building sites (the rates are mostly affected by seasonal and regional factors). It is safe however to assume that the typical rate is around £L 1.200. The important point is that it is significantly higher than in agriculture and oil.

It seems that the government employs unskilled labour at rates that vary between £L 0.700 and £L 0.800 save for agricultural work where the rates, as noted earlier, are significantly higher. The available data do not allow us to reach categorical conclusions, but there are strong indications that the average wage is in the range £L 0.700 – 0.800 (except for NASA). The legal minimum wage is £L 0.500 and it is significant that everywhere actual rates are higher than those prescribed by the law.

Our data on manufacturing industry and transport are incomplete. We feel, however, that the wages in manufacturing are not significantly different from those prevailing in the oil industry (they may be somewhat lower). The transport sector which has been expanding considerably in recent years generally hires at higher rates. And workers engaged in long-haul transport may benefit from a number of incentive schemes affording comparatively large premiums.

The sectoral wage-structure displayed in Table 6.2 puts Libya in a rather different category than most developing countries. In most countries wage-rates (for unskilled workers) are higher in the modern sector than in agriculture. The differential is of the order of 50% to 100%. The evidence suggests that in Libya agricultural wage-rates were higher than industrial rates by some 30 to 50%. This requires a word of explanation.

Before the oil era, Libya did not constitute an exception to the general rule that wages are lowest in agriculture. The wage level in agriculture was very depressed (£L 0.100 - 0.150 in 1952-54) and the rural/urban wage differential, although small, favoured the emerging modern sector.*

When, in 1956, oil companies started exploring the desert they offered employment at wages substantially higher than the rates prevailing either in agriculture or industry and the wage-gap between the traditional and modern sectors widened considerably (between 1956 and 1959, wage rates in agriculture rose from £L 0.140 to 0.180 but oil companies were recruiting unskilled labour at rates varying between £L 0.250 and £L 0.400). In later years - 1960/62 - agricultural wage-rates rose sharply to 0.400 but it is doubtful whether the increase represented a real gain to the workers, for prices were rising sharply too. These were very difficult years for the State: the level of expectations was high, the operations of the oil industry were exerting strong pressures on the price-level and the government was facing demands for higher wages and for the opening up of new employment opportunities. The State, however, was not in a position to satisfy these demands, not having received as yet any substantial revenues from oil (production and exports began in 1961). Rural migrants were flowing to the towns, amplifying a movement that seems to have started before the beginning of the oil era and that gained momentum in later years.

The result is familiar: the rural surplus of labour was transferred into the towns. Because of their small size, neither manufacturing nor oil could be expected to absorb the urban surplus. The "services" sector (private) may have expanded somewhat, offering means of subsistence to the newcomers; it is wrong to assume, however, that the capacity of this sector is unlimited. There seems to be no other option for the State but to create new jobs in its own departments. When oil revenues started to flow into the Treasury, the Government found itself able to respond to the demands. It might have responded too much: the salary scales were revised and adjusted upwards in 1964 and in 1966, and official employment considerably expanded. Recruitment was not restricted to the towns but extended to the rural areas also. To a large extent, the policy was aimed at distributing the oil revenues to some segments of the population.

---

* *A time series of agricultural wages (median) derived from the records of a large farm in Libya will be used in the discussion. The series is as follows:*

Year	Wage £L/day	Index
1953	0.135	100
1954	0.140	103
1955	0.140	103
1956	0.145	107
1957	0.150	111
1958	0.170	126
1959	0.180	133
1960	0.250	185
1961	0.300	222
1962	0.300	222
1963	0.300	222
1964	0.400	296
1965	0.500	370
1966	0.600	444
1967	0.650	481
1968	0.800	592

From then on, wages paid by the government to unskilled workers were as high - if not higher - than the wages paid by oil firms. As from 1964 -65, the oil industry ceased to be the wage-leader of the economy - the role being taken over by the State. The reversal of the agriculture/industry wage differential, which seems to have taken place around 1964/65, can be easily explained by a combination of three factors: (a) internal migration, which created a small surplus and some unemployment in the towns; (b) the wage and employment policies of the State, which established the rate of £L 0.700 - 0.800 as the minimum reward for a relatively easy job. Agricultural wage-rates were bound to rise above this level especially during the seasonal peak when labour is short and the work irksome; and (c) the stagnation of employment in the oil sector. After 1964 employment in the oil industry failed to expand significantly for at least two reasons. First, the passage from exploration to production that took place during this period is labour-saving in character. Second, oil firms started to contract out a number of auxiliary operations such as transport, catering and construction. In earlier years these activities were undertaken by the firms themselves.

The oil sector was thus facing favourable conditions in the labour market: excess supply and a stagnant demand. There were no pressures for higher wages.

The construction sector is in a different position. Construction is a very large employer and demand for labour is expanding continually. The conditions of work on building sites are not very attractive because of instability of employment and the nature of the physical effort required. Building contractors encounter great difficulties in recruiting Libyan labour and wages are consequently high. (Their only alternative is within the limits set by the allocation of work permits to foreign labour). It is clear that the Government is employing so many workers that shortages of labour for construction, the private services, as well as for transport and trade are created. The sectoral structure of wage-rates suggest that these shortages are also felt in agriculture.

If workers were leaving agriculture - where both water and land are scarce and the markets fragmented and isolated - to find employment in more productive pursuits in the modern sector, we would conclude that internal migration is performing a useful economic function. In such circumstances we would expect higher wage-rates in agriculture than in other sectors of the economy because of the seasonal character of employment, the longer hours of work and the type of physical effort required. In Libya the situation is somewhat different. Workers who could be easily absorbed in agriculture and in other productive sectors, are employed by the State, and it is difficult to believe that the Government sector is free from disguised unemployment in an economy where jobs and wages are the most convenient means of distributing oil revenues.

6.4 Qualitative Aspects of the Labour Force

It is widely acknowledged that in the early stages of development, the problems of recruiting, training and stabilising an industrial labour force may seriously hinder the efficient performance and the expansion of the modern sector. In other words, the issue of quantitative supplies may be complicated by problems arising from the qualitative aspects of workers' attitudes and behaviour. High rates of absenteeism and labour turnover, seasonal migration of urban workers to the family farms, social barriers to mobility and the difficulties of assimilating workers of recent rural extraction into the technological environment are often identified as major obstacles facing employers in industry. Is this the case in Libya?

We have studied with some care problems of labour stability in the petroleum industry for the period 1964-68 and the analysis of data supplied by some of the largest firms suggests the following results.

1. It seems that the average age of the Libyan labour force employed by the oil industry is relatively low. The majority of workers were born in the rural areas, but since recruitment generally takes place in the towns, we may infer that most workers are recent migrants. The ratio of skilled to unskilled labour is alarmingly low. There is a clear correlation between "skills" and "urban origin" (born in the towns).

2. The rates of labour turnover are extremely high (60% to 80% in 1964) and have shown a marked tendency to fall in recent years. Greater stability seems to be due to higher average earnings and to an improvement in the quality of the labour force, which is clearly revealed by a steady decrease in the number of dismissals for unsatisfactory performance over the years.

3. There is no correlation between the time-pattern of voluntary resignations in any given year and the seasonal profile of agricultural work.

4. It seems that certain categories of semi-skilled workers, such as drivers, who happen to be of predominantly urban origin, are more unstable than unskilled labour of rural origin.

5. The highest rates of turnover in oil firms are recorded among "trainees" who have acquired their skills in vocational programmes sponsored by the companies.

The results suggest that it may be wrong to attribute labour instability in the emerging modern sector of a developing economy to the persistence of traditional values or to the existence of a tie that attracts rural workers to their villages after a short period of employment in industry. It seems that labour stability is related to employers' policies and may be improved through the provision of economic incentives. The mobility of skilled workers is a reflection of their scarcity in Libya.

6.5 Conclusion

The most serious problem facing the Libyan economy is the shortage of skilled labour. In order to provide the country with its growing requirements of professionals, technicians and craftsmen, it is important to invest considerable resources in training and education. Impressive efforts have already been made and no doubt even greater attention will be given in future to this problem. But education is not sufficient; greater incentives are needed to induce the acquisition and improvement of skills. A large proportion of the skilled labour force finds employment in various Government administrative agencies. The shortage of unskilled labour for industry is not primarily due to a quantitative deficiency in manpower reserves, since institutional factors affect the allocation of labour as between the private and public sector.

The apparent shortage of labour in agriculture is not the cause of the unsatisfactory performance of this sector. It may be argued that the reverse is true: labour is leaving the rural areas because the prospects appear bleak. Wages are high in agriculture because the opportunity cost of labour is high in a booming economy where Government employment offers attractive wages and conditions of work.

It seems that the importance of agriculture to the Libyan economy is bound to decline still further in the future unless new sources of water supplies are discovered and new technological improvements introduced and adopted on a large scale. With adequate water and technological changes, employment in agriculture might expand, for it cannot be assumed that capital (in the form of new techniques) would displace labour. In a dynamic context, capital and labour are complementary factors rather than substitutes (see Symaps 8.1 and 9.1, Appendix 9) where investment per unit of land seems to be correlated with man/land ratio). If the prospects of a major hydrological and technological revolution in agriculture are deemed to be slim, the long-run employment problem in Libya would consist in finding alternative occupations in other productive sectors of the economy. It seems that the provision of jobs would have to be made in the towns, since a reversal of the rural/urban drift is not likely to occur. The process of economic development may follow the sequence "oil revenues - services - manufacturing" rather than the usual progression "agriculture - industry - services". The discussion of policies aiming at the fulfilment of these twin objectives - development with full productive employment - is beyond the scope of this paper. One thing is certain: education and skills will be required whatever the options.

Reference

1 See W. C. WEDLEY "Unemployment and Underemployment in Libya" *The Libyan Economic and Business Review* vol II, no. 2, 1966.

APPENDICES

MAPS

LIBYA CROP SURVEY MAPS
GENERAL LAND USE MAPS
AND
AN ANALYSIS OF THE AGRICULTURE
OF WESTERN LIBYA
BY COMPUTER MAPS

APPENDICES

		Page
1.	The Crop Survey - Libya	
	1.1. Introduction.	173
	1.2. Criteria considered in selecting case study areas.	176
	1.3. Comments and results.	176
2.	The General Agricultural Land Use Map of Northern Libya	
	2.1. Definitions and sources.	182
	2.2. The maps and the patterns of land use.	182
3.	Computer Maps - Western Libya	
	3.1. Introduction.	186
	3.2. The data.	186
	3.3. An explanation of SYMAP.	186
	3.4. Comments and results.	188
4.	An Interpretation of the Variables Presented in Symap Form	
	4.1. The method of treatment.	188
	4.2. The SYMAPS in relation to the farm classification.	189
	4.2.1. The distribution of irrigated and non-irrigated farming.	189
	4.2.2. The distribution of traditional and modern farming.	189
	4.3. Some general trends in agriculture in Western Libya as indicated by the SYMAPS.	192
	4.4. Conclusion.	194

  Page

5.   Figures

          Libya - Field Areas
                    July – August 1967 and February 1968.   174

          Libya - Western Provinces
                    1968 Survey – Sample Points.   187

          Western Libya - 1968
                    Selected Symaps.   196-207

6.   Tables

     Table 1. Rainfall at selected stations.   175

     Table 2. 1967 Field areas listed by farm type in
               the three regions of the country.   178-181

     Table 3. Areas of particular and mixed land use
               types for the areas shown on the
               LIBYA-LAND USE MAP (Map 8 – lower part.)   183

     Table 4. LIBYA – CROP SURVEY 1967/68 – Summer and
               Winter. Total area of particular crop
               or groups of crops.   184

9. Contents of Computer Map Series

The following maps will be found according to the numerical sequence after page 195.

1.1   Farm size.
1.2   Fragmentation of holdings.
2.1   Total residents per farm.
2.2   Rural population density.
3.1   Length of occupation of the farm.
3.2   Type of dwelling of the farmer.
4.1   Percentage cultivated.
4.2   Percentage cereals.
5.1   Percentage irrigated.
5.2   Percentage vegetables.
6.1   Irrigation − Hectares per electric pump.
6.2   Irrigation − Hectares per diesel pump.
6.3   Spray pipes per irrigated hectare.
7.1   Trees per hectare.
7.2   Mechanisation − tractors per cultivated hectare.
8.1   Labour intensity − permanent workers per total farm hectares.
8.2   Labour intensity − permanent workers per cultivated hectare.
9.1   Investment − per total farm hectares, including house and car.
9.2   Investment − per cultivated hectare, including house and car.
9.3   Investment in rural housing − total investment per farm.
10.1 'Off-farm' employment of the farmer.
10.2 'Off-farm' employment of farmer's first son resident on the farm.

INTRODUCTION

1.1 Introduction

The purpose of the crop survey was to record the distribution of crops in diverse parts of Libya and to present this information in map form, to highlight differences between individual farms and between private and state sponsored agriculture, as well as to record regional contrasts in cropping patterns.

Farms in all except Southern Libya were visited twice in order to map both summer and winter crops. The main part of the survey, carried out in the Summer of 1967, came at the end of a 12-month period during which rainfall had been close to average. The following figures, for selected stations in all provinces, show that the September 1966 - August 1967 agricultural year was one in which actual rainfall was close to the mean.

	Mean rainfall mm.	Sep'66- Aug'67 mm.	Rainfall deficit/surplus for winter season '67/'68 up to February 1968		
			mm.	out of	%
Tripoli	361.9	372.2	-136.1	279.3	49
Gharyan	312.6	372.2	+ 36.0	189.7	19
Benghazi	265.8	315.8	- 12.9	198.9	6
Shahhat	587.8	675.3	+ 56.2	267.0(Jan)	21
Sabhah	9.1	0.0	not applicable		

The above figures also show details for the winter season up to February 1968 when rainfall varied considerably from place to place, in relation to the respective mean figures. Tripoli and much of the irrigated and semi-irrigated Gefara was in deficit (Tripoli 49%) by the beginning of February. The coastal area of the Eastern Provinces received rainfall close to the mean, as did the jabal areas of both provinces (Gharyan +19% at the beginning of February, and Shahhat +21% at the beginning of January). These rainfall data have been quoted at length to establish that the crop survey information was collected during reasonably representative seasons. The main serious deficit was that for Tripoli for the February 1968 survey. Even this is less serious than it might seem, as the Tripoli area is one where supplmentary irrigation is generally undertaken. Other places on the coast to the east and west of Tripoli fared better. For example Zuwarah had a deficit up to the beginning of February 1968 of 15.3 mm. (i.e. only 10% of the 157.4mm., the mean for this period), while at al Khums (Valdagno) there was a surplus of 25.9 mm. (i.e. 15% of the 173.1 mm., the mean for the period).

The survey was organised to examine agricultural land-use only, in such a way that all plots of individual crops were identified. In order to carry out this work in the field, maps, normally at a scale of 1:5,000 (1 cm. represents 50 metres) were prepared, although in some cases maps of 1:1,000

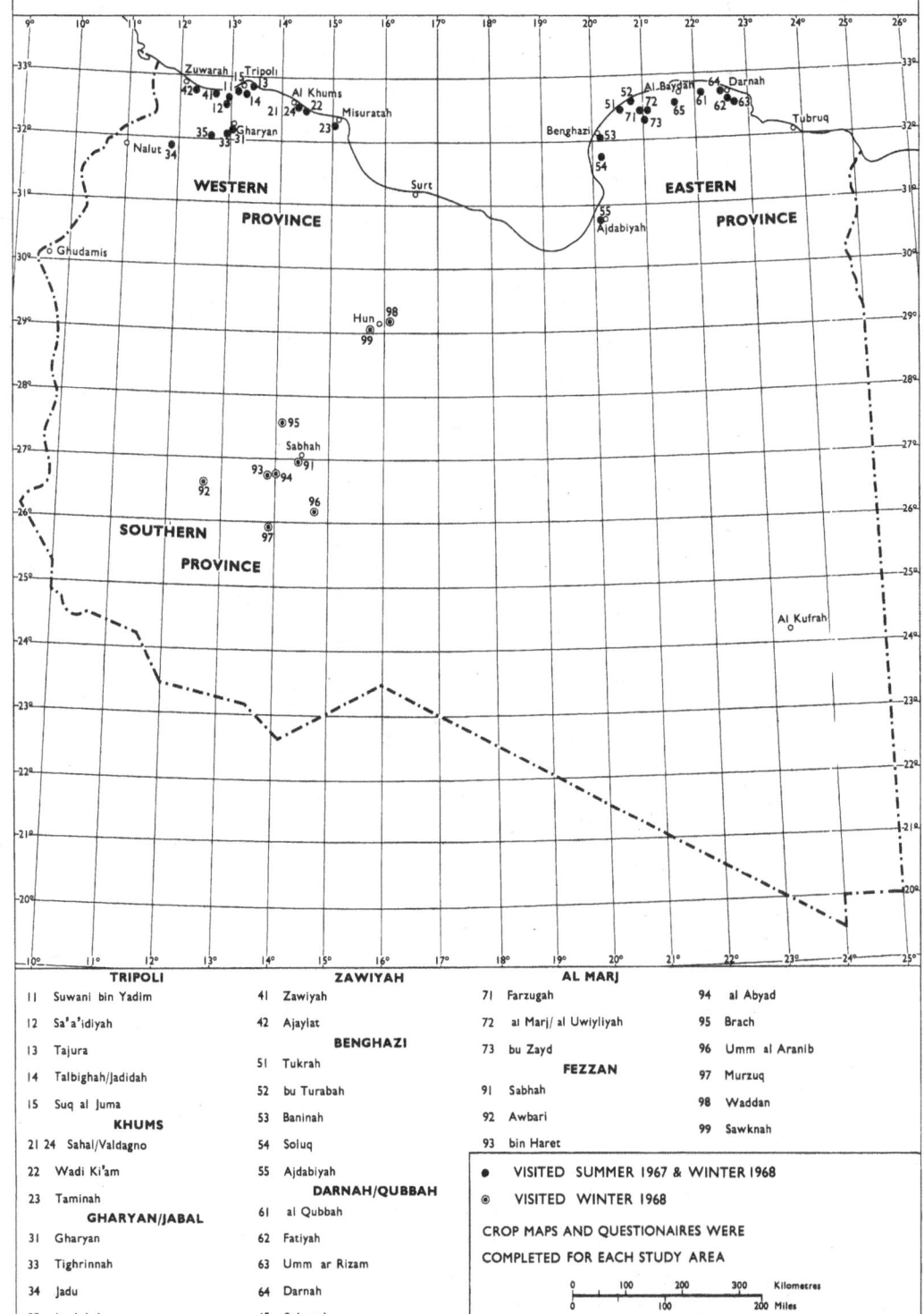

TABLE 1

RAINFALL AT SELECTED STATIONS - MEAN MONTHLY AND ANNUAL PRECIPITATION - MILLIMETRES

		J	F	M	A	M	J	J	A	S	O	N	D	TOTAL Jan.-Dec.	TOTAL Sept.-Aug.	PERIODS OF RECORDINGS
WESTERN LIBYA																
TRIPOLI	MEAN	73.4	40.6	23.5	10.9	5.2	1.3	0.5	0.6	9.7	36.2	64.9	95.1	361.9		(84 Years)
	1966	6.5	3.8	48.0	32.4		0	0	0	1.8	71.9	21.7	122.7	308.8	(372.2)	
	1967	57.3	16.0	49.2	1.7	24.3	5.6	0	0	3.5	30.4	33.6	38.9	260.5	(198.7)	
	1968	35.6	41.2	0.3	7.6	0.2	7.4	0	0	1.3						
GHARYAN	MEAN	66.5	49.1	39.1	21.1	10.2	2.4	0.4	0.6	9.4	22.7	34.0	57.1	312.6		(42 Years)
	1966	20.5	15.1	146.3	238.5	0	9.0	1.5	0	25.3	41.2	33.0	9.0	509.6	(331.5)	
	1967	81.5	32.5	81.5	0	18.0	7.5	0	2.0	47.0	88.5	13.2	22.5	394.2	(328.2)	
	1968	56.5	75.0	0	5.5	7.0	15.0	0	0							
EASTERN LIBYA																
BENGHAZI	MEAN	67.2	40.4	19.4	4.6	2.0	0.4	0.1	0	2.9	16.8	46.4	65.6	265.8		(54 Years)
	1966	30.3	2.7	32.9	0	0	0	0	0	4.8	0	47.5	196.0	314.2	(315.8)	
	1967	16.5	8.5	40.0	0	2.5	0	0	0	8.0	45.5	38.5	27.0	186.5	(226.0)	
	1968	67.0	17.0	8.5	0	7.5	7.0	0	0	0						
SHAHHAT	MEAN	145.1	83.5	60.8	16.3	11.6	1.1	0.6	1.8	7.9	44.6	78.7	135.8	587.8		(13 Years)
	1966	217.4	35.0	109.9	22.5	0	4.5	0	0	62.0	46.0	33.5	167.5	698.8	(675.3)	
	1967	128.5	85.1	108.9	33.1	5.9	0	0	4.5	7.5	145.5	54.8	115.4	689.5	(-)	
	1968															
SOUTHERN LIBYA																
SABHA H	MEAN	1.3	1.3	0.4	0.7	2.4	0.1	0	0	0	0	2.3	0.7	9.1		(21 Years)
	1966	0	0	0	0	13.0	0	0	0	0	0	0	0	13.0	(0)	
	1967	0	0	0	0	0	0	0	0	0	0	0	0	0	(0)	
	1968	0					-	-	-							

▼ ▲ Fieldwork months

Source. Meteorological Department, Ministry of Communications, Tripoli.

were already available, while in other districts it was only possible to use 1:10,000 or 1:20,000 maps. All field and base map details are shown in the compilation notes which appear on each colour map.

1.2 Criteria Considered in Selecting Case-Study Areas

Six main farming types have been identified, as listed in Table 2, and it was considered important to cover these as far as possible for the three major administrative (and at the same time geographical) units in the country. Table 2 shows that at least one area of each farming type has been included among the case-study areas, but it is also clear that there is an emphasis on the smaller more intensive types of traditional and modern farming. Few very large farms were covered. In the Southern Provinces where agriculture is restricted to small oasis areas, only irrigated agriculture has been examined. The emphasis in coverage in West and South Libya has been, therefore, upon irrigated and semi-irrigated agriculture, although considerable areas of mainly dry land cultivation have been included in the examination of Eastern Libya.

A second condition which had to be considered was the availability of maps and air photographs. Case-study areas were selected where maps and air photographs were available during the period of preparation to July 1967. Recent aerial survey carried out on behalf of the Ministry of Planning and Development and the National Agricultural Settlement Authority (NASA) were generously made available to the joint project by the respective departments, and were extensively utilized in preparation of field sheets.

Field recording.

Work in the field was carried out on Ozalid type prints, which were produced from traces made in the Tripoli office of the project. A minimum of general topographical detail was included on field sheets to leave adequate space for annotations in districts where tiny areas of crops are grown intercropped. Crops were recorded by alphabetical symbols, for example:-

```
        W ......... Wheat          O ......... Olive

        B ......... Barley         A ......... Almond
```

and each enumerator was provided with a list of such symbols in both Arabic and English. Maps were annotated in the field, and later either overdrawn in ink or transferred to a second neat map in the Tripoli office. These compilations were later redrawn by a cartographer. In the field the various levels of cropping were recorded in full, including tree as well as field crops, though tree crops (except citrus) were omitted from the final maps to ensure clarity of presentation.

1.3 Comments and Results

The results of the surveys are summarised in the eight maps (Appendix 7) which form part of this volume. The work has been finally drawn at 1:10,000 for irrigated and semi-irrigated areas, and at 1:50,000 for dry land farms. All irrigated areas, except Umm ar Rizam, are shown for both the summer 1967 and the winter 1967/68 seasons (Maps 1. 2, 3, 4, 5, and 6). Extensive dry land farming areas of the Eastern Province and one area of the Western Province,

Jandubah, are shown for one season only, February 1968. It was not felt to be necessary to show both seasons, as only one crop per year is normally grown in these areas. In 1967 spring-sown dry land crops had not been harvested by the time that summer field-work was completed, and to have re-recorded these areas would have been unnecessary duplication.

Within the limitation of the case-study method adopted, the main patterns of Libyan farming are demonstrated by the crop survey maps. Traditional farms of both dry and irrigated types contrast strongly with the larger farm and field pattern, laid down between 1911 and 1939.

The high intensity of land-use is also clear for NASA (government) farms, and also on some recently (after 1960) acquired Libyan farms, where intensive irrigation is being applied to formerly mainly dry farming areas, for example Talbighah/Jadidah and Suwani bin Yadim.

The pattern of winter and summer cropping is also demonstrated, with cereals figuring predominantly in the winter, and more valuable irrigated crops in summer, for example tomatoes and ground nuts.

Full descriptions and analysis of the crop maps are made in Chapter 5.

Special note.

>Area No. 64 Darnah - shown on MAP 1 and 2.
>A distortion was introduced into this map during fieldwork, and it was not possible to reconcile exactly the summer and winter versions in respect of field boundaries. It was felt, however, that despite this inaccuracy the results of both seasons should be included, as they do give a picture of the seasonal differences and relative crop distribution in Darnah.

TABLE 2

1967/68 Field Areas Listed by Farm Type in the Three Regions of the Country.

Farm type	Name of field area	Farm description	Total area surveyed Km²	Area shown on map Km²	Area No.	See map No.
WESTERN LIBYA						
1 Irrigated and semi-irrigated traditional	Tajura	Small farms (under 10 ha) close to the coast. All farms Libyan owned and run.	0.75	0.72	13	1 and 2
	Suq al Jumah		1.25	1.08	15	1 and 2
	Sahal (Al Khums)		10.05	9.80	21	5 and 6
	Zawiyah		3.15	2.85	41	1 and 2
	Ajaylat		1.60	1.53	42	1 and 2
			16.80	15.98		
2 Irrigated and semi-irrigated modern-Private (ex-Italian farms.)	Suwani bin Yadim	Ex-Italian farms, both Libyan and Italian owned. Average size of farm in field areas over 20 ha. Farms over 100 ha in some places.	9.75	4.40	11	3 and 4
	Talbighah/Jadidah		5.50	4.46	14	3 and 4
	Valdagno		6.25	6.01	24	5 and 6
	Taminah		7.80	4.83	23	3 and 4
			29.30	19.70		
3 Irrigated and semi-irrigated modern - N.A.S.A.	Wadi Ki'am	N.A.S.A. Farms. Small farms of between 2 and 4 hectares. Very intensive and densely populated	3.35	3.27	22	3 and 4
	Sa'a'idiyah		1.25	1.06	12	3 and 4
			4.60	4.33		
4 Non irrigated traditional - Jabal	Gharyan	Small average farm size and fragmented.	3.00	2.88	31	1 and 2
			3.00	2.88		

TABLE 2 (cont'd)

Farm Type	Name of field area	Farm description	Total area surveyed	Area shown on map	Area No.	See map No.
WESTERN LIBYA (continued)			Km²	Km²		
5 Non-irrigated modern – ex-Italian Jabal	Tighrinnah Jandubah (part)	Ex-Italian. Tobacco farms average 10 ha. Other large farms at Jandubah.	2.50 28.30	2.08 28.30	33 35	1 and 2 7
			30.80	30.38		
6 Non-irrigated modern – ex-Italian Jabal – N.A.S.A.	Jandubah (part)	Ex-Italian farms, administered by N.A.S.A. Not yet developed.	*(incl'd. above)	*(incl'd above)	35	7
			–	–		
		TOTAL WESTERN LIBYA	84.50	73.27		
EASTERN LIBYA						
1 Irrigated and semi-irrigated traditional	Tukrah Umm ar Rizam Darnah	Small farms (under 10 ha). All farms Libyan owned and run.	1.62 0.50 0.60	0.29 0.50 0.57	51 63 64	1 and 2 7 1 and 2
			2.72	1.36		
2 Irrigated and semi-irrigated modern ex-Italian	Baninah	Partially irrigated (Less than 10%).	5.75	1.70	53	1 and 2
			5.75	1.70		

TABLE 2 (cont'd.)

Farm type	Name of field area	Farm description	Total area surveyed	Area shown on map	Area No.	See map No.
			Km²	Km²		
EASTERN LIBYA (continued)						
3 Irrigated and semi-irrigated N.A.S.A.	Bu Turabah	N.A.S.A. run scheme commenced by Italian administration for Libyan farmers. Small farms.	0.50	0.23	52	1 and 2
			0.50	0.23		
4 Non-irrigated traditional	Sulumtah	Partly developed by Italians still some tractor farming. Dispersed plots.	18.75	18.75	65	7
			18.75	18.75		
5 Non-irrigated modern - Private	Fatiyah Al Marj (part) Bu Zayd	Extensive grain farms mechanised. Farm size 100 ha to over 2000 ha.	12.50 30.00 56.25	12.50 30.00 56.25	62 72 73	7 7 7
			98.75	98.75		
6 Non-irrigated modern - N.A.S.A.	Al Qubbah Farzugah al Marj, Al Uwiyliyah	N.A.S.A. administered ex-Italian farms.	5.50 37.50 82.50	5.50 37.50 82.50	61 71 72	7 7 7
			125.50	125.50		
		TOTAL EASTERN LIBYA	251.97	246.29		

TABLE 2 (cont'd.)

Farm type	Name of field area	Farm description	Total area surveyed	Area shown on map	Area No.	See map No.
			Km²	Km²		
SOUTHERN LIBYA						
1 Irrigated traditional	Sabhah, Awbari Bin Haret, Al Abyad, Umm al Aranib, Waddan, Sawknah.	Oasis farms, irrigated dependent small farms 1 to 10 hectares.	TOTAL 10.00 (approx.)	3.19	91,92 93,94,95, 97, 98,99.	8 8 8 8
	TOTAL SOUTHERN LIBYA		10.00	3.19		

2. The General Agricultural Land-Use Map of Northern Libya

2.1 Definitions and Sources

In order to give an outline of the distribution of main farming types, a general land-use map of northern Libya has been compiled at a scale of 1:1,000,000. The types of land-use are shown as follows:-

CROPLAND 1. IRRIGATED - including semi-irrigated

                1.1. TRADITIONAL GARDENS

                1.2. MODERN SECTOR

         2. NON - IRRIGATED

                2.1. TRADITIONAL GARDENS

                2.2. MODERN SECTOR

UNIMPROVED GRAZING WITH SHIFTING CULTIVATION

TREE CROPS

WOODLAND - OPEN WOOD AND SCRUB

SABKHAH - SALT FLAT

AGRICULTURALLY UNPRODUCTIVE LAND

It has been necessary to choose symbols and colours which allow the mixed characters of Libyan agriculture to be shown, for example the very common situation of unimproved grazing, interspersed with shifting cultivation, which may occur in a predominantly unproductive area. As far as possible, the colours used approximate to those of the World Land Use Survey.

A number of sources have been found useful. The 1:400,000 map produced by Rowland and Robb of the British Military Administration was utilized in compiling the general land-use map of the Western Provinces (1945). The whole of the area was covered relatively recently by the US Army Map Service, which annotated photographs for the P761 1:50,000 series, during the period 1958-1962. This map series gives a valuable impression of the extent of agriculture at that time. Finally, extensive travelling, necessary to complete the various seasons of fieldwork for the joint project survey, brought most of agricultural Libya to the attention of those compiling the maps.

2.2 The Maps and the Patterns of Land Use

The general land-use maps indicate clearly the important characteristics of Libyan agriculture despite the constraint imposed by the 1:1,000,000 scale. For Northern Libya as a whole, it is apparent that settled agricultural areas comprise only small and discontinuous islands either close to the coast or on the hills immediately inland. The predominant land-use type throughout even the better watered areas of the country is shifting cultivation and unimproved pasture.

Regional variations clearly demonstrated by the maps include the much greater areal coverage of irrigated lands in Western Libya than in the East, indicative of a higher proportion of settled agriculture and more intensive use of land. Extensive open forest and scrub in Eastern Libya, interspersed with patches of grazing and shifting cultivation, serves to emphasise the considerable visual contrast between the hill areas of the East and the West. On the other hand, the orchard and plantation developments of Western Libya have no real counterpart in the East as yet.

The following table has been compiled by measuring the areas of the various types of land use shown on the land use maps on the lower part of Map 8.

TABLE 3

Areas of particular and mixed land use types for the areas shown on the LIBYA - LAND USE map (Map 8 - lower part).

Land use type	Area Square kilometres					
	West Libya	%	East Libya	%	Total	%
Cropland - Irrigated traditional gardens	535	1.4	124	0.5	659	1.1
Irrigated modern sector	1389	3.6	-*	-	1389	2.2
Non-irrigated traditional gardens	1228	3.2	128	0.5	1356	2.1
Non-irrigated modern sector (and tree crops)	508	1.3	319	1.3	877	1.3
Unimproved grazing with shifting cultivation	20513	53.7	4731	18.7	25244	39.8
Unimproved grazing with shifting cultivation and unproductive land	9970	26.1	-	-	9970	15.7
Unimproved grazing with unproductive land	1804	4.8	13495	53.3	15297	24.0
Woodland	191	0.5	25	0.1	216	0.4
Woodland - Open woods and shrubs, with unimproved grazing	-	-	5971	23.6	5971	9.4
Unproductive land (including settlements)	382	1.0	278	1.1	660	1.0
Sabkhah	1680	4.4	228	0.9	1908	3.0
Total	38198		25274		63472	

* *The irrigated modern farming in East Libya is very limited in extent and could not be shown on the map at the 1:1,000,000 scale.*

Note:- The areas listed as West and East Libya are not the same as the Western and Eastern Muhafadat.
Statistical discrepancies due to rounding.

TABLE 4

LIBYA CROP SURVEY. TOTAL AREA OF PARTICULAR CROPS OR GROUPS OF CROPS.   PER CENT (%)   SUMMER (JULY/AUGUST) 1967

(See page following the table for a full list of crops)   ' - ' = none

FARM TYPE			Type of Crop/Land Use. ▶	Map No.	No info.	01 Cereal	02 Alfalfa	03 Beans	04 Root veg.	05 Other veg.	06 Artichoke	07 Pepper etc.	08 Tom ato	09 Tobacco	10 Squash	11 Henna	12 Vine	13 Citrus	14 Fallow	15 Pasture	16 Trees	17 Abandoned	18 Non-Agric.	19 Houses	20 Graves
IRRIGATED AND SEMI-IRRIGATED																									
1	Traditional Intensive	W. Province	13 Tajura	1		3.7	10.4	-	0.3	-	-	1.0	2.3	5.0	2.0	1.3	-	2.7	43.9	-	-	2.7	17.4	0.3	7.0
			15 Suq al Jumah	1	(1, 5)	4.4	7.7	0.4	-	-	2.8	2.8	1.5	0.4	2.5	0.2	-	9.5	40.8	-	-	0.8	22.5	0.2	2.1
			21 Sahal (Al Khums)	5	(0, 2)	2.7	6.6	0.1	0.2	0.1	-	1.4	0.8	-	1.5	-	0.2	0.1	73.5	-	0.3	0.3	0.3	1.5	1.0
			41 Zawiyah	1		1.4	1.2	1.1	0.2	0.7	-	0.5	1.6	-	1.2	-	0.4	1.4	74.7	-	-	7.6	4.2	1.9	1.9
			42 Al Ajaylat	1		2.2	2.5	-	-	-	-	0.3	1.0	-	-	-	1.3	0.3	81.6	-	8.5	6.3	1.0	1.0	-
		E. Prov.	51 Tukrah	1		1.7	10.9	1.2	-	-	-	-	2.3	-	1.7	-	3.5	-	70.6	-	-	6.1	-	2.0	-
			64 Darnah	1		15.3	-	-	-	-	-	-	-	-	0.4	-	0.4	1.2	22.2	-	0.9	0.9	48.0	2.4	-
			63 Umm ar Rizam	1		not recorded			0.4	1.6	-	6.5	-	-	-	-	-	-	-	-	-	-	-	-	-
2	Modern Private Intensive and Extensive	W. Prov.	11 Suwani bin Yadim	3		0.1	3.8	4.1	-	0.3	-	0.8	4.2	-	2.2	-	13.5	9.5	52.7	-	1.7	-	7.0	0.1	-
			14 Taibighah/Jadidah	3		0.9	8.4	1.0	-	0.1	-	0.1	0.7	-	1.3	-	0.1	30.1	51.9	-	3.9	-	1.5	-	-
			22 Taminah	3		2.9	18.3	-	-	-	-	0.5	1.2	-	2.8	-	0.7	-	71.7	-	-	-	1.4	0.5	-
			24 Valdagno	5	(4, 2)	1.9	1.0	-	-	-	-	0.4	-	0.7	-	2.0	-	1.0	77.6	-	9.6	0.2	1.4	-	-
		E. Pr.	53 Baninah	1		0.6	-	-	-	-	-	3.4	-	12.9	-	-	6.4	-	76.7	-	-	-	-	-	-
3	Modern NASA Intensive (Govt)	W. Prov.	12 Sa'a'idiyah	3	(4, 2)	0.3	3.9	19.4	5.7	-	-	3.6	7.5	-	16.1	-	-	37.5	-	-	1.1	-	1.8	0.3	-
			22 Wadi Ki'am	3		17.9	11.5	0.3	-	-	2.0	12.4	1.8	0.4	0.8	-	1.4	-	42.1	-	-	5.0	3.0	-	-
		E. Pr.	52 Bu Turabah	1		5.3	-	-	-	6.1	-	4.5	13.6	-	20.4	-	2.3	-	47.8	-	-	-	-	-	-
NON IRRIGATED																									
4	Trad. Intensive	W. Prov.	31 Gharyan	1	(5, 3)	-	-	-	-	-	-	-	8.1	0.6	-	1.1	-	-	54.4	-	0.3	2.7	26.5	1.0	-
5	Modern Private Intensive	W. Prov.	33 Tighrinnah	1	(3, 0)	0.2	-	-	0.4	-	-	-	2.1	36.2	-	-	0.4	0.2	55.8	-	-	0.2	1.1	0.4	-

Note: Extensive dry land areas have not been included for the summer seasons; only one crop per year is grown.

IRRIGATED AND SEMI-IRRIGATED   **WINTER (FEBRUARY) 1967/68**

						01	02	03	04	05	06	07	08	09	10	11	12	13	14	15	16	17	18	19	20
1	Traditional Intensive	W. Province	13 Tajura	2		11.1	8.5	3.0	1.0	-	-	-	-	-	-	1.4	-	3.3	46.9	-	-	2.7	17.4	0.3	7.0
			15 Suq al Jumah	2	(1, 1)	0.2	3.2	3.0	0.4	0.8	-	0.2	0.2	-	0.2	1.3	0.4	12.1	50.8	-	-	1.2	22.5	0.2	2.1
			21 Sahal (Al Khums)	6		27.5	2.9	7.1	0.2	0.1	-	0.6	0.1	0.1	-	-	0.1	0.2	56.9	-	0.5	0.3	0.5	2.0	0.6
			41 Zawiyah	2		1.9	5.6	3.9	0.5	0.2	-	0.2	-	-	-	-	-	2.3	69.8	-	-	7.6	4.2	1.9	1.9
			42 Al Ajaylat	2		13.1	5.8	3.4	-	0.9	-	0.9	-	-	-	-	0.9	-	64.3	-	8.2	0.3	1.0	1.0	-
		E. Prov.	51 Tukrah	2		23.3	-	4.7	1.3	7.3	-	2.0	-	-	-	-	3.0	-	51.4	-	5.0	-	-	2.0	-
			64 Darnah	2		5.2	0.9	3.0	5.2	15.9	-	0.5	0.5	-	-	-	1.3	-	16.4	-	0.9	-	48.0	2.3	-
			63 Umm ar Rizam	7		21.8	-	12.2	-	1.4	-	-	-	-	-	-	-	-	32.0	-	-	19.0	13.6	-	-
		Southern Province	91 Sabhah	8		13.1	13.6	0.5	7.9	0.9	-	0.5	-	-	-	-	-	-	54.3	-	0.6	0.1	8.5	-	-
			92 Awbari	8		15.5	4.1	1.1	5.3	2.7	-	-	1.3	-	-	-	-	-	52.6	-	13.9	3.7	0.2	-	-
			93 Bin Haret	8		31.1	1.5	0.3	2.6	4.9	-	-	0.3	-	-	-	1.9	-	50.6	-	-	3.4	3.4	-	-
			96 Umm al Aranib	8		19.6	4.5	-	12.8	5.7	-	-	-	-	-	-	-	-	55.1	-	-	1.4	-	0.5	-
			97 Murzuq	8		15.9	6.5	1.9	7.5	4.2	-	0.9	-	-	-	-	-	-	61.2	-	-	-	-	-	-
			98 Waddan	8		1.4	14.8	0.2	-	3.9	-	-	0.7	-	-	-	-	-	61.9	-	-	0.5	15.9	0.7	-
			99 Sawknah	8		5.1	21.5	-	-	0.5	-	-	0.9	-	-	-	-	-	59.9	-	-	-	11.2	0.9	-
2	Modern Private	W. Prov.	11 Suwani Bin Yadim	4		10.9	2.4	1.2	-	-	-	0.2	-	-	-	-	10.7	8.3	60.4	-	1.5	-	4.3	0.1	-
			14 Taibighah/Jadidah	4		4.5	8.1	5.0	0.6	-	-	-	-	-	-	-	-	30.2	45.6	-	4.6	-	1.2	0.2	-
			22 Taminah	4		42.2	4.8	13.2	-	0.2	-	-	0.6	-	-	-	-	-	37.0	-	-	-	1.4	0.4	-
			24 Valdagno	6	(3, 8)	23.8	1.1	0.1	0.4	-	-	-	-	-	-	-	2.0	0.6	56.7	-	10.1	0.1	1.3	-	-
	Intensive and Extensive	E. Pr.	53 Baninah	2		1.2	-	-	-	-	-	-	-	-	2.3	-	-	6.4	90.1	-	-	-	-	-	-
3	Modern NASA Intensive	W. Prov.	12 Sa'a'idiyah	4		26.4	4.0	10.3	-	3.3	3.3	-	0.2	-	-	-	-	0.7	50.6	-	-	-	1.2	-	-
			22 Wadi Ki'am	4		36.4	11.1	10.5	0.2	0.2	2.0	0.9	0.6	-	-	-	-	0.2	28.0	-	0.8	4.9	3.0	0.6	-
		E. Pr.	52 Bu Turabah	2		13.1	-	3.4	2.8	6.2	-	3.4	-	-	-	-	-	0.7	70.4	-	-	-	-	-	-
NON IRRIGATED																									
4	Trad'l. Inten.	W. P.	31 Gharyan	2		36.3	-	2.6	-	-	-	-	-	-	-	1.7	-	-	29.3	-	0.5	2.7	26.0	0.9	-
5	Modern Private Extensive	W. Prov.	33 Tighrinnah	2	(3, 0)	43.9	-	5.8	-	-	-	0.2	0.2	-	-	-	0.8	-	45.2	-	-	0.2	1.1	0.4	-
			35 Jandubah	7		46.6	-	0.4	-	-	-	-	0.1	-	-	-	-	-	38.8	-	-	13.1	0.2	-	-
		E. Pr.	72 Al Marj/Al Uwiliyah	7		86.2	-	0.5	-	-	-	0.5	0.5	-	0.8	-	0.5	-	5.9	1.7	0.5	-	2.9	-	-
			73 Bu Zayd	7		56.8	-	-	-	-	-	-	-	-	-	-	-	-	18.7	24.2	-	0.1	0.1	-	0.1
			62 Fatiyah	7		83.3	-	-	-	-	-	-	-	-	-	-	-	-	11.3	0.2	-	3.4	1.8	-	-
6	Modern NASA (Gov't.) Extensive	W. Pr.	71 Farsugah	7		27.9	-	0.2	-	-	-	-	0.2	-	-	-	-	4.4	64.9	-	-	1.1	0.9	0.2	-
			72 Al Marj/Al Uwiliyah	7		82.7	-	0.1	-	-	-	-	0.1	-	-	-	1.2	3.2	12.2	-	-	0.3	5.3	-	-
			61 Al Qubbah	7		43.0	-	0.5	-	-	-	-	-	-	-	-	5.3	33.8	-	1.6	-	8.1	-	-	-
			65 Suluntah	7		14.4	-	-	-	-	-	-	-	-	-	-	-	1.6	81.7	1.6	0.7	-	-	-	-

All figures in the table are percentages. The term intensive is intended to indicate an area of irrigated agriculture; such farming may be continuous throughout the year, with high labour inputs. Extensive agriculture is non-irrigated, with farming taking place for short periods of the year and involving low labour inputs.

LIST OF CROPS AND TYPES OF OTHER LAND USE
REFERRED TO BY NUMBER THROUGHOUT TABLE 4

01	Wheat, barley, oats, millet, sorghum and maize.
02	Alfalfa.
03	Broad beans, runner beans, peas and ground nuts.
04	Carrot, potato, turnip and radish.
05	Cabbage, cauliflower, lettuce, onion and fenugreek.
06	Artichoke.
07	Pepper, pimento and aubergine.
08	Tomato.
09	Tobacco.
10	Cucumber, marrow, pumpkin and squash.
11	Henna.
12	Vine.
13	Citrus.
14	Fallow.
15	Rough Pasture.
16	Trees.
17	Abandoned.
18	Non-agricultural and built up areas.
19	Houses.
20	Graves.

These have been listed in the same order as in the legend which accompanies each map.

3. Computer Maps - Western Province

3.1 Introduction

A number of computer maps have been produced in the process of analysing the data collected by questionnaire survey, and a selection of these maps is reproduced in this volume to show the geographical distributions of various basic farm characteristics, as well as of important inter-relationships, for example the number of farm residents or tractors per hectare.

The maps have been extremely useful as 'tools' in the writing of descriptive and analytical material in the main text. Those reproduced here have been photographically reduced to improve visual interpretation, and to permit the inclusion of more material.

3.2 The Data - refer to the map facing page opposite.

In July 1968 a questionnaire survey was conducted throughout the settled agricultural areas of the Western Provinces. As well as collecting information with reference to farm investment, labour, wages, and migration, more than 30 items relating to farm inventory were also recorded. The survey utilized a systematic sampling technique in which data points were selected at the intersections of grid lines (Universal Transverse Mercator Grid) two kilometres apart, as shown on the US A.M.S. P761 Series, 1:50,000. In some areas a ten kilometre grid was adopted, covering lands where farming was discontinuous, dispersed and carried out by dry farming methods, as for example on the Gefara and Jabal areas, totalling approximately 25% of the total. The US A.M.S. maps were a convenient and suitable basis for sample point selection, and proved excellent for map reading purposes in the field.

Some 450 farms were selected and visited, from which 371 complete and adequate sets of individual farm data were obtained. Of the 450 farms, 51 were found to have been selected first on large farms for which data had already been enumerated at another grid intersection or secondly, where agriculture was no longer carried out. 28 completed questionnaires were found to be unreliable when checks were carried out in the Tripoli office, and these have been rejected.

Since coordinate references of all farms were recorded, and finally coded on punch cards along with the other farm data, it was found that the data could readily be used in a programme for the production of computer maps, a method known as SYMAP, devised in the Laboratory of Computer Graphics at Harvard University.

3.3 An Explanation of Symap

The Synagraphic Mapping System (SYMAP) is a computer programme which allows the graphic output of spatially distributed data, after complex computer manipulation of these data.[1] The programme is devised to operate with a standard line printer, which permits the use of standard computer equipment but has the disadvantage that the symbolisation possible from such a printer is limited.[2] However, by overprinting the normal typographic characters of the line printer, it is possible to produce an acceptable range of contrasting symbols with an increasing density of tone where this is desirable.

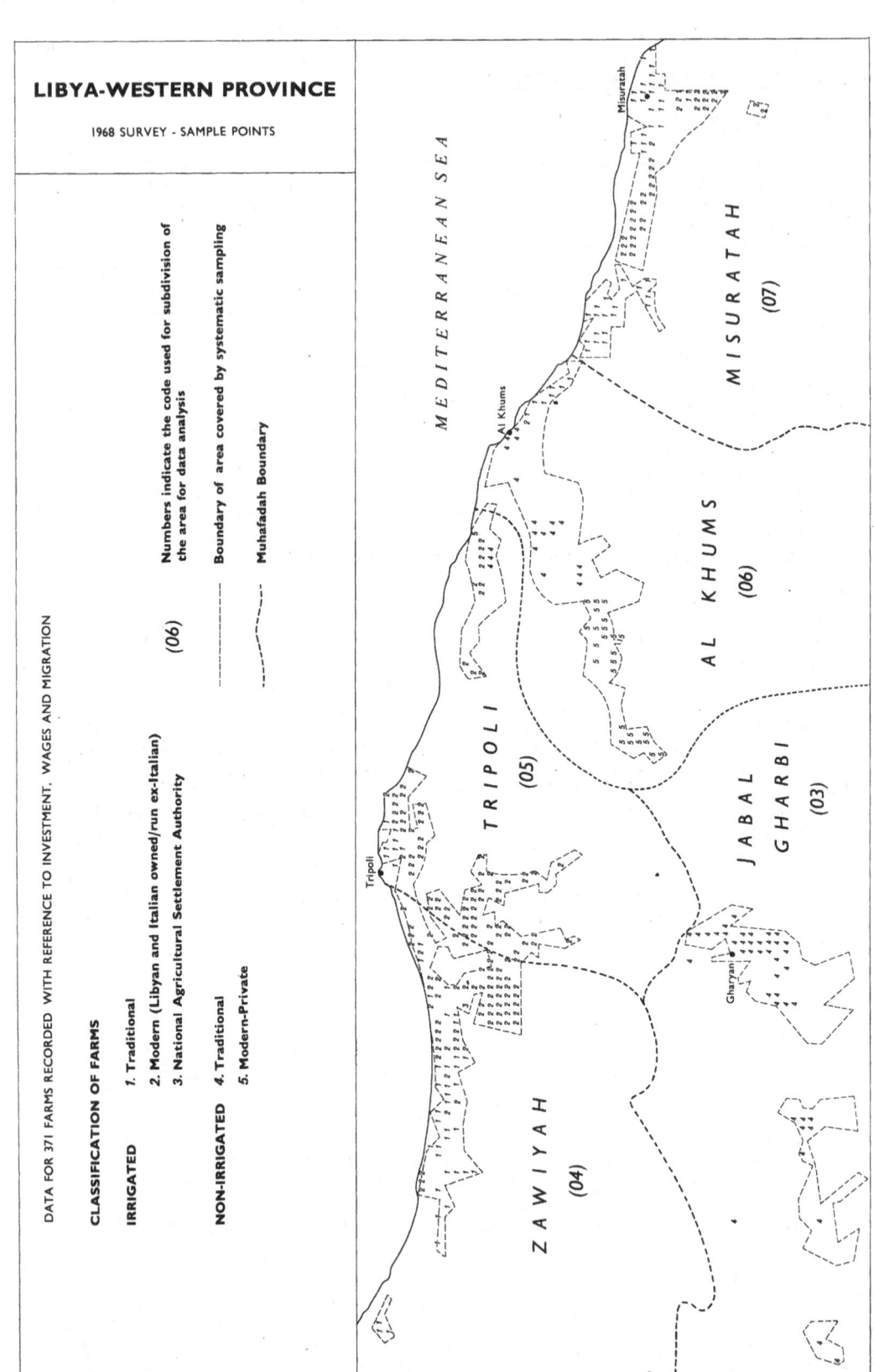

The type of map used for Western Libya is of the 'Contour' type; that is, it is based on the interpolation by the computer of 'slopes', by means of complex weighted averages. For each 1/8 inch by 1/10 inch position of the line-printer, reference is made to surrounding data points, and a symbol of the required density is printed out, the mathematical relationship of which is consistent with the nearest data points. Such extensive manipulation is only possible in a computer, and the map print-out which requires only a few further seconds saves many hours of cartography and interpretation.

It will be seen for Libya, that well-defined 'islands' of agricultural activity have been considered. The limits of these islands can be accurately described within the limitations of the 1/8th by 1/10th symbolisation.

A transparent overlay has been used in the final reproduction of the maps, to show details of coast, settlement and roads, and to assist in the interpretation of the maps. Legends and place names can be printed by the line-printer within the limits of its symbolisation, but the overlay method permitted easier map interpretation, neater presentation, and added little to the total effort and cost, since one overlay was sufficient for all maps.

3.4 Comments and Results

The maps speak for themselves in term of usefulness, and it is hoped that this method of mapping, which is capital rather than labour intensive, will in the future assist other surveys of Libya, on agricultural and other subjects, as in Libya there is a shortage of correctly sampled material, as well as a shortage of the skills to present this information quickly.

One very useful aspect of the SYMAP is its ability to highlight errors in data. As the area of influence of each item of data is symbolised, any incongruities with reference to the general trends displayed on the map stand out. If these are 'unreasonably' inconsistent or more commonly, if they contradict personal knowledge of the area, (for example a water pump recorded in an area where irrigation is never carried out), then the data can be checked and amended. Normal tabulation and data classification do not always reveal such errors.

4. An Interpretation of the Variables Presented in Symap Form

A number of farm characteristics have been presented in Symap form, not only to illustrate this information most clearly in terms of space, but also to determine whether location and related physical characteristics (e.g. the dry character of the jabal hills), have influenced settled farming throughout Western Libya.

4.1 The Method of Treatment

First in section 4.2 the maps will be discussed in terms of the farm type classification used throughout this report. The farm types relevant to Western Libya are as follows: -

Irrigated and semi-irrigated	Traditional	(Coded as Type 1)
	Modern	(Coded as Type 2)
Non-irrigated	Traditional	(Coded as Type 4)
	Modern	(Coded as Type 5)

The distribution of these farm types is shown on the map facing page 186 Government farms which have elsewhere been coded as farm types 3 and 6, have not been considered, as significant samples of these farms were not collected during the 1968 period of fieldwork.

In section 4.3 a number of general propositions will be confirmed by making reference to the maps. Other material will be drawn on to a minor extent.

4.2 The Symaps in Relation to the Farm Classification

4.2.1 The distribution of irrigated (and semi-irrigated) and non-irrigated farming.

(Non-irrigated farming will be referred to frequently as dry farming).

A number of maps justify the basic classification of irrigated (and semi-irrigated) and dry farms. Maps 6.1, 6.2 and 6.3, which refer to the distribution of pumps and other irrigation equipment, indicate clearly the dry character of the farming on the jabals, that is the Jabal Nafusah and Jabal Tarhunah, the latter including the area known as Mslata. The Jabal Tarhunah and Mslata are not marked on the map, but should be identified as the area between Tarhunah and al Khums, which are both shown.

Maps 4.1 and 4.2, showing respectively the percentage of the farm cultivated, and that under cereals, indicate that a higher proportion of a dry farm is cultivated, and a much higher proportion of these same farms are used for cereals. Map 4.2 shows that this concentration on cereals is found mainly on the traditional farms located around al Qassabat, and on the western jabal, between Gharyan and Yafran. This pattern was also observed in flights over these areas.

Conversely Map 5.1 shows the predominance of irrigated farming in the Ajaylat, Aziziyah, Tripoli triangle, as well as at Zliten and Misuratah. Elsewhere irrigated farming even in coastal areas is not so important, generally being undertaken on less than 20% of the farm area.

The larger average farm size of the dry farms is also indicated on Map 1.1.. In the eastern jabal farms are rarely less than 25 hectares, and near Tarhunah the modern farms average 68 hectares. Further west around Gharyan the dry farms are much smaller, averaging only 8 hectares, but this is still twice the size of traditional irrigated farms, and the 68 hectare average size for the Tarhunah farms is again more than twice the size of irrigated and semi-irrigated farms (31.3 hectares) of the coast.

4.2.2 The distribution of traditional and modern farming.

The general distribution of traditional and modern farms is also highlighted by a number of the symaps.

Irrigated and semi-irrigated farms.

Traditional irrigated farming is mainly confined to areas north of the main road in the Tripoli triangle,* to the low plain (sahal) between Al Khums and Zliten, and to the farms within a radius of approximately ten kilometres of Misuratah. This distribution is reflected in Map 1.1. (farm size) which shows the predominance of small farms in these areas. Larger farms of more than 25 hectares predominate in the areas former Italian settlement, for example at Taminah, Dafniyah (Between Zliten and Misuratah), near Qarahbulli and in the southern part of the Tripoli triangle.

An important distinguishing feature of modern irrigated farming is the spray pipe method of irrigation, and the intensity of the use of such equipment is mapped on symap 6.3. Scarcely any of this equipment is owned by farmers previously defined as traditional, while modern farms in the Tripoli area and farms in the Dafniyah area show up as important users.

Fragmentation of holdings would appear to be a feature of traditional irrigated farms, as shown on Map 1.2, with high levels of fragmentation occuring close to the main coastal towns, for example near Ajaylat, Zawiyah, Zliten and Misuratah. Data from the questionnaire survey showed that 44% of the sampled farms had more than one parcel in the traditional irrigated category, while the figure for the modern irrigated farms was 28%.

The length of occupation of the farm by the farmer is another variable which distinguishes modern and traditional irrigated farms. Map 3.1 indicates that the ownership of modern farms has changed hands in many cases in the very recent past. The area to the south-east of Zawiyah and to the south-west of Tripoli demonstrates this trend most clearly. This is the area known as az Zahra, a former Italian settlement where farms have been bought since independence and especially since the discovery of oil in Libya. Fifteen per cent of the sampled modern irrigated modern farms were acquired in 1960 alone. These developments are also reflected in the average length of ownership of the farms, which for modern irrigated farms is only 13.3 years compared with 25.6 years for the traditional irrigated farm. Centres of traditional farming can be seen on Map 3.1 (Length of occupation around the main urban centres). However, many modern farms were still run by Italian farmers at the time of the questionnaire survey and so the highest classification on the map including up to 24 years of ownership has within it many areas where Italian farmers were still active, since no Italian farmer could have been in Libya for less than 24 years.

As a result of the smaller average size of traditional irrigated farms, four hectares as opposed to 31.3 hectares for modern farms, the investment and expenditure per hectare appears to be much higher on the smaller farms. (Maps 9.1 and 9.2). This mainly arises from the high allocations which the farmers are making to housing in all areas, and so small farms show as having a higher rate of investment when investment is related to area. The allocation is especially high on the traditional irrigated farms at 49% of total investment, compared with a level of 17% on modern irrigated farms for the same period 1967-1968. In order to illustrate the distribution of investment in rural housing Map 9.3 has been included and it shows that it is on

---

* *The Tripoli triangle is the area of settled farming located in the Muhafadat of Tripoli and Zawiyah, coded as areas 05 and 04.*

the generally small irrigated traditional farm that house replacement is going on. These small farms are often highly valued for their residential qualities, especially if they are near a town   (Map 6.3).

Non-irrigated farms.

Some of the important distinctions between modern and traditional farms on the dry jabal areas of Western Libya are also demonstrated on the symaps.

The area of modern dry farming is around Tarhunah, as far as a point half way to al Qassabat. Other modern farms around Gharyan have been classified as traditional, as they are generally small, i.e. ten hectares or less, which is an average size for a traditional dry farm. Also, apart from the raising of tobacco on these ex-Italian farms, and the European type of dwelling upon them, they differ little from the traditional farms which surround them.

Map 1.2 showing the fragmentation of holdings clearly confirms the definition, with the traditional western jabal and the al Qassabat areas being most fragmented. The average number of parcels per holding on traditional dry farms (farm type 4) was found to be 3.8., while for modern dry farms the figure was 2.4.

Rural population density is shown to be higher on traditional dry farms than on modern in Map 2.2, with between one and four residents per hectare on the traditional farms and under 0.25 per hectare on the modern farms around Tarhunah.

Because some of the modern farms on the jabal were still Italian owned at the time of the questionnaire survey the length of occupation of the farm does not appear to be an important distinguishing characteristic, although the area of traditional farming on the eastern jabal around Al Qassabat does have farms with a predominantly lengthy ownership. The appearance of a short ownership pattern around Gharyan can be accounted by the departure of the Italian farmers from the tobacco farms near the town. It was these farms which were mainly sampled in the survey of the Gharyan area.

It is Maps 4.1 and 4.2 and especially the latter, which are most useful in defining the limits of modern farming on the jabal. The percentage of the farm utilised in total and for cereals is generally much higher on the traditional dry farms. Conversely the degree of mechanisation is higher on the modern farms, with mainly 16 to 60 cultivated hectares per tractor on the modern farms, while the traditional farms around al Qassabat show a negligible tractor usage, certainly over 60 cultivated hectares per tractor. The information for the western jabal has been erased from the map as it had been misrepresented. Scarcely any western jabal farms have tractors. Field visits showed that tractors were often used, but these were usually hired for the very short ploughing season in September or October.

Investment follows the same pattern as on irrigated farms. Traditional dry farms average 8.0 hectares in size while their modern counterpart averages 68.2 hectares, and since rehousing is going ahead rapidly, especially near Gharyan (Map 9.3) it is these smaller traditional farms which appear on the maps to have the highest rate of investment per hectare (Map 9.1 refers to total farm area, and Map 9.2 refers to the cultivated area of the farm).

The significance of the proximity of the main centres upon farm and housing investment is also demonstrated by these maps. Investment is at the rate of over £L 400 per cultivated hectare near Gharyan and is everywhere else lower, declining with distance from this main centre. One exceptional area is that of al Khadra, which shows up on Maps 9.1 and 9.2, just to the east of Tarhunah. Here the ex-Italian farms have been taken over and are being developed by Libyan farmers.

4.3 Some general trends in agriculture in Western Libya as indicated by the symaps.

4.3.1 The Tripoli triangle is the most vigorous agricultural area in Western Libya.

In terms of the degree of mechanisation of irrigated agriculture and the general levels of investment, it has already been shown to some extent that the Tripoli triangle is the most important area of irrigated agriculture in Western Libya, (see Maps 6.1, 6.2, 6.3, 9.1, 9.2 and 5.1), and therefore the most important farming region in the whole of Western Libya, since yields are so much higher on irrigated than on dry farms.*

Other characteristics indicate a higher level of agricultural activity in the Tripoli region, such as the high percentage of the areas of the sample farms irrigated, generally over 40% of the farm (Map 5.1), and the emphasis on vegetables as a crop (Map 5.2). Tree crops are also grown more intensively in the region, and mechanisation often associated with tree crops is also most advanced in the Tripoli area (Map 7.2).

Farm investment, both on housing and on irrigation and other machinery, is most general and highest in the Tripoli area, especially in terms of investment per cultivated hectare (Map 9.2).

4.3.2. A higher proportion of the farm is cultivated on the dry jabal than on the irrigated and semi-irrigated farms near the coast.

Maps 4.1 and 4.2 indicate that the traditional dry farmers of the jabal raise crops on a higher proportion of their farm area than do farmers near the coast. Certainly in 1968, the traditional dry farmers utilised a high percentage of the farm for cereals, mainly barley, for which there is still a strong demand, in that barley bread is very much valued. Cereals covered over 40% of these farms. This proportion is confirmed by the crop survey map, map number 2, Appendix 7 - see the maps for Gharyan and Tighrinnah. However, since these are dry farms from which yields are poor and unreliable, the absolute importance of the grain yield is uncertain, and is certainly less important than yields of irrigated crops from the better watered coast.

That such activity is being maintained on the jabal is, however, an important indication that jabal farmers still have an incentive to utilize their resources.

---

* *Irrigated yields can be as much as five times those from dry land methods.*

4.3.3 Towns have an important influence on farming activities on farms located within 30 kilometres.

Farms which are located near towns are generally small. This is shown on Map 1.1, except for the town of Zawiyah, where one large farm is located very close to the town. Likewise fragmentation of holdings is much more obvious close to towns (Map 1.2), while rural population density falls off away from urban and large village centres. Certain exceptional situations, such as that around al Qassabat have already been discussed in section 4.2.3 and 4.2.4.

Investment is especially marked near towns throughout Western Libya (Map 9.3).

One very significant fact is revealed in Map 10.1 and 10.2, which is relevant to this discussion of the influence of urban centres on agricultural activity. It concerns 'off-farm' employment, and the maps show that 'off-farm' employment by either the farmer or his first son is unrelated to the distance of the farm from the town. Such activity is evenly spread throughout all farms, whether dry or irrigated. Some resided as much as 40 kilometres from the city, sometimes living some distance from the main roads, yet they still relied on casual 'lifts' for transport to work.

Since approximately 30% of farmers have a second job, and a similar proportion of farms had first sons with 'off-farm' employment, it is likely that this 'off-farm' income is significant in terms of farm investment. However, the distribution of these investment resources is general rather than related to urban centres, and their significance on farms further from the towns is less obvious on Maps 9.1 and 9.2 because these more distant farms are generally larger, and on maps 9.1 and 9.2 investment is expressed in terms of area.

4.3.4 Development of irrigated agriculture is taking place on the modern farms rather than on the traditional irrigated farms.

The above contention is confirmed by the position revealed in Map 6.3 showing the length of spray pipes per irrigated hectare for the sample farms. The Tripoli region is shown to be the most heavily involved in this modern method of irrigated farming, and most spray pipes are owned by farmers living south of the main coastal highway, which has previously been suggested as a convenient divide between traditional and modern farming in the Tripoli triangle. The series of air photographs showing changes in Libyan agriculture referring specifically to Talbighah, West of Ajaylat, Sabratah and Suwani bin Yadim, where many areas of new irrigation show up, confirm this idea. There is additional evidence from other areas, such as modern farming at Dafniyah between Zliten and Misuratah.

4.3.5 Character of labour usage.

There are no very clear patterns to be seen on the two maps which refer to labour intensity (Maps 8.1 and 8.2). Traditional farms, both irrigated and dry, would appear to have a rather higher labour intensity, almost always with more than 2.5 workers (including residents) per cultivated hectare. An exception is the al Qassabat region where there is generally less than one worker per hectare. Modern irrigated and dry farms very rarely employ more than one worker per cultivated hectare.

4.3.6 Mechanisation.

In addition to the higher proportion of modern irrigation equipment on modern farms than on traditional, mechanisation, reflected in the number of tractors per hectare, is shown to be more advanced on modern farms. A few examples from Map 7.2 confirm this, such as the Taminah area, Dafniyah (between Zliten and Misuratah), and south of the coastal road in the Tripoli triangle. Mechanisation is also shown to be higher on the modern dry farms to the east and west of Tarhunah.

4.3.7 Rural housing is being replaced rapidly.

The Libyan farming community is mainly housed in permanent dwellings. In 1968 there were still about 6% of the total sampled farms with underground dwellings, these being located exclusively on the western part of the Jabal Nafusah, and a similar number were shown to have temporary dwellings. Temporary dwellings were found mainly in the Tripoli area, where large modern farms have been sold to a number of farmers, and some had not yet constructed a house. The housing stock created by the Italian administration is almost everywhere used.

Throughout areas of settled agriculture house replacement is taking place, and especially near the towns. (Map 10.3 shows house investment per farm). The underground dwellings of the western part of the Jabal Nafusah, a type of dwelling used by 50% of sampled farmers in 1968 in that area, are being rapidly replaced, as are the houses of farmers living on the small coastal traditional gardens. The extent of such changes is illustrated on the diagram of 'Changes in rural housing - Talbighah', page 98. New houses are also being erected on modern farms, but on sites less closely situated than on traditional farms. Such an area is shown on the photographs of Talbighah page 98, where some 200 hectares have been sold in lots of four hectares approximately. A large number of new dwellings can be seen on these new small farms.

4.4 Conclusion.

This summary of the main farm variables and their distributions revealed by the symaps, has been intended to supplement and confirm the conclusions reached as a result of the discussion of the land-use and crop maps, and of the studies of changes in farming deducted from air photographs.

It is felt that the symap method of presenting data has been shown to be valid for the Libyan situation, and to have been invaluable in relating and understanding a number of important variables.

References:

[1] *A team led by Howard T. Fisher produced the SYMAP program at the Laboratory of Computer Graphics, Harvard University.*

[2] *Robertson, J.C. 'The Symap Programme for Computer Mapping' pp 108-113* Cartographic Journal *December 1967.*

Appendix 9

Contents of Computer Map Series

		Page
1.1	Farm size.	196
1.2	Fragmentation of holdings.	196
2.1	Total residents per farm.	197
2.2	Rural population density.	197
3.1	Length of occupation of the farm.	198
3.2	Type of dwelling of the farmer.	198
4.1	Percentage cultivated.	199
4.2	Percentage cereals.	199
5.1	Percentage irrigated.	200
5.2	Percentage vegetables.	200
6.1	Irrigation – Hectares per electric pump.	201
6.2	Irrigation – Hectares per diesel pump.	201
6.3	Spray pipes per irrigated hectare.	202
7.1	Trees per hectare.	203
7.2	Mechanisation – tractors per cultivated hectare.	203
8.1	Labour intensity – permanent workers per total farm hectares.	204
8.2	Labour intensity – permanent workers per cultivated hectare.	204
9.1	Investment – per total farm hectares, including house and car.	205
9.2	Investment – per cultivated hectare, including house and car.	205
9.3	Investment in rural housing – total investment per farm.	206
10.1	'Off-farm' employment of the farmer.	207
10.2	'Off-farm' employment of farmer's first son resident on the farm.	207

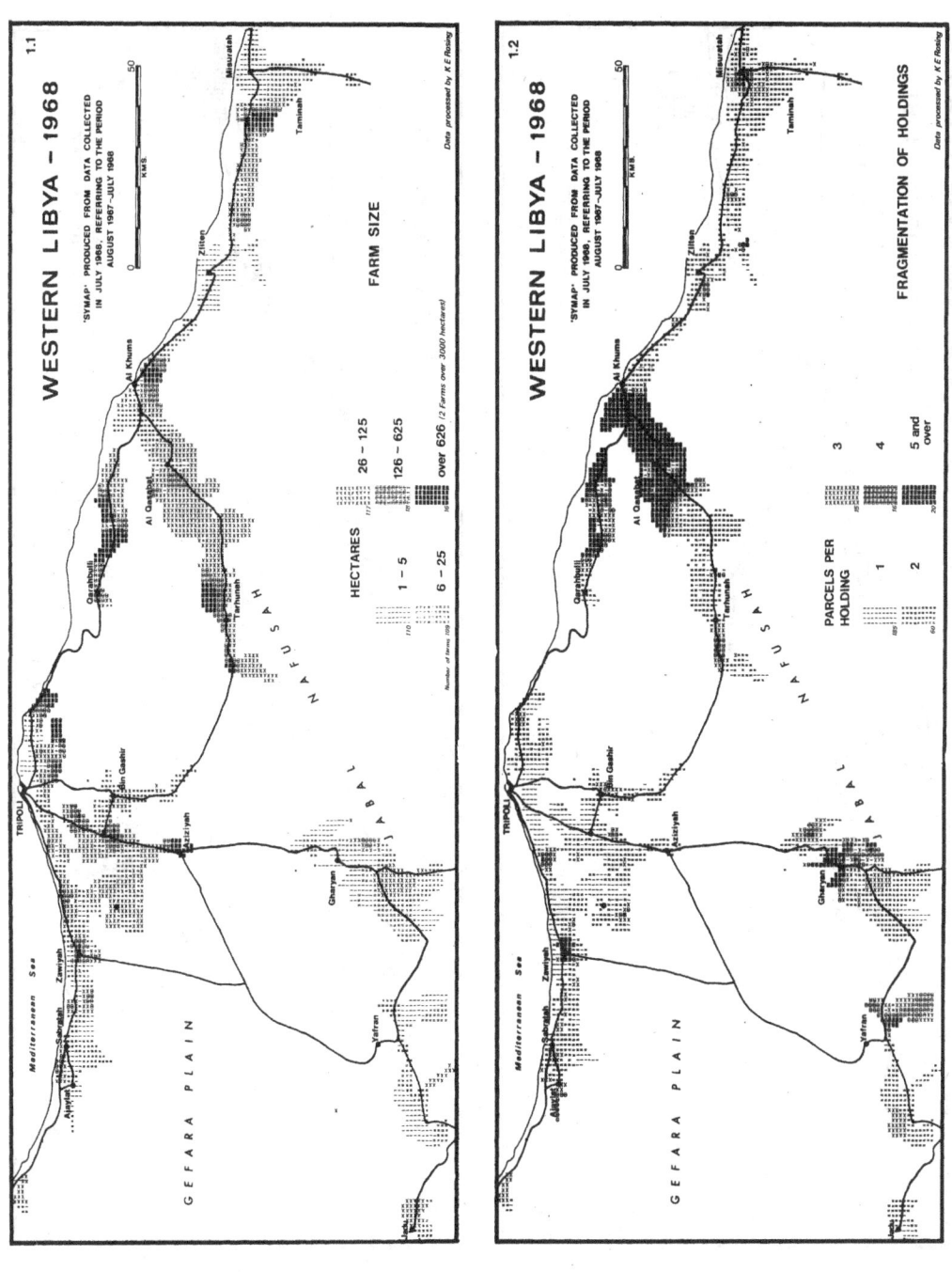

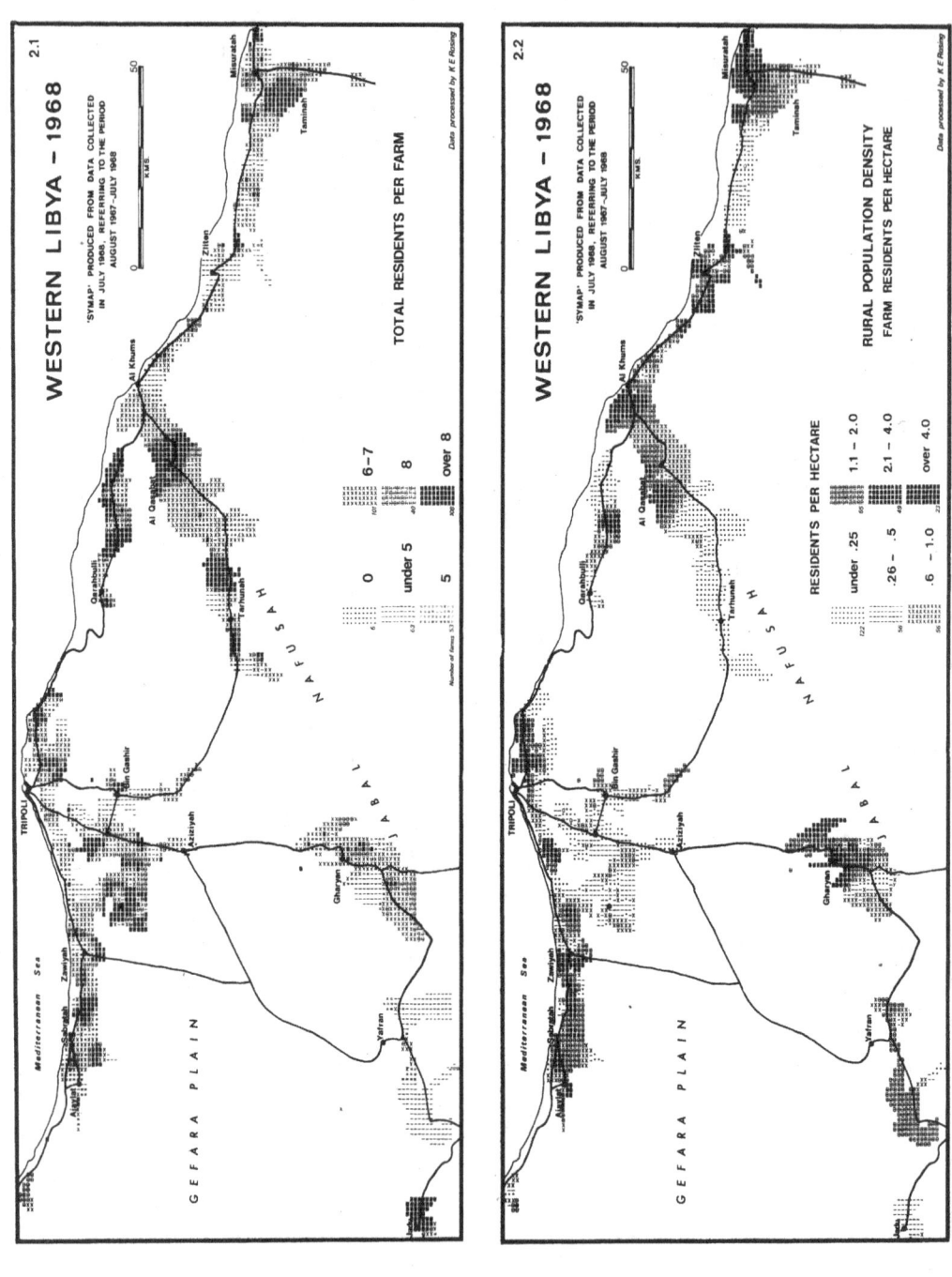

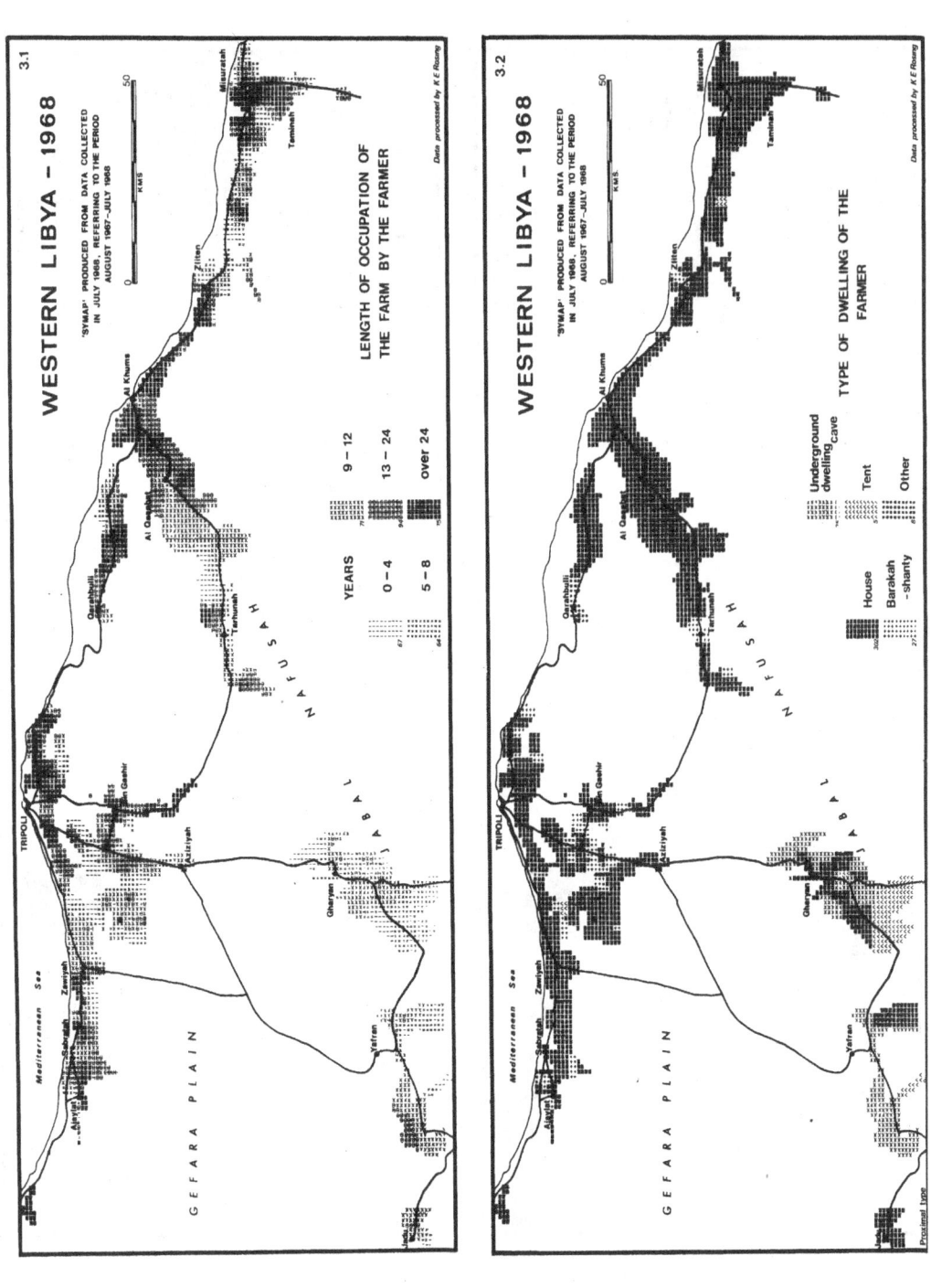

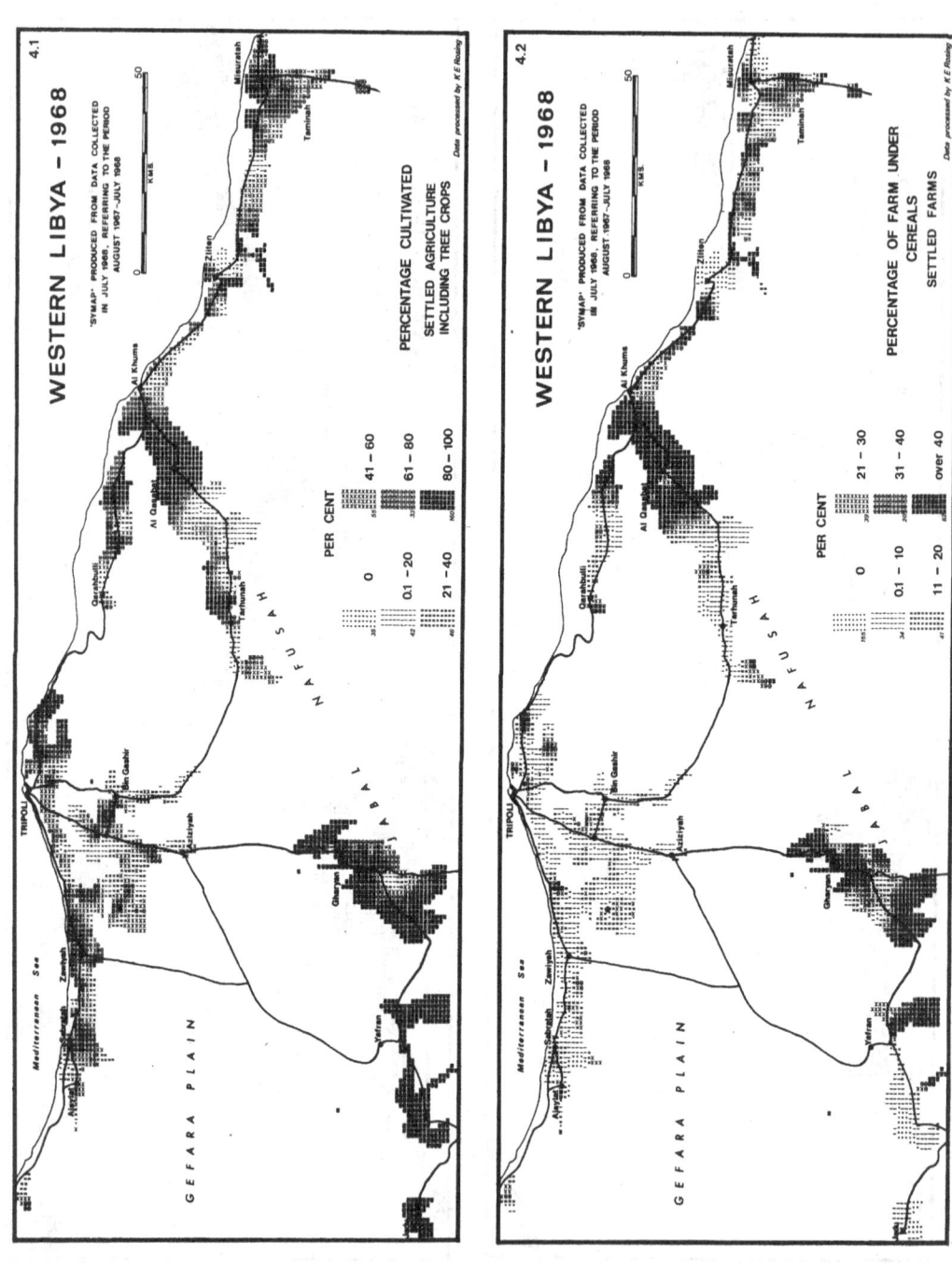

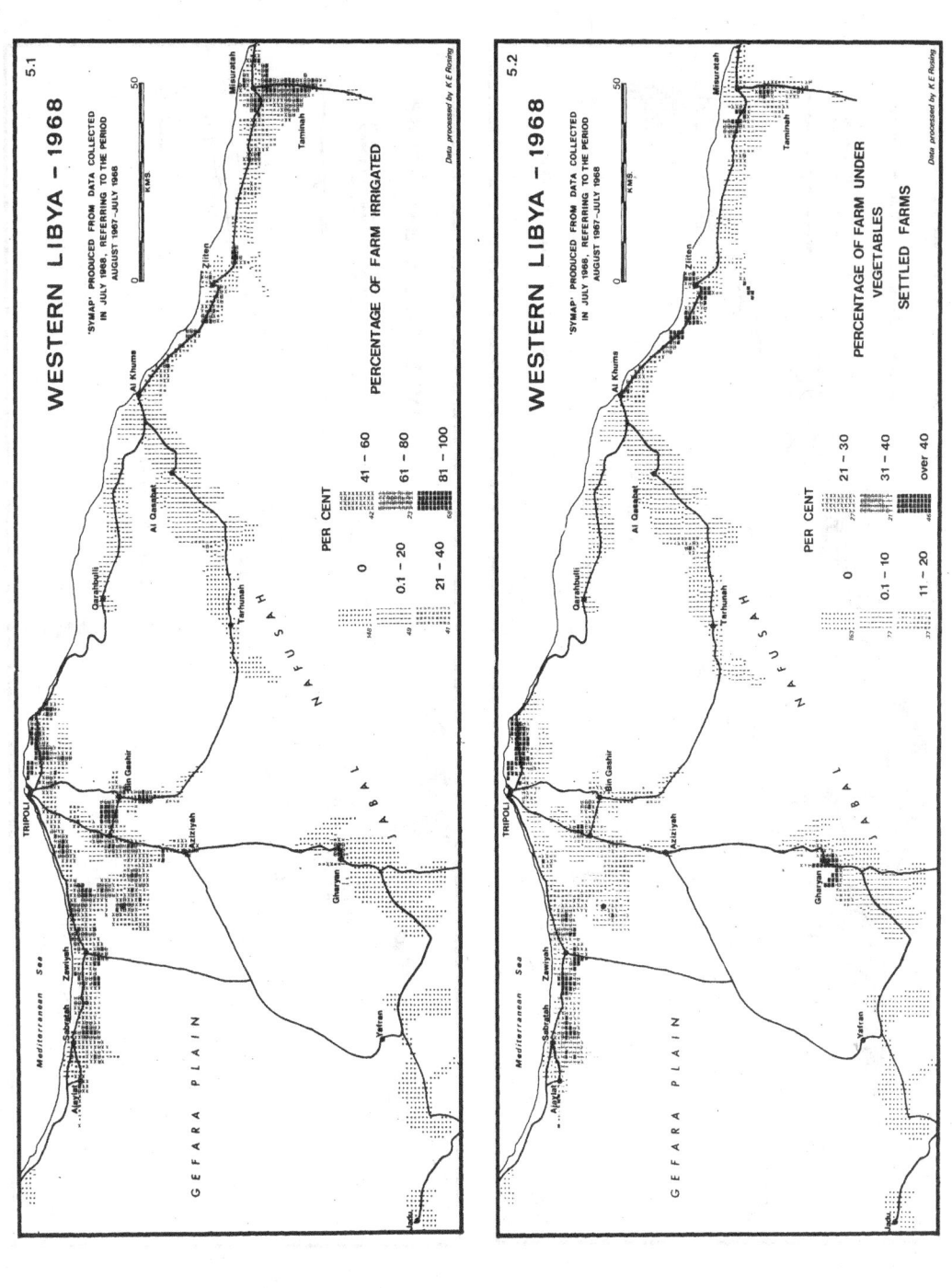

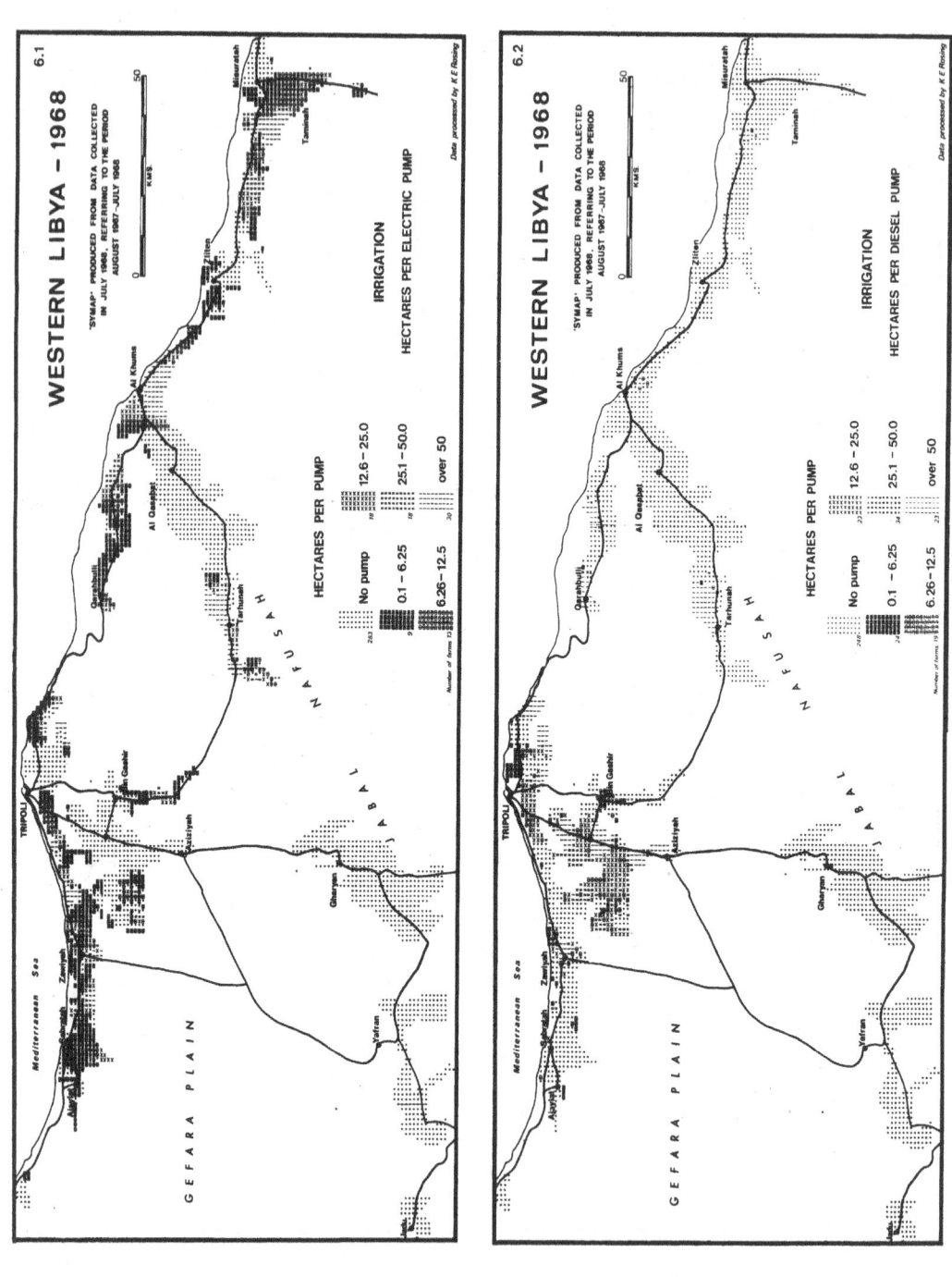

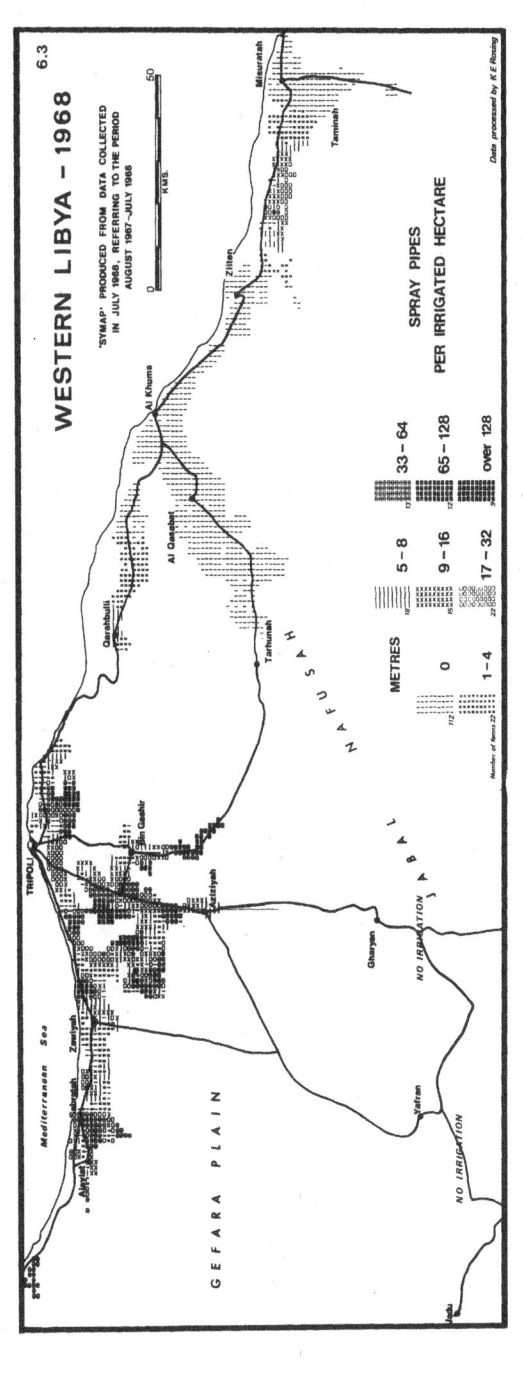

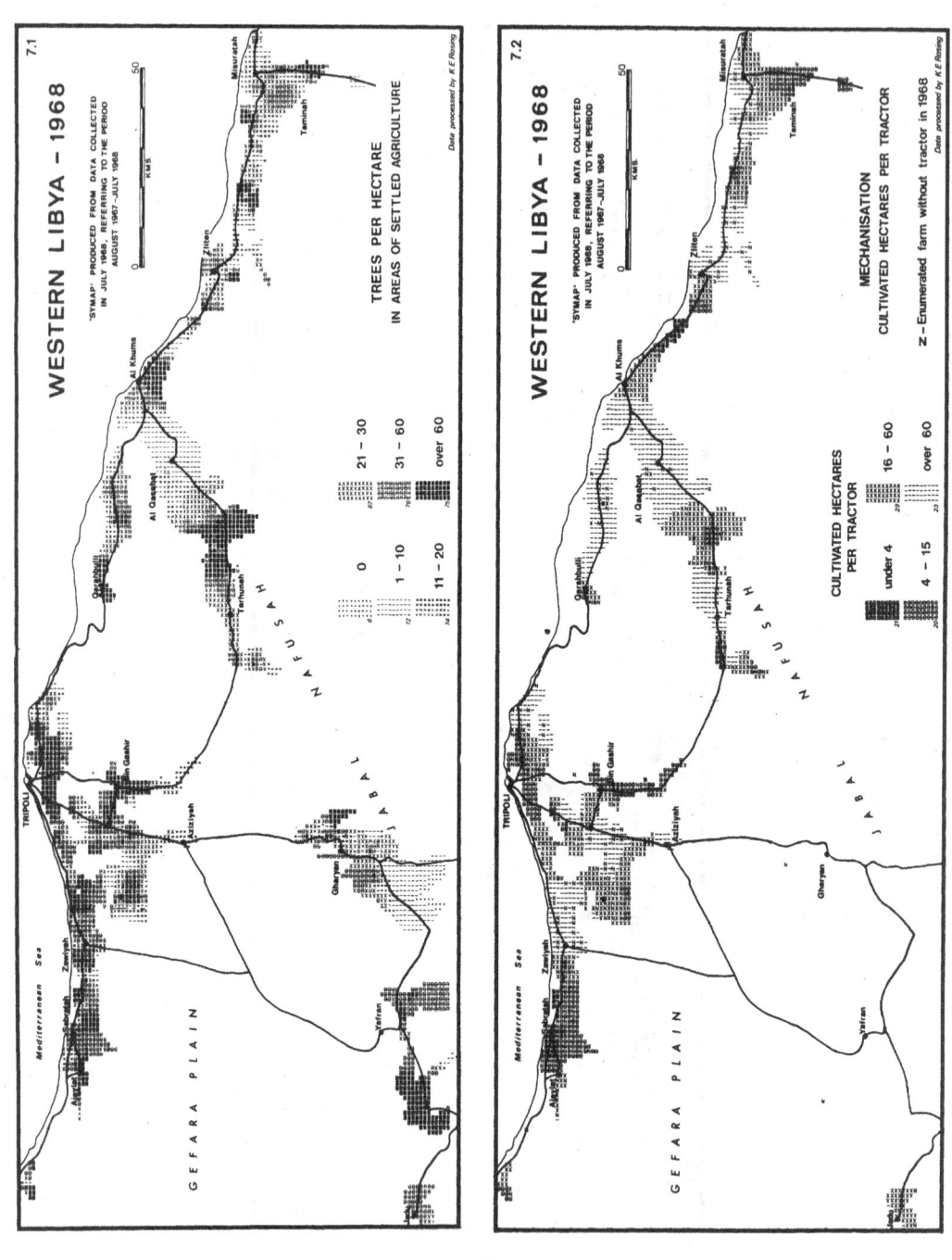

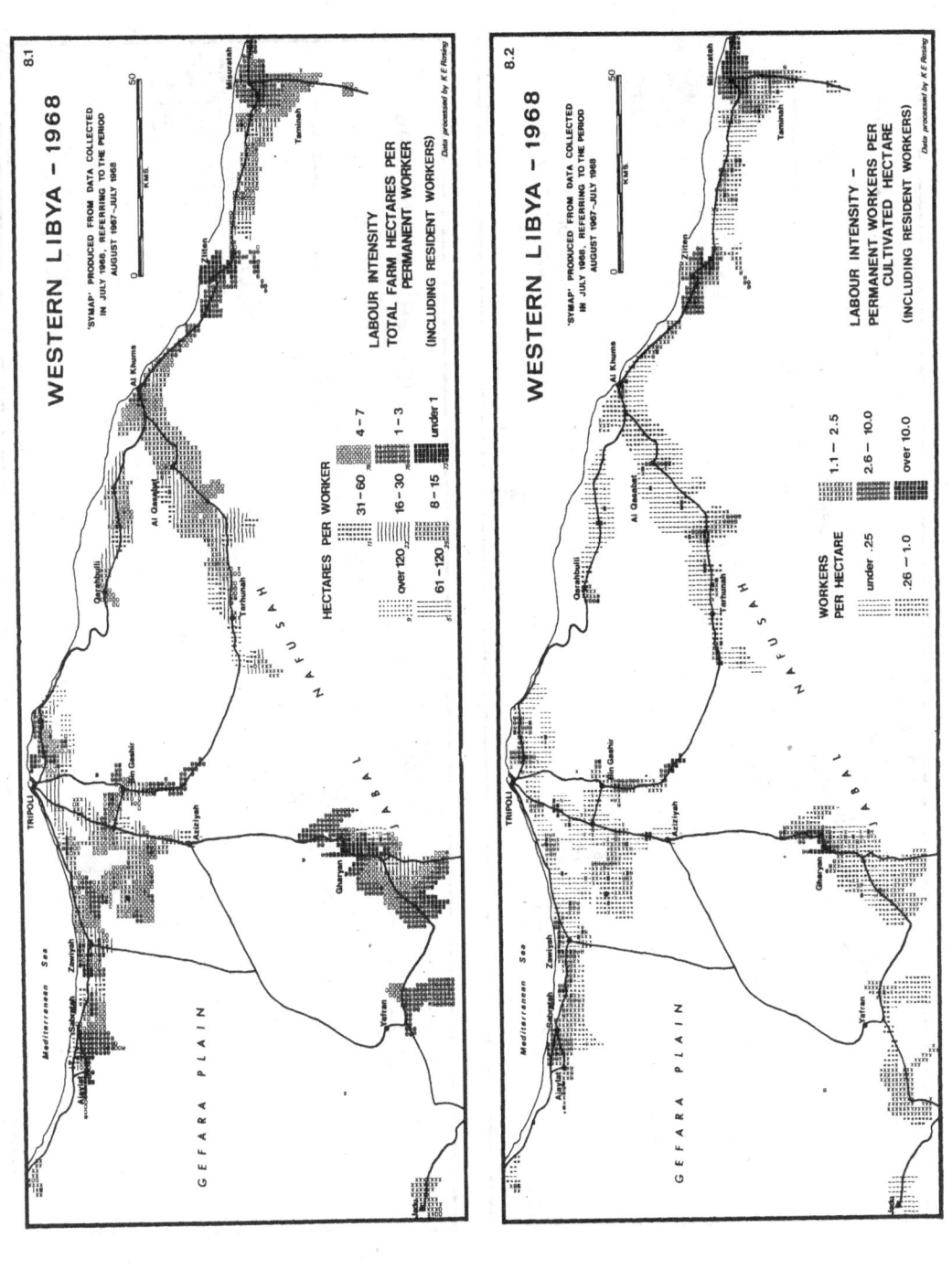

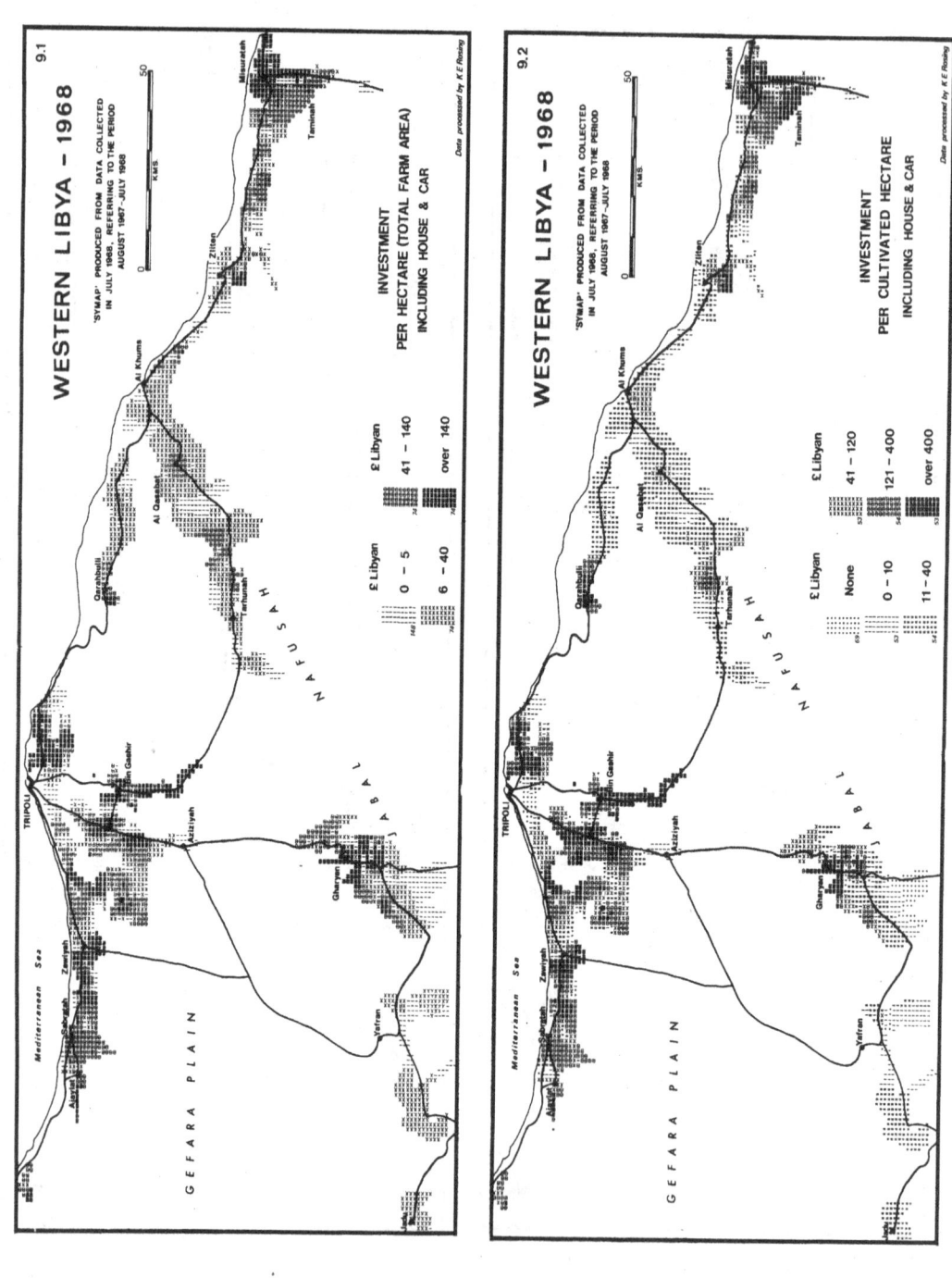

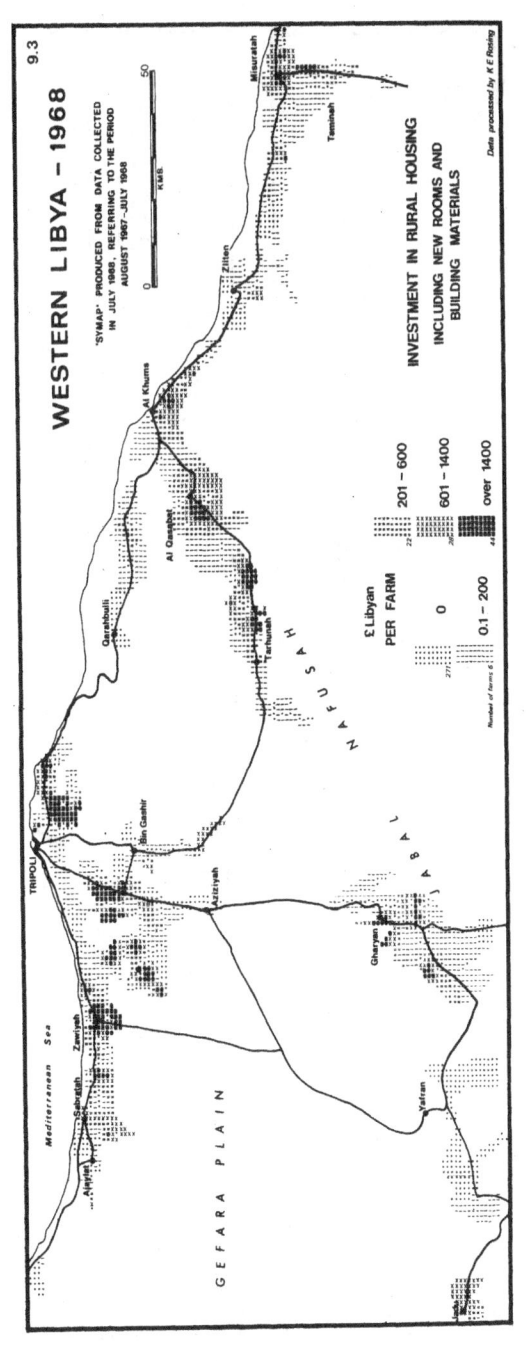

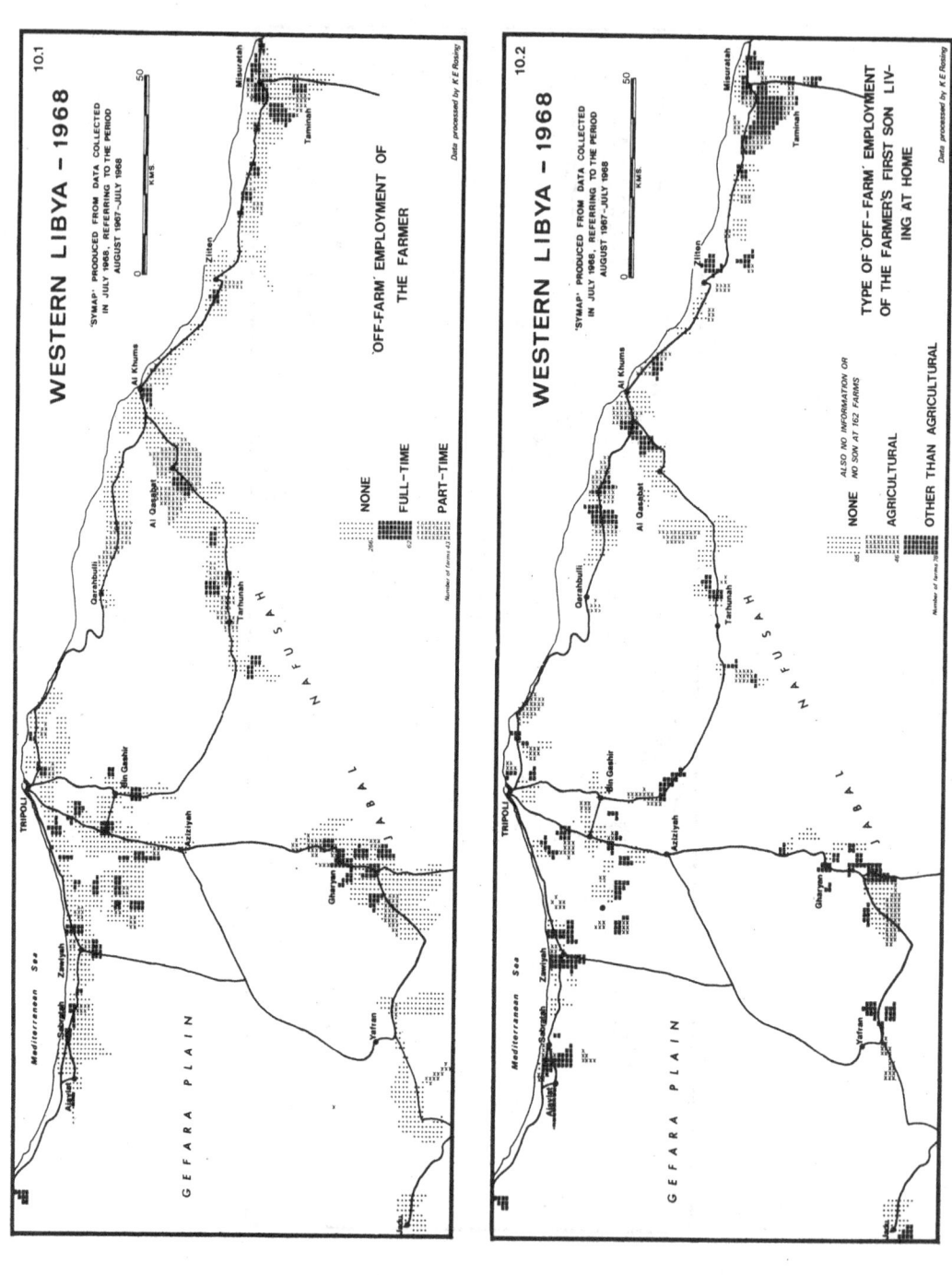

INDEX

Agricultural bank	99,130.
Agricultural production	9, 10, 11, 13, 14, 15, 16, 17, 53, 54, 55, 57, 58, 60, 61, 110, 126.
Agricultural sector	7, 8, 17,162.
Agriculture (traditional)	11, 12, 13, 53, 54, 55, 56, 57, 58, 60, 61, 67, 68, 70, 72, 73, 74, 76, 78, 79, 82, 84, 88, 89, 91, 92, 93, 97, 99, 101, 108, 110, 112, 116, 118, 124, 126, 132, 134, 138, 141, 142, 155, 182, 189, 193, 194.
Ajaylat	68, 76, 80, 94, 100-104,126, 171, 178, 183, 189, 193.
Almond	15, 50, 57,58, 59, 60, 85, 176.
Apple	58.
Apricot	58.
Awbari	28, 38, 40, 80, 124, 172, 181,184.
Aziziyah	27, 38, 189.
Balance of payments	3.
Baninah	80, 171, 184.
Barley	9, 50, 52, 54, 55, 56, 57, 58, 91, 110, 176, 192.
Baydah	35, 38.
Benghazi	19, 35, 36, 38, 48, 116, 117, 163, 173, 175.
Bin Gashir	40, 78, 82, 84.
Brack	28.
British Military Administration (B.M.A.)	51, 52, 53, 56, 61, 62, 64, 182.
Broad beans	57, 60.
Bu Turabah	81, 120, 171, 180,184.
Bu Zayd	81, 117, 180,184.
Camels	9, 52, 61, 62, 63, 131.
Cattle	9, 52, 61, 62, 63, 64, 131.
Cereals	9, 15, 45, 50, 51, 52, 54, 56, 83, 89-91, 93, 108, 110, 114, 116, 122, 126, 172, 184, 185, 191, 192.
Citrus	58, 60, 85, 91, 94, 97, 176, 183, 184.
Climate	20, 26, 28, 34, 35,73.
-------, regions	30.
Colonisation	48-51, 58.
Construction	2, 3, 130, 131, 133, 137, 139, 160, 162, 163, 165.
------------ sector	11, 17, 165.
Co-operatives	130.
Credit	12, 13, 14, 15, 17.
------ loans	13, 99, 130, 136.

Dafiniyah	112, 190, 194.
Dalu	40, 53, 57, 112, 124.
Darnah	19, 35, 38, 48, 80, 116, 117, 118, 126, 171, 177, 184.
Daryanah	116.
Date palm	9, 45, 53, 56, 57, 58, 59, 76.
Demographic settlement	53, 60, 74, 76, 85, 116, 120.
---------------------, decrees	57.
Development plans	7, 12, 13, 14, 15.
Economy, state of	1.
Education	1, 7, 14, 17, 35, 42, 157, 166, 167.
Employment	10, 15, 131, 157- 167.
un--------	161- 162.
Ente (ENTE)	50.
Exports	2, 9, 11, 14, 18, 164.
Fallow	79, 80, 81, 118, 184, 185.
Family	
extended-----	110.
------labour	131.
Farm size	74-78, 90, 108-110, 117, 131-134, 136-156, 172.
Farzugah	68, 81, 94, 116, 117, 118, 119, 120, 122-124, 127, 180, 184.
Fatiyah	81, 117, 172, 180, 184.
Fertilizer	15, 130, 131.
Fezzan	23, 38, 43.
Fig	58, 59.
Forests	50, 53, 184.
afforestation	99.
Fragmentation	13, 74, 108, 172, 190, 193.
Fruit	14, 50, 53, 56, 58, 59, 74.
Gefara	19, 26, 28, 60, 61, 68, 74, 78, 82, 88, 94, 104-108, 110, 117, 124.
Gharig	52, 57,120.
Gharyan	26, 57, 58, 59, 74, 81, 82, 89, 90, 104, 108, 110, 118, 171, 173, 175, 178, 183, 188, 190, 191.
Ghibli	30, 33.
Ghudamis	51.
Ginan	45, 82.
Girnadah	117.
Goats	9, 52, 61, 62, 63, 131.
Groundnuts	15, 53, 60, 104.
Housing	7, 97, 99, 101, 116, 132, 190,192.
Horse	52, 62, 131.
Hun	38, 124.
Imports	3, 7, 11, 17, 110, 130.
Income	3, 10, 11, 12, 13, 15, 17. 112.
------, Gross National	2, 3.
------, national	1, 7, 67.
------, per capita	1.
Independence	1, 13, 52, 53, 67.
Inflation	4, 11, 13.
Insecticide	131.

Investment   8, 10, 12, 13, 14, 15, 93, 97,
                99, 110, 124, 126, 130-156, 172,
                186, 190, 191, 192, 193.
Irrigation   8, 19, 40, 42, 50, 51, 53, 57,
                73, 74, 82, 83, 84, 93, 104, 112,
                114, 116, 122, 124, 126, 131, 132,
                133, 134, 135, 136, 137, 139, 140,
                143, 144, 145, 146, 147, 148, 149,
                150, 151, 152, 192.
Italians   1, 9, 12, 13, 19, 48-51, 59, 60,
                74, 84, 88, 97, 116, 117, 120,
                122, 130.

Jabal Akhdar   19, 23, 24, 26, 28, 32, 33, 35,
                36, 38, 40, 45, 54, 57, 61, 116,
                117, 120, 122, 124.
Jabal Gharbi   see Jabal Nafusah
Jabal Nafusah   19, 23, 26, 28, 30, 32,
                35, 40, 45, 54, 58, 59, 61, 68,
                73, 82, 83, 88, 90, 92, 94, 104,
                108-110, 111, 118, 124, 127,
                130, 132, 135, 136, 137, 138,
                148, 151, 153, 156, 188, 193.
Jadu   26, 74, 88.
Jandubah   81, 89, 118, 171, 177, 179, 184.
Jufrah   57, 124, 126.

Kararim   52, 112.
Khadra   88.
Khums   19, 50, 52, 54, 77, 78, 80, 83,
                88, 90, 91, 92, 110, 112, 130,
                132, 135, 136, 137, 138, 151,
                153, 156, 171, 174, 179, 184,
                187, 190.
Kitchen garden   58.
Kufrah   20, 38.

Labour
------ force   2, 9, 10, 157, 167.
------, foreign   14, 162, 163, 164, 165.
------, hired   131.
------, mobility   157.
------, participation   158-159.
------, permanent   160, 161, 162.
------, shortage   157, 158, 165, 166.
------, temporary   160, 161, 162.
------, utilisation   159-160.
Laghbe   56.
Land abandonment   10, 52, 74, 81, 184, 185.
Land concessions   48, 49, 50, 52, 58, 76.
Land ownership   12, 13, 17.
Land reclamation   131, 133, 134, 139, 140,
                   143, 144, 145, 146, 147,
                   148, 149, 150, 151, 152.
Land tenure   12.
-----------, insecurity   53.
Land use   1, 45-56, 67-127, 182, 193.
Livestock   9, 12, 36, 53, 56, 60-63, 73,
                83, 112, 131.

Loans   see Credit

Lucerne   57.

Ma'murah   50.
Marj   36, 38, 44, 52, 53, 57, 68,
                81, 94, 116, 117, 118, 119,
                120-122, 127, 172, 180, 183.
Marketing   12, 17, 97.
Meat   14, 63.
Mechanisation (of Agriculture)   8, 15, 117,
                130, 133, 136, 139, 140, 141,
                142, 143, 144, 145, 146, 147,
                148, 149, 150, 151, 152, 172,
                                      192, 194.
------------, combined harvesters   131, 133.
------------, ploughs   131, 133.
------------, tractors   114, 130, 131, 133,
                           136, 172, 185, 190.
Melon   57, 60, 120.
Migration   48, 157, 165, 185.
----------, rural-urban   10, 15, 130, 158,
                                      164, 167.
----------, seasonal   165.
----------, war-time   51.
Milk   9, 63.
Ministry of agriculture   12, 13, 62, 63.
Misuratah   19, 51, 73, 78, 82, 83, 88,
                90, 92, 126, 130, 132, 135,
                137, 138, 152, 153, 155, 156,
                           189, 190, 193, 194.
Mizdah   28, 38.
Money supply   6, 7, 10.
Murzuq   20, 43, 80, 172, 184.
Nalut   58, 59.
National Agricultural Settlement Authority (NASA)
                70, 76, 79, 84, 85, 89, 91,
                93, 114, 116, 120, 122, 124,
                127, 163, 171, 172, 176, 177,
                                      179, 180.
Natural resources   1, 9, 12.
Nomadism   9, 12, 45, 48, 60, 61, 112.
Nutrition   14.
Off-farm employment   108, 110, 172, 192.
Oil   1, 9, 10, 12, 13, 14, 17,
                18, 19, 61, 78, 114, 130,
                131, 158, 162, 164, 166, 190.
--- revenues   1, 3, 7, 15, 52, 70, 73,
                99, 130, 164, 165, 167.
Olive, tree   45, 50, 52, 57, 58, 59, 60,
                           76, 85, 89, 104, 176.
-----, harvesting mats   131.
-----, oil   9, 15, 53, 59.
Orchard   45, 50, 51, 53, 57, 58, 59,
                60, 73, 78, 83, 85-89, 183.

Part-time farming   52.
Peach   58, 59.
Pear   58.

Pepper	60, 183, 185.
Plum	58.
Pomegranate	58.
Population	1, 14, 20, 45, 48, 93, 130, 158, 159, 172, 191, 193.
Potato	57, 60.
Poultry	131.
Prickly pear	58.
Productivity	9, 10, 11, 13, 14, 56, 74, 100.
Pumps, diesel	53, 112, 131, 133, 172.
-----, electric	53, 131, 133, 172.
-----, motor	40, 57, 124, 130.
Qassabat	38, 54, 57, 76, 78, 82, 90, 118, 188, 190, 192.
Jabal al -------	58, 78.
Qubbah	52, 68, 81, 94, 117, 120, 124-125, 180, 184.
Rainfall	9, 19, 27, 28, 29, 34, 55, 56, 60, 61, 73, 74, 78, 89, 108, 110, 112, 114, 116, 117, 120, 122, 173, 175.
Real property	11, 14, 131, 132, 134, 135, 136, 137, 139, 140, 143, 144, 145, 146, 147, 148, 149, 150, 151, 152.
Remittance	130.
Sa'a'idiyah	67, 81, 120, 171, 178, 184.
Sabhah	24, 38, 80, 95, 124, 125, 126, 127, 172, 173, 175, 181, 184.
Sabratah	32, 78, 84, 85, 86, 87, 91, 101, 104, 193.
Sahal al Ahmad (Sahal)	36, 77, 80, 90, 91, 110, 112, 114, 171, 178, 184, 190.
Salinization, of aquifers	39, 40.
Sample	67, 70, 130, 137, 186, 192.
Saving	15, 130.
Sawknah	80, 124, 126, 172, 181, 184.
Sedentarisation	60.
Service sector	2, 3, 10, 11, 164, 167.
Shahhat	31, 45, 122, 175.
Sheep	9, 52, 61, 62, 63, 131.
Shifting cultivation	45, 48, 51, 53, 60, 72, 73, 74, 90, 116, 117, 182, 184.
Suani (Suwani)	45, 57.
Subsidies	11, 15, 17, 110, 130.
Suluntah	81, 117, 120, 180, 184.
Suq al Jumah	40, 42, 80, 91, 171, 178, 184.
Suq al Khamis	32, 112.
Surman	57, 91.
Surt	20, 23, 30, 32, 33, 38, 61, 73.

Suwani bin Yadim   40, 41, 68, 78, 80, 82, 84,
                    94, 104-106, 129, 171, 177,
                    178, 184, 193.

Tajura   50, 80, 91, 171, 178, 183.
Talbighah   68, 78, 80, 82, 94, 96,
                    97-101, 104, 171, 177, 178,
                    184, 193, 194.
Taminah   80, 82, 112, 171, 178, 184,
                    190, 194.
Tarhunah   36, 54, 57, 74, 89, 118,
                    192.
   Jabal ----------   26, 58, 78, 189, 194.
Tariffs   11.
Taxation   11, 15, 54.
Tibesti   20, 23, 33, 43.
Tobacco   74, 82, 108, 110, 118, 184,
                    185, 191.
Tobruq   35, 38.
Tomato   53, 57, 60, 104, 183, 185.
Tractors   see Mechanisation
Trade, sector   10, 11, 17, 130, 158.
Transport   1, 2, 3, 7, 131, 133, 134,
                    135, 139, 140, 143, 144, 145,
                    146, 147, 148, 149, 150, 151,
                    152, 158, 163, 165, 193.
Tripoli   12, 20, 28, 29, 30, 31, 32,
                    35, 40, 50, 60, 64, 78, 82,
                    83, 84, 85, 88, 90, 91, 92,
                    97, 99, 101, 104, 129, 130,
                    132, 133, 135, 136, 137, 138,
                    150, 153, 156, 163, 172, 173,
                    175, 186, 189, 190, 192, 193,
                    194.
Tukrah   80, 116, 120, 171, 179, 184.
Turkish administration   45, 55.
Umm ar Rizam   80, 116, 176, 184.
Vegetables   14, 50, 52, 57, 78, 89,
                    91-93, 172, 184, 185, 192.
Vine   50, 57, 58, 59, 60, 88,
                    104, 117, 184, 185.
Waddan   80, 124, 126, 172, 181, 184.
Wadi al Ajal   36, 45.
Wadi Ki'am   35, 36, 53, 67, 68, 81, 82,
                    94, 110-116, 120, 171, 178,
                    184.
Wadi Ash Shatti   36, 38.
Wages   99, 131, 157-167, 185.
-----, rates of   131, 160-165.
Water resources   20, 34, 35, 42, 44, 85, 99,
                    104, 114, 116, 130.
Weddings   131, 133, 134, 137.
Wheat   9, 50, 52, 53, 55, 56, 58, 176.
Woodland   46, 50, 51, 53, 72, 94, 97,
                    104, 116, 182, 184.
Wool   9, 63.
World Bank (IBRD)   12, 13, 14, 18.

Yafran	28, 32, 59, 74, 88, 90, 189.
Zawiyah	40, 44, 57, 58, 64, 73, 80, 83, 88, 90, 91, 92, 112, 126, 130, 132, 135, 137, 138, 149, 153, 156, 171, 178, 184, 190, 193.
Zliten	82, 90, 91, 110, 112, 189, 190, 193, 194.
Zuwarah	19, 51, 82, 173.